Linguistic Landscapes Beyond the Language Classroom

Advances in Sociolinguistics Series
Series Editor: Tommaso M. Milani

Since the emergence of sociolinguistics as a new field of enquiry in the late 1960s, research into the relationship between language and society has advanced almost beyond recognition. In particular, the past decade has witnessed the considerable influence of theories drawn from outside of sociolinguistics itself. Thus rather than see language as a mere reflection of society, recent work has been increasingly inspired by ideas drawn from social, cultural, and political theory that have emphasized the constitutive role played by language/discourse in all areas of social life. The Advances in Sociolinguistics series seeks to provide a snapshot of the current diversity of the field of sociolinguistics and the blurring of the boundaries between sociolinguistics and other domains of study concerned with the role of language in society.

Titles in the series include:

Becoming a Citizen: Linguistic Trials and Negotiations in the UK, Kamran Khan

Language Ideologies and the Globalization of "Standard" Spanish, Darren Paffey

Making Sense of People and Place in Linguistic Landscapes, edited by Amiena Peck, Christopher Stroud and Quentin Williams

Multilingual Encounters in Europe's Institutional Spaces, edited by Johann Unger, Michał Krzyżanowski and Ruth Wodak

Multilingual Memories: Monuments, Museums and the Linguistic Landscape, edited by Robert Blackwood and John Macalister

Negotiating and Contesting Identities in Linguistic Landscapes, edited by Robert Blackwood, Elizabeth Lanza and Hirut Woldemariam

Remix Multilingualism: Hip-Hop, Ethnography and Performing Marginalized Voice, Quentin Williams

The Discursive Construction of Identity and Space among Mobile People, Roberta Piazza

The Languages of Global Hip-Hop, edited by Marina Terkourafi

The Language of Newspapers: Socio-Historical Perspectives, Martin Conboy

The Tyranny of Writing: Ideologies of the Written Word, edited by Constanze Weth and Kasper Juffermans

Voices in the Media: Performing Linguistic Otherness, Gaëlle Planchenault

Linguistic Landscapes Beyond the Language Classroom

Edited by
Greg Niedt and Corinne A. Seals

BLOOMSBURY ACADEMIC
LONDON • NEW YORK • OXFORD • NEW DELHI • SYDNEY

BLOOMSBURY ACADEMIC
Bloomsbury Publishing Plc
50 Bedford Square, London, WC1B 3DP, UK
1385 Broadway, New York, NY 10018, USA
29 Earlsfort Terrace, Dublin 2, Ireland

BLOOMSBURY, BLOOMSBURY ACADEMIC and the Diana logo
are trademarks of Bloomsbury Publishing Plc

First published in Great Britain 2021
This paperback edition published in 2022

Copyright © Greg Niedt, Corinne A. Seals, and Contributors 2021

Greg Niedt and Corinne A. Seals have asserted their right under the Copyright,
Designs and Patents Act, 1988, to be identified as Editors of this work.

For legal purposes the Acknowledgments on p. xviii constitute
an extension of this copyright page.

All rights reserved. No part of this publication may be reproduced or transmitted in
any form or by any means, electronic or mechanical, including photocopying,
recording, or any information storage or retrieval system, without prior
permission in writing from the publishers.

Bloomsbury Publishing Plc does not have any control over, or responsibility for,
any third-party websites referred to or in this book. All internet addresses given
in this book were correct at the time of going to press. The author and publisher
regret any inconvenience caused if addresses have changed or sites have
ceased to exist, but can accept no responsibility for any such changes.

A catalogue record for this book is available from the British Library.

Library of Congress Cataloging-in-Publication Data
Names: Niedt, Greg, editor. | Seals, Corinne, editor.
Title: Linguistic landscapes beyond the language classroom / edited by
Greg Niedt and Corinne A. Seals.
Description: London ; New York : Bloomsbury Academic, 2020. | Series: Advances in
sociolinguistics | Includes bibliographical references and index.
Identifiers: LCCN 2020034855 (print) | LCCN 2020034856 (ebook) | ISBN 9781350125360
(hardback) | ISBN 9781350195356 (paperback) | ISBN 9781350125384 (ebook) |
ISBN 9781350125377 (epub)
Subjects: LCSH: Second language acquisition. | Informal language learning. |
Non-formal education.
Classification: LCC P118.2 .L545 2020 (print) | LCC P118.2 (ebook) | DDC 418.0071–dc23
LC record available at https://lccn.loc.gov/2020034855
LC ebook record available at https://lccn.loc.gov/2020034856

ISBN: HB: 978-1-3501-2536-0
       PB: 978-1-3501-9535-6
       ePDF: 978-1-3501-2538-4
       eBook: 978-1-3501-2537-7

Series: Advances in Sociolinguistics

Typeset by Integra Software Services Pvt. Ltd.

To find out more about our authors and books visit www.bloomsbury.com
and sign up for our newsletters.

For all educators, both formal and informal, and all those who seek to learn

Contents

List of Figures	ix
List of Tables	xiii
List of Contributors	xiv
Acknowledgments	xviii
Introduction *Greg Niedt and Corinne A. Seals*	1

Part 1   Other Forms of Language Classroom

1. From Part of the Scenery to Curricular Resources: Authentic Signs as Portals to Cultural Practices within a Residential German Language Immersion Program *Justin Quam and Heidi E. Hamilton*   13
2. Unveiling Sign Languages in the Linguistic Landscape: Representations of Sign Languages in Nonsigning and Signing Milieux *Jami Fisher, Donna Jo Napoli, and Gene Mirus*   37
3. New Caledonia: A Semiotic Analysis of the Landscape as an Opportunity for Learning *Diane de Saint Léger and Kerry Mullan*   57

Part 2   Structured Spaces Becoming Classrooms

4. The Linguistic Landscape of Public Health Institutions in Tanzania *Paschal Mdukula*   77
5. Information, Education, and Language Policy in the Linguistic Landscape of an International Airport in New Zealand *Una Cunningham and Jeanette King*   97
6. English Learning Experience in a Textile Company in Turkey *Yasemin Kırkgöz*   117
7. The Public Discourse and Presentation of Migrant Groups within a Museum Space *Barbara Loester*   133

Part 3   LLs as Activist Education

8. Exploring Multimodal Story Houses in the Indigenous Paiwan-Rukai Post-Disaster Reconstruction *Chun-Mei Chen*   155

9	Activist Teaching through the Linguistic Landscape in Göttingen and Lviv *Corinne A. Seals and Greg Niedt*	177
10	Educating the Public? Affective and Epistemic Stances as Approaches to Campaigning during Ireland's Eighth Amendment Referendum *Louis Strange*	197
11	Dynamic Walking Tour Methodology for LL Research: A Case Study in Jaffa *Amir Michalovich, Sarah Naaman, Moraia Trijnes, Iman Agbaria, and Elana Shohamy*	217

Index 238

List of Figures

The companion website hosting all figures in color is available at (www.bloomsbury.com/linguistic-landscapes-beyond-the-language-classroom).

1.1	Photo of question signs along the road leading to the *Bahnhof* building	14
1.2	*Bahnhof* from *Parkplatz*	online
1.3	Aerial map of *Waldsee*	online
1.4	Recycling bins	online
1.5	Drawer labels	online
1.6	A sign on the door of the health center reading *Wo sind die Krankenschwestern?* [Where are the nurses?] and listing times of day when they can be found	online
1.7	Price labels in the camp store	online
1.8	*ZIEHEN* [PULL] on a door handle	online
1.9	A warning sign near the door to the sauna	online
1.10	*Albert Hohmann Turmuhr: In Anerkennung der vielen Beträge der Familie Hohmann, Waldsee, Juni 1986* [Albert Hohmann Clock Tower: In recognition of the many contributions of the Hohmann family, *Waldsee*, June 1986]	online
1.11	A villager-created poster encouraging fellow students to pick up trash	online
1.12	Panels adorning a central stone fountain painted by villagers as part of an elective course	online
1.13	Photos of "word art" purchased in Germany	online
1.14	A sign reading *Wieviel kostet … ?* [How much does … cost?]	online
1.15 and 1.16	Signs in the dining listing example phrases for requesting food	online
1.17	Signposts featuring questions of the day that underpin the *Waldsee* curriculum	online
1.18	A sign on an official yellow German mailbox reading *Eilsendungen bitte bei den Postämtern einliefern*	online
1.19	A parking sign reading *Nur für Besucher* [Visitors only]	online
1.20	A bus stop sign	online

x *List of Figures*

1.21	A sign denoting a *Naturschutzgebiet* [nature reserve]	online
1.22	A sign listing distances to hiking locations in Switzerland	online
1.23	A sign listing safety rules on the beach	online
1.24	How to call for help on a landline	online
1.25	Recycling bins	28
1.26	Sign reading "You are leaving the American sector"	30
2.1	Examples of deaf peddler cards	43
2.2	Italian bank advertisement featuring the LIS alphabet	45
2.3	SLLL examples around Gallaudet campus	online
2.4	Gallaudet Starbucks signage	50
3.1	Typical signposting in Noumea	online
3.2	Place des Cocotiers	online
3.3 and 3.4	Street art photographed in 2015, *Fédération des oeuvres laïques* (FOL), Nouméa	65
3.5	Local market, Noumea	66
3.6	Église du Sacré-Cœur, Bourail	online
3.7	European Union, French, and Kanaky flags on the *Centre de formation en alternance* (i.e., TAFE school)	online
3.8	Fontaine Céleste, Places des Cocotiers, Noumea	online
4.1	Top-down sign indicating administrative information	87
4.2	Top-down sign indicating regulatory information at MNH	online
4.3	Monolingual English sign	online
4.4	Monolingual Kiswahili sign communicating administrative information	89
4.5	Monolingual Kiswahili sign communicating client's responsibilities	90
4.6	Monolingual English sign about regulatory discourse	online
5.1	Wayfinding sign inside terminal in English, Chinese, Japanese, and Korean, Christchurch International Airport, September 2016	online
5.2	From left: "no spitting" sign in Chinese and Korean outside terminal; sign outside terminal for Chinese Language Week; staff buttons for Chinese Language Week, Christchurch International Airport, September 2016	104
5.3	Chinese biosecurity sign before customs, Chinese biosecurity amnesty bin, English biosecurity amnesty bin, Chinese biosecurity sign before customs, Christchurch International Airport, September 2016	106

5.4	Tourist information before passport control (above); *kia ora* (informal greeting) sign between airbridge and duty free (below), Christchurch International Airport, September 2016	108
5.5	From left: *Taonga* (treasure) and *Haere mai* (welcome) signs between customs and landside, Christchurch International Airport, September 2016	online
6.1	Placement of the posters of textile terms	121
6.2	Placement of a poster of a dialogue in the corridor	122
7.1	Description of Judith de la Motte	143
7.2	Interactive display	144
7.3	Storybox "Ten Pound Poms"	146
7.4	Gateway exhibition—opening display	online
7.5	Gateway exhibition—migrant profiles	online
7.6	Gateway exhibition—transmigrants	online
7.7	Storybox "Pakistan"	online
7.8	Storybox "Caribbean"	online
7.9	Storybox "Poland"	online
7.10	Storybox "Cookery Exchange"	online
8.1	Distribution of story houses in this study	online
8.2	Modalities of the story houses	online
8.3	Slate story house and multilingual signs in the playground	164
8.4	The learning system of the slate story house in the linguistic landscape	online
8.5	Rukai shoes-off tribal houses, murals, and the chieftain's house	166
8.6	Quinoa story house and the "Silent Protest"	169
8.7	Murals of the workshop houses	online
9.1	Graffiti on the walls of Göttingen (left) and Lviv (right)	184
9.2	Some of many stickers found in the streets of Göttingen (left) and Lviv (right)	186
9.3	Local flags hung from buildings in Göttingen and poetry mural in Lviv	189
10.1	Donnybrook Road, Dublin	206
10.2	Dorset Street, Dublin	210
10.3	Together for Yes leaflet	212
10.4	St. Stephen's Green, Dublin	online
11.1	Distinguishing features of the dynamic walking tour methodology: a comprehensive framework	225

11.2	Hebrew dominance on signage along Yefet Street	228
11.3	Members of the walking tour discussing the lack of Arabic on signage along Yefet Street	229

List of Tables

1.1	Languages appearing in the *Waldsee* linguistic landscape	23
4.1	Summary of interview respondents' profile	85
4.2	Linguistic landscape actors	86
4.3	Language preference on top-down vs. bottom-up signs	87
7.1	2011 census figures according to ethnicity in percent	135
7.2	Wards with the highest percentages of non-white and non-UK-born residents	136
10.1	Epistemic stance(s) in "No" poster messages	207
10.2	Affective stance(s) in "Yes" poster messages	207

List of Contributors

Iman Agbaria is an MA student at the multilingual education program at the School of Education, Tel Aviv University. She is currently working on her thesis entitled "Language activists' engagements with linguistic landscape." Iman is an English teacher at high school in Jaffa and a lecturer at Ono Academic College. Her research interests include multilingual education, minority language preservation, language rights, linguistic landscape, and language activism.

Chun-Mei Chen is Associate Professor of linguistics in the Department of Foreign Languages and Literatures at National Chung Hsing University, Taiwan. Her research interests include phonetics, phonology, and language education of Indigenous languages in Taiwan and L2 Chinese learners' acquisition in multilingual contexts. She has published articles in journals and edited volumes. Her most recent book chapter is "Social network, dual identity, and agency in the implementation of indigenous language education in migration communities" (2019).

Una Cunningham is Professor at Stockholm University, Sweden, in the Department of Language Education, and Adjunct Professor at the University of Canterbury, New Zealand, in the Department of Educational Studies and Leadership. Her research interests are in language learning, education, and technology in various permutations. Her most recent book is the fourth edition of *Growing Up with Two Languages* (2020).

Diane de Saint Léger is Lecturer in French Studies at the University of Melbourne. Her research interests focus on the perception of self and others in the language classroom as well as on the circulation of discourse about self and others in public spaces. She has published in the areas of language teaching, motivation, class-based assessment, and discourse analysis.

Jami Fisher is the Director of American Sign Language (ASL) and Senior Lecturer in foreign languages in the Department of Linguistics at the University of Pennsylvania, a position she has held since 2005. Her current academic interests include finding ways to integrate meaningful, collaborative, community-based activities into ASL and Deaf Studies coursework as well as documenting and analyzing the Philadelphia variety of American Sign Language. She is a native ASL user and CODA (Child of Deaf Adults), born and raised in Philadelphia.

Heidi E. Hamilton is Professor in the Department of Linguistics at Georgetown University, where she explores interrelationships between discourse and health. Her recent books are *Language, Dementia and Meaning Making: Navigating Challenges* of *Cognition and Face in Everyday Life* (2019), the *Wiley-Blackwell Handbook of Discourse Analysis* (2015, with Tannen and Schiffrin), and the *Routledge Handbook of Language and Health Communication* (2014, with Chou). Awards include Fulbright Distinguished Chair in Linguistics (Innsbruck), DAAD *Gastdozentin* (Berlin), and Humboldt Research Prize (Potsdam). For the past 40+ summers she has taught German and conducted research at Concordia Language Villages in northern Minnesota.

Jeanette King is Professor at the University of Canterbury in the School of Māori and Indigenous Studies. She has published widely in areas relating to the Māori language and languages spoken by Māori—from aspects of linguistic change, particularly in the phrasal lexicon, through to language revitalization. She leads the bilingualism theme of the New Zealand Institute of Language, Brain and Behaviour (NZILBB) and is a member of the MAONZE (Māori and New Zealand English) project examining change over time in the pronunciation of Māori. She is also a founding editor of the *Journal of Home Language Research*.

Yasemin Kırkgöz is a professor in the English Language Teacher Education Department of Çukurova University. She completed her master's and PhD at Aston University, England. Her main research interests focus on English medium instruction in higher education, pre-service and in-service teacher education, school-university partnership, language policy, and teaching English to young learners. She has published on these topics in various international journals. In 2013, she received the IATEFL award for her work on *Initiating and Managing the Process of Curriculum Innovation* from the IATEFL's Leadership and Management Special Interest Group. She is the co-editor of the book *Key Issues in English for Specific Purposes in Higher Education* (2018).

Barbara Loester received her PhD from the University of Aberdeen (Scotland) in 2009 and is a senior lecturer in English linguistics in the Department of English, Creative Writing and American Studies at the University of Winchester, UK. Her research interests lie in the field of sociolinguistics, with a key focus on language and identity, minority and contested languages, and language policy and planning. She has published on Scots and Bavarian (2010), their roles in regional and national identity construction, and the cultural representation of minority language speaker groups and their perception by society (2017).

Paschal Charles Mdukula is a lecturer at the University of Dar es Salaam in the Centre for Communication Studies. His research interests focus on linguistic landscapes, language access, and sociolinguistics. He has published on linguistic landscapes. His most recent publication is "The linguistic landscape of Muhimbili National Hospital: Its implication to information access in the public space" (2018) in the *Journal of Linguistics and Language in Education*.

Amir Michalovich is a PhD Candidate at the University of British Columbia in the Department of Language and Literacy Education. He completed his MA studies in the Multilingual Education Program at Tel Aviv University, and published the findings of his master's thesis in the journal Linguistic Landscape: "Reframing the linguistic to analyze the landscape: The role of metaphor elicitation for the critical interpretation of multimodal advertising media" (2019). His research interests focus on multimodal composition, participatory video, linguistic landscape, and qualitative data analysis.

Gene Mirus is Associate Professor at Gallaudet University in the Department of ASL and Deaf Studies. As a deaf linguistic anthropologist, he takes interest in understanding how understudied deaf groups take advantage of various linguistic and paralinguistic resources and how they creatively incorporate those resources in their communicative interactions among themselves.

Kerry Mullan is Associate Professor and Convener of Languages at RMIT University in Melbourne. Her main research interests are cross-cultural communication and differing interactional styles, particularly French and Australian English. She has published in the areas of intercultural pragmatics, discourse analysis, language teaching, and conversational humor. Her most recent book is *Studies in Ethnopragmatics, Cultural Semantics, and Intercultural Communication, Volumes 1–3* (2020) with Bert Peeters and Lauren Sadow.

Sarah Naaman is a high school English as a Foreign Language teacher and has been teaching for eight years. She is currently writing her thesis to conclude her MA studies on the topic of "Students' perspectives of classroom pedagogies in EFL classrooms" for the Multilingual Education Program at Tel Aviv University. She is also working as a research assistant for the department on the research project for a new multilingual language policy for Israeli schools. Her research interests include linguistic landscapes and multilingual and translanguaging perspectives of second and foreign language teaching.

Donna Jo Napoli is a professor of linguistics and social justice at Swarthmore College. Her research is primarily on the linguistic analysis of sign languages, as well as on the syntax of spoken languages, sociolinguistics, historical linguistics, bilingual education, and similarities between linguistics and other fields such as yoga and dance. She is on a team that advocates for the language rights of deaf children, through publishing in medical journals. And she codirects a project on e-books for deaf children. In 2019, she (co-)authored twelve journal articles and co-edited one book.

Greg Niedt received a PhD in Communication, Culture, and Media from Drexel University and is currently a lecturer in liberal arts at the Pennsylvania Academy of the Fine Arts (PAFA) in Philadelphia. Greg's research is focused on the manifestation of minority Discourses in the linguistic/semiotic landscape, in particular those involving ethnolinguistic diversity and/or queer identity.

Justin Quam is a PhD candidate in the Department of German at Georgetown University and currently teaches at the St. Paul's Schools in Brooklandville, Maryland.

His dissertation research explores the ways in which learners of German express evaluative meanings in narrative writing.

Corinne A. Seals is a senior lecturer of applied linguistics at Victoria University of Wellington (New Zealand) and director of the Wellington Translanguaging Project and Translanguaging Aotearoa. Her research interests include the linguistic landscapes of mass-scale protests and activist movements, language and identity, heritage language education, translanguaging, and forensic linguistics. Her publications include the books *Embracing Multilingualism across Educational Contexts* (2019) with Vincent Olsen-Reeder, *Choosing a Mother Tongue: The Politics of Language and Identity in Ukraine* (2019), and *Heritage Language Policies around the World* (2017) with Sheena Shah. She was recently awarded a prestigious Royal Society Marsden Fund Fast-Start Grant (2020–2023).

Elana Shohamy is a professor of multilingual education at Tel Aviv University, where she teaches and researches multiple issues in sociolinguistics as they relate to testing and assessment, language policy, immigration, language rights, and linguistic landscapes. She authored *The Power of Tests* (2001), *Language Policy: Hidden Agendas and New Approaches* (2006), and two volumes of *The Encyclopedia of Language and Education* (2009, 2018) as well as numerous chapters and articles on the above topics. Elana is the founder and current editor of the journal *Linguistic Landscape*. In 2010 she was granted the ILTA Lifetime Achievement Award.

Louis Strange is a PhD student in the Department of Linguistics at Queen Mary University of London, funded by the ESRC. He is interested in the intersection of language, national identity, and gender, issues which he looks at from a linguistic landscape perspective. His doctoral project focuses on the recent (and ongoing) debates surrounding the legalization of abortion in Ireland and how questions of national identity and gender surface in signage commenting on or advocating either for or against the liberalization of abortion laws.

Moraia Trijnes is a summa cum laude graduate of the MA at the program of multilingual education at the School of Education, Tel Aviv University. She has been an English as a Foreign Language teacher for the Ministry of Educations since 1994, specializing in learning difficulties, and also counsels English teachers for youth at risk. Her research interests focus on linguistic landscapes and specifically the predicament of the Arab language in Jaffa.

Acknowledgments

We first and foremost thank the authors who put so much thought, time, and critical analysis into their work. We also recognize that having to choose through such meaningful photographs is difficult work, and we appreciate the care you have put into doing so. Additionally, we thank the editorial team at Bloomsbury for taking interest in this work and for supporting all of us to make it a reality. Thanks also go to the grants, organizations, and institutions that have made it possible for many of us to collect the data for these chapters and to have the opportunity to discuss our ideas with each other and with other linguistic landscape scholars. A major thanks also to the many informants (both formal and informal) so many of the authors of this book had along the way, who provided insight, viewpoints, and wonderful conversation to go along with it. Finally, thank you to our friends, families, and networks for your patience and support throughout this journey. This includes the wonderful Elana Shohamy, from whom both editors first learned about linguistic landscapes many years ago at Georgetown University and who has remained a treasured mentor and friend still.

Introduction

Greg Niedt and Corinne A. Seals

In 2017, the biannual International Symposium on Bilingualism (ISB) was held in Limerick, Ireland, with the topic "Bilingualism, Multilingualism, and the New Speaker." Our panel, entitled "Exit through the Language Classroom," in homage to Banksy's 2010 documentary, *Exit through the Gift Shop,* concerned itself with the role of linguistic landscapes (LL) and how the unstructured built environment can provide opportunities to educate those who move through it. The chapters focused especially on language learners in unfamiliar places, such as immigrants and refugees, in light of *new speakers* as a different kind of subject in traditional frameworks of the language shift process (cf. Jaffe, 2015; O'Rourke & Ramallo, 2013). Yet as we developed our chapters and eventually delivered them, this seemed like one piece of an even larger puzzle. Surely, people can learn more from the LL than simply new words in the local languages? And isn't it possible that even long-term residents, speakers who are familiar with the landscape and its particularities, might continue to acquire new insights from their environments? The discussions between ourselves and the other panelists, both at the conference and over dinner the following evening, were the first seeds that led to the development of the present volume.

As a discipline, study of the LL is usually traced back to Spolsky and Cooper's (1991) study of language visibility in Jerusalem and how it reflects sociolinguistic patterns, and to Landry and Bourhis's (1997) analysis of French and English in Montreal as a measure of ethnolinguistic vitality (it is in the latter article that *paysage linguistique* first appeared as a term). The interdisciplinarity of the field is further reflected by LL researchers' incorporation of theories from scholars in geography, sociology, anthropology, philosophy, literature, and elsewhere (e.g., Henri Lefebvre, Yi-Fu Tuan, Mikhail Bakhtin, etc.), who have contributed to deeper understandings of space, place, language, and identity. All of these factors have contributed to developing the key idea that the discourses that define the world around us, and the ones about culture and society that they manifest through their use of language, have a demonstrable impact upon the sense we have of ourselves. Following the ongoing call to "expand the scenery" (Shohamy & Gorter, 2009), the scope of what is included in the definition of a meaningful *landscape* has grown tremendously in the past decade. While individual studies are still often based in cities, given their density of texts and images at the street level, researchers working within the LL paradigm have lately accounted for other kinds of space, and more dynamic constructions of landscape, increasingly often. This volume features several permutations of how an educational space might form and be recognized, and how the teachable moments it conveys differ in their tenor and impact. We present throughout the chapters of this volume these naturalistic, everyday encounters that are the hallmark of LL studies.

Additionally, we are certainly not the first ones to argue for the specifically educational benefits of exploring the LL across a variety of contexts. For example, Brown (2012), Cenoz and Gorter (2014), Gorter (2017), and Seals (forthcoming), among others, have done extensive research on multilingual schoolscapes. Sayer (2010) and Malinowski (2015) have outlined strategies for integrating LL into language learning curricula, and Chesnut, Lee, and Schulte (2013) have challenged LL researchers to specifically consider how learners' unique backgrounds contribute to how they find meaning in the LL projects in their language learning classroom. Also of particular note, Gorter (2017) surveyed published LL research to uncover four key trends in research involving education and LL: (1) schoolscapes, (2) elements of the LL from outside brought into the classroom, (3) the use of LL for EFL teaching, and (4) school trips into the community to examine the LL in an effort to build critical language awareness. These studies, and many more like them, have laid the groundwork for demonstrating the landscape's utility for teachers; our purpose here, however, is to invert things a bit. Rather than thinking about how explorations in the landscape can support a specific pedagogical program, the chapters gathered here discuss how those explorations themselves can be a form of education, often in nontraditional educational settings.

In principle, schools feature several components that individually have much variation, but that are recognizable enough to function as pieces of the whole (e.g., the teacher, the student, the classroom, etc.). Each has a certain idealized purpose: the teacher is there to transmit the information, the student to receive, the classroom to contain (Bourne, 2008). However, as self-contained as the classroom ecosystem may appear to be at one level, it is intimately tied to external ones (Morgan & Martin, 2014), both physically and discursively. Blurring the boundary between the classroom and the world is not our goal; instead, we want to re-conceptualize the streets and neighborhoods and other spaces that make up the LL *as* types of classroom in their own right and as loci for learning of different kinds. Most of all, we are motivated by the unintentional creation of these spaces that occurs whenever a passerby unexpectedly learns something about the world from an element in the landscape. They may become a student every time they pause and look at an unfamiliar artifact, whose producer becomes a momentary teacher. For new speakers, this could simply be a new word or point of grammar, but for speakers of any level, a raised awareness of the sociocultural dynamics happening around them is also a crucial part of learning through observation.

This approach is not intended to denigrate the good-faith efforts of teachers in traditional classrooms, who look for every opportunity to foster a better experience for their students. But aside from the fact that not everyone who learns (or needs to learn) has access to a traditional classroom setting, the whole structure of formal schooling is subject to numerous complications. The ideologies about the "best" way to teach students—who already have highly divergent learning styles—change regularly.

Students, particularly minority students, have identities and roles defined for them in ways that may reflect problematic Discourses and minimize their contributions to the learning environment (Bourne, 2008; Levine, 2013; Seals & Peyton, 2017). Although we do not presume to solve these issues, we believe that they can be eased by supplementary, independent learning from the LL (cf. Chesnut, Lee, & Schulte, 2013), which makes it a worthy topic for research.

Naturally, attending to supplementary education from the LL to support all students' educational experiences requires different outlooks and tools than a research program whose end goal is to re-conceptualize the determined environment of a "proper" school. Rather than calculate the quantifiable impact of the LL on things like grades and testing results, the chapters in this volume deal with the experience itself of learning in and from alternate settings. Interviews, narratives, and ethnographic approaches help to unpack the myriad resonances between a landscape rich with texts and images, and the personal effects on the individuals who move through it. In this sense, our approach here has more in common with Marton's (1981, 1986) phenomenography tradition in education studies, where the goal is not to record "statements about the world as such, but about people's conceptions of the world" (1986: 32). When the world in question is limited to a (geographically or abstractly) bounded space, and the conceptions are limited to those that arise from interactions with the unfamiliar object—that which can teach something to the onlooker—we find as many possible examples as there are people, multiplied by the number of semiotically rich locations available to them.

To unsee the specific boundary between a school and the outside world requires an open mind and a certain flexibility to where such a space begins and ends. The typical schoolscape consists of recognizable objects—desks, chalkboards, perhaps posters, or other visual aids on the walls—and the defining teacher/student relationship. Understanding the form and placement of these signifiers is perhaps more important than the textual content that they complement, forming a *semiotic* landscape more than a purely linguistic one (Jaworski & Thurlow, 2010). It is difficult to break down these assumptions about where and how learning should take place. But the polysemy of a landscape means that where some observers may see merely a wall of graffiti, others learn the social structure of a particular local street culture. Architecture and the condition of buildings teach something of a neighborhood's historical and economic position; political signage and propaganda attempt a more nefarious kind of education. So many of the impressions these aggregated signs create rely on how well we understand the discourses they represent and how they are "meant" to be read (Scollon & Scollon, 2003)—and in turn, how we choose to interpret them.

As with other work in the discipline, we want to further situate this volume's case studies in relation to identity, politics, and social justice. It is impossible to read a sign in the landscape without being keenly aware of your own subjectivity in relation to it (and if it is illegible, you are still positioned as an outsider with respect to whoever produced it). An encounter with an individual sign may not have a lasting impact on the viewer, but over time, and given enough signs, a geodiscursive identity begins to form that the individual may embody while in that landscape. One could argue that even learning something unpleasant is a net positive, as it is still knowledge gained, but when the result is a feeling of alienation, ostracism, or prejudice, it leads to the "symbolic violence" that Bourdieu (1991) speaks of as a more accepted stand-in for other forms of violence. An education about who holds power and who does not, who is "acceptable" and who is not, is made manifest in the form and content of signs within the bounds of a given landscape. This fact underlies discussions of how the LL can facilitate both positive and negative identity formation in a space (cf. Blackwood, Lanza, & Woldemariam, 2016) but also enables us to critique its mechanics and the psychic impact they have on those who move through them. We do not always ask to become students of the things that LLs have to teach us; nevertheless, their information is impressed upon us, so we might as well do our best to comprehend it.

Through this lens, we begin in the classroom and exit through it.

Structure of the Book

The arrangement of this volume is intended to lead the reader from more standardized (though still fairly nontraditional) educational spaces to those that provide specific knowledge in specific circumstances. Of course, all of the contributors' offerings cross and connect with other landscapes, other forms of teaching and learning, and other ways of conceptualizing language. The focus on landscape allows us to narrow down such a massive topic to one set of effects that can be grasped: the interaction of speakers with texts and how they variously manage it.

Part One of the book is dedicated to landscapes that are structured for the purposive goal of teaching something to their occupants, or that have been re-purposed to this end, placed within a formal pedagogical discourse. We begin with Quam and Hamilton's examination of a German-language summer camp in Minnesota. They discuss the typology and distribution of texts around the space ranging from the functional to the playful, and how they serve the broader purpose of immersing residents in an experience meant to feel as authentic as possible. Importantly, they consider not only each sign in isolation but the cumulative multilingual impact of the diverse range of signs in toto. The chapter posits that in addition to conveying new vocabulary, the camp's signage offers connections to German culture and history, providing a subtextual layer to the education taking place. Regardless of the fact that this linkage takes place in a somewhat artificial environment, with key differences from the organically created environment of an "actual" study abroad program, it conveys the idea that learning these aspects of the landscape is an invaluable part of the process.

In their contribution, Fisher, Mirus, and Napoli discuss some of the representations of American Sign Language (ASL) in the landscape of Gallaudet University, an institution in Washington, DC, that primarily serves a deaf student body. Their study moves outside the classroom to the passageways and gathering places of the campus and compares the representations of ASL visible there, on paper and video screen alike, to examples found elsewhere (such as ASL alphabet cards). Providing this sociohistorical context emphasizes the inequality in the built environment between dominant languages with a written tradition and the minority languages they subsume. Given that ASL is often textually rendered into English—despite its rather different grammar and status as a language in its own right—the authors' focus on handshapes, photos and videos, and other more direct forms of representations is a necessary expansion of LL studies.

This section is concluded by de Saint Léger and Mullan's chapter on a two-week Australian study abroad program in New Caledonia, a French territory in Polynesia. In some ways, this chapter is a mirror image of the first: a lived-in, diverse landscape perceived through the lens of the students who occupy it. While the linguistic benefit for students is clear from the presence of French and Kanak, the authors point out that the trip's main focus is the recent social and political changes in the territory, particularly a postcolonial awakening that has taken place. The LL becomes a tool to expose the stances of members of the community, raising the awareness of privileged visitors with respect to their neighbors. The authors focus on the blurry boundary between linguistic and semiotic, including not only textual signage in their analysis but also artifacts like flags and architecture that are loaded with meaning, as well as the layout of spaces themselves. Their data are drawn primarily from students' observational journals, giving an ethnographic angle to the work that directly shows the significant educational impact this kind of program can have.

In Part Two, we proceed through a series of spaces that are as structured (or in some cases, even more so) by institutional authority as formal schools but are not primarily intended for educational purposes. In Mdukula's chapter, he turns the reader's attention to the composition of linguistic landscapes in public health institutions in Tanzania. He characterizes the nation as triglossic, with English, Swahili, and local languages interacting in a complex arrangement, plus the recent influx of Chinese due to foreign investment. The LL reflects this situation and the power dynamics involved. The examples presented come from hospitals around the country and illustrate three divisions in the production and consumption of texts. There are medical vs. nonmedical signs in a medicalized space; signs that present information and signs that are merely directive, which teach the reader norms of behavior; and signs produced from official figures positioned against those that are more bottom-up. Mdukula moves through different configurations of these dichotomies as he presents numerous examples of text, each of which has something to instruct hospital visitors, even if it is as simple as who has the authority to say what, to whom, and in which language(s).

This is followed by Cunningham and King's exploration of informative landscapes in the international airports of New Zealand, particularly focusing on Christchurch. As places that mix the infrastructural with the touristic, where the violation of established norms can have serious legal consequences, airports provide many opportunities to expose the interaction of political and commercial interests with high discursive weight. Here we see the question extend from *what* and *how* the relevant groups (e.g., government, marketing boards, airlines themselves) are trying to teach passersby, to *why* they are doing so. From a practical standpoint, the movement and management of bodies is the airport's primary concern, but the authors point out the recent rebranding of airports as destinations in their own right. Their examples illustrate how the Indigenous Māori language is appropriated for touristic purposes rather than used for practical ones. A visitor to New Zealand thus gains a perception of language use that may or may not resemble the sociolinguistic reality, depending on where they travel within the country.

We continue with Kırkgöz's chapter on English teaching strategies pursued in a Turkish textile factory, where the organizers rely on simple signage scattered around the workplace to supplement formal lessons. As many researchers have pointed out (cf. Cook, 2014; Scollon & Scollon, 2003), the design and material used to create signage often play a part in how they are interpreted. The paper printouts with individual words and pictures serve to reinforce basic, occupational vocabulary (such as the names of textiles and parts of clothing) for the workers, along with simple phrases. Yet the low production value and low student participation in the creation of the LL raise the question, how helpful are these signs to the learning process? Kırkgöz combines her survey of the signs with interviews that gather the workers' opinions; many of them express appreciation for the additions to their work environment but seem unsure about their impact. The chapter situates the research within the pedagogical paradigm of peripheral learning and asks whether this method is effective.

Finally, this section closes with Loester's chapter on a museum space in Southampton, UK, where a recent exhibition highlights the role immigrants have played in the city's development. Even though museums are probably the space closest to the pedagogical context without necessarily being part of it, the author demonstrates how they can more flexibly meet the need for commentary on the ideologies about people, culture, and language that arise from current events (in this case, both the refugee crisis and Brexit). This has not always been the role of the museum, and Loester is careful to lay out the evolution of their landscapes, as well as the Discourses they manifest. As a site of alternative education, two factors in the Southampton case stand out: the framing device of "story boxes" that combine oral histories with objects and the social, interactive nature of the space. Like the New Caledonia chapter, the semiotic is at least as important as the linguistic here, if not more so, yet the purposefully constructed exhibit develops in the viewer a visual language that enables them to read and comprehend the different stories in an engaging, personal way.

Part Three moves away from structured sites and refocuses on educational artifacts and moments scattered through mixed-purpose landscapes. In particular, these studies highlight attempts by small organizations and groups, as well as individuals, to explore issues of equality and social justice in the everyday cityscape. Chen describes "story houses" in Taiwan, constructed and put forward into the landscape by Indigenous Paiwan and Budai Rukai peoples. After being resettled into Chinese-speaking communities after natural disasters, some of these groups elected to build the houses as a way of preserving their traditions and educating others about them. The builders seek to actively tell stories through the material, arrangement, and naming of these houses. In the author's study, the houses in question make use of multilingual written texts, oral explanations from tour guides, murals, and the architecture itself to create an alternate cultural system, embedded within the community. Even the organization of space reflects the Indigenous discourses of what a house and its functions are, which may differ significantly from that of their neighbors or international visitors. Most of the cases presented here echo the existing sociolinguistic situation in their area; Chen's chapter provides an example of an attempt to save a threatened way of life by teaching it to others.

Our chapter on political and activist signage in two European cities (Lviv, Ukraine, and Göttingen, Germany) continues this section, with attention to the multimodal use of graffiti, stickers, and other types of media to convey messages to the public. The discursive meanings of the signs' content, form, and placement are contextualized by the historical and political situations of each city. We perform a deep analysis of selected cases to unpack how the casual observer might regard this messaging and illustrate how it resembles bottom-up alterations to the landscape elsewhere in the world. Aside from any active language learning facilitated by the LL, these signs reveal the dynamic social fabric through the careful deployment of text and image. The content does not pretend to be unbiased in the same way a standard language classroom's curriculum does but instead displays the social dynamics that take place under an otherwise innocuous and static landscape.

Following this theme, Strange's contribution looks at political messaging surrounding the recent repeal of the Eighth Amendment banning abortion in the Republic of Ireland. The flyers, billboards, and other media that make up the author's dataset are loaded with ideology, given the sensitive nature of their topic. Therefore, the chapter uses epistemic and affective stance as a framework to discuss how the education taking place between sign producer and sign consumer happens along two dimensions: conveyance of information and appeal to emotions. Regardless of any given sign's intention, they had the combined effect of opening a conversation on a subject taboo in Ireland. The visual data are supplemented by interviews with creators and readers from both sides of the debate, showing that the strategies used cut across the ideological spectrum (and at times veer rather close to the tactics used for propaganda). Aside from the content of the signs, Strange also discusses the multimodality of their form; the incidental education that takes place upon the encounter with a text is facilitated by a pop of color or a certain positioning in the landscape.

We close our volume with a methodological chapter by Michalovich, Naaman, Trijnes, Agbaria, and Shohamy, centered on a walking tour of Jaffa. As this area has been slowly integrated into the modern city of Tel Aviv, the long-standing Arab presence and its manifestation in the landscape have been eroded due to politics and demographic changes. The authors focus on one multilingual commercial street in the neighborhood, moving in and out of shops to speak with owners and noting the disappearance of Arabic on publicly visible texts. Like some of the other chapters, this one draws its data from field notes, but importantly, the participants in data collection worked as a group, interacting with each other as much as with residents of the space. It is this dynamic that lies at the heart of the methodology that the authors craft and define in terms of several qualities that add nuance to the experience of moving through the landscape. With their assertion that this kind of mobile activity can provide a useful framework for educating students—or indeed, anyone—about the sociolinguistic situation and potential injustices of a given place, we come full circle, returning to the language classroom armed with what has been learned out in the world.

Overall, we hope these chapters provide you, the reader, with examples that resonate with your own experience and process of education, in a formal context or otherwise, as a student, teacher, or both. We must also note that no one book could contain the full breadth of any one case study, let alone eleven, particularly for researchers in the LL discipline who are so fond of photographing and analyzing every piece of the puzzle they can. To this end, we provide a companion site online (www.bloomsbury.com/linguistic-landscapes-beyond-the-language-classroom) where we have added additional photos from the studies to elaborate on the work that has been done here. Our gratitude goes out to the authors for their contributions, and we ourselves have learned a lot through the process of reading them. With that, we leave you to explore at your own pace, in the hopes that you too will come away from this book (dare we call it a portable LL?) feeling that you have gained something, too.

References

Blackwood, R., Lanza, E., & Woldemariam, H. (Eds.). (2016). *Negotiating and Contesting Identities in Linguistic Landscapes*. London: Bloomsbury.

Bourdieu, P. (1991). *Language and Symbolic Power*. Cambridge, MA: Harvard University Press.

Bourne, J. (2008). Official pedagogic discourses and the construction of learners' identities. In M. Martin-Jones, A. M. de Mejia, & N. H. Hornberger (Eds.), *Encyclopedia of Language and Education. Vol. 3: Discourse and Education* (pp. 41–52). New York: Springer.

Brown, K. D. (2012). The linguistic landscape of educational spaces: Language revitalization and schools in southeastern Estonia. In D. Gorter, H. F. Marten, & L. Van Mensel (Eds.), *Minority Languages in the Linguistic Landscape* (pp. 281–98). Basingstroke: Palgrave-Macmillan.

Cenoz, J., & Gorter, D. (2014). Linguistic landscapes in multilingual schools. In B. Spolsky, O. Inbar-Lourie, & M. Tannenbaum (Eds.), *Challenges for Language Education and Policy* (pp. 239–54). New York: Routledge.

Chesnut, M., Lee, V., & Schulte, J. (2013). The language lessons around us: Undergraduate English pedagogy and linguistic landscape research. *English Teaching*, 12(2), 102–20.

Cook, V. (2014). Meaning and material in the language of the street. *Social Semiotics*, 25(1), 81–109.

Gorter, D. (2017). Linguistic landscapes and trends in the study of schoolscapes. *Linguistics and Education*, 44, 80–5.

Jaffe, A. (2015). Defining the new speaker: Theoretical perspectives and learner trajectories. *International Journal of the Sociology of Language*, 231, 21–44.

Jaworski, A., & Thurlow, C. (2010). Introducing semiotic landscapes. In A. Jaworski, & C. Thurlow (Eds.), *Semiotic Landscapes: Language, Image, Space* (pp. 1–40). London: Continuum.

Landry, R., & Bourhis, R. Y. (1997). Linguistic landscape and ethnolinguistic vitality: An empirical study. *Journal of Language and Social Psychology*, 16(1), 23–49.

Levine, G. S. (2013). The case for a multilingual approach to language classroom communication. *Language and Linguistics Compass*, 7(8), 423–36.

Malinowski, D. (2015) Opening spaces of learning in the linguistic landscape. *Linguistic Landscape*, 1(1–2), 95–113.

Marton, F. (1981). Phenomenography—describing conceptions of the world around us. *Instructional Science*, 10(2), 177–200.

Marton, F. (1986). Phenomenography—a research approach to investigating different understandings of reality. *Journal of Thought*, 21(3), 28–49.

Morgan, B., & Martin, I. (2014). Towards a research agenda for classroom-as-ecosystem. *Modern Language Journal*, 98(2), 667–70.

O'Rourke, B., & Ramallo, F. (2013) Competing ideologies of linguistic authority amongst new speakers in contemporary Galicia. *Language in Society*, 42(3), 287–305.

Sayer, P. (2010). Using the linguistic landscape as a pedagogical resource. *ELT Journal*, 64(2), 143–54.

Scollon, R., & Scollon, S. W. (2003). *Discourses in Place: Language in the Material World*. London: Routledge.

Seals, C. A. (forthcoming). Classroom translanguaging through the linguistic landscape. In D. Malinowski, H. Maxim, & S. Dubreil (Eds.), *Language Teaching in the Linguistic Landscape: Mobilizing Pedagogy in Public Space*. Springer.

Seals, C. A., & Peyton, J. K. (2017). Heritage language education: Valuing the languages, literacies, and cultural competencies of immigrant youth. *Current Issues in Language Planning*, 18(1), 87–101.

Shohamy, E., & Gorter, D. (2009). Introduction. In E. Shohamy, & D. Gorter, *Linguistic Landscape: Expanding the Scenery* (pp. 1–10). New York: Routledge.

Spolsky, B., & Cooper, R. L. (1991). *The Languages of Jerusalem*. Oxford: Oxford University Press.

Part One

Other Forms of Language Classroom

1

From Part of the Scenery to Curricular Resources: Authentic Signs as Portals to Cultural Practices within a Residential German Language Immersion Program

Justin Quam and Heidi E. Hamilton

Introduction

Traveling along *Hauptstraße* into the small village of *Waldsee*, visitors drive by many signs: one directs drivers to watch out for children at play (*Achtung! Spielende Kinder*) on the adjacent soccer field; another warns of the possibility that toads might be crossing the road (*Vorsicht! Krötenwanderung*) within the surrounding nature preserve (*Naturschutzgebiet*). Turning right onto *Ruppstraße*, one passes by the official town sign, just before coming to an indication that one needs to stop to clear customs (*Zoll/Douane*). Guided by a one-way street (*Einbahnstrasse*) sign, one arrives at a parking lot marked by signs that demarcate reserved parking spots (*Privatparkplatz*) from those available to employees (*Mitarbeiter*), visitors (*nur für Besucher*), and to those planning to stay only a short time (*Kurzparkzone*).

    Exiting the car, one's eye is captured by the assortment of signs on the nearby soccer field, one simply labeling the area (*Fußballplatz*); others in the form of large colorful posters displaying grammatical rules and sample sentences that demarcate the soccer field as a "language area" (*Sprachzone Fußballplatz*); and still others in the form of hand-painted signposts (see Figure 1.1) that contain questions related to soccer, such as "What is the score?" (*Wie ist der Spielstand?*) and "How long have you been playing soccer?" (*Wie lange spielst du schon Fußball?*). Turning back across the parking lot toward a large official-looking building, one notices a large number of signs in close proximity, indicating a bus stop (*Autobus*); giving directions to *Erlach* and *Jolimont-Gampelen*; providing the name of the dedicatee of the building's clock tower (*Albert Hohmann Turmuhr*) (see the website for Figure 1.2: *Bahnhof* from *Parkplatz*); listing pick-up times for letters dropped into a yellow mailbox (*Briefkastenleerung*); declaring "You are leaving the American sector" in four languages (English, Russian, French, and German); and announcing "All are welcome here" (*Alle sind hier herzlich willkommen*) on rainbow-colored paper, among many others.

14   *Linguistic Landscapes Beyond the Language Classroom*

Figure 1.1 Photo of question signs along the road leading to the *Bahnhof* building

This highly unusual collection of signs indexing disparate times and places comprises a segment of the linguistic landscape (LL) of *Waldsee*, the sixty-year-old[1] German language and cultural immersion program of Concordia Language Villages located in the wooded lake country of northern Minnesota (USA). Consisting of thirty-five buildings spread across 46 acres of land, *Waldsee* emulates a full-fledged village, as well as being accredited both as a residential summer camp (through the American Camping Association) and as an educational institution (through accrediting agency AdvancEd) at the elementary and secondary levels. *Waldsee* shares with all fourteen[2] Language Village programs the mission of "inspir[ing] courageous global citizens"; in the service of this mission, *Waldsee* provides its participants with a wide range of opportunities to learn and practice German; to directly experience cultural practices and products of German-speaking Europe; and to explore issues of relevance to the world at large, such as the environment, war/peace, justice, literacy, health, and human rights.

Waldsee's focus on living life in the target language within a village outside the classroom might remind some readers of the "language learning in the wild" initiative by Johannes Wagner and colleagues (Clark et al., 2011); in that program, adult migrant learners in Nordic countries are encouraged to navigate the disconnect between the content of classroom instruction and the requirements of everyday communicative needs by engaging with employees of cafés and other nearby small businesses who have been specially sensitized to the linguistic and cultural needs of these learners. In contrast to the *actual* neighborhoods that surround the classrooms of these learners, the village of *Waldsee* was intentionally designed and built as a village that could serve as a decentralized learning environment for its residents. It is the role of physical signs within this constructed village that centers our attention in this chapter.

Given the complexity associated with this hybrid community, we were guided most profoundly by the perspective of historically informed deep ethnography as articulated and illustrated by Blommaert (2013) and Scollon and Scollon (2003). Following this approach, we aim to exemplify how linguistic landscape research may provide a concrete way to understand abstract philosophies that underlie decentralized language education, i.e., to help us discern order out of the "genuine jungle of signs" (Ben-Rafael, Shohamy, & Barni, 2010: xv). Because *Waldsee* is neither an actual German village nor a traditional school, our resulting study of its linguistic landscape displays characteristics of both "cityscape" (Aiestaran, Cenoz & Gorter, 2010; Gorter, 2006) and "schoolscape" (e.g., Dressler, 2015; Gorter, 2018; Joselit, 2019; Savela, 2018) research.

Using both quantitative and qualitative methods, we identify and examine patterns and semiotic processes related to the 722 physical signs visible within the public areas of *Waldsee* to illuminate how these signs function to constitute this highly unusual community of practice. In what follows, we situate our work in relation to previous research; characterize the sociolinguistic context of the *Waldsee* German Language Village; and describe our decisions regarding the demarcation of our research area, our definition of "sign," and our cataloguing practices. We then report on our three-tiered analysis: first, we provide an inventory with quantitative details related to the signs' languages, locations, and functions; next, we characterize the overlapping discourses that form what Scollon and Scollon (2003: 168) call the "semiotic aggregate" of the scaffolded "playworld" (Hamilton & Cohen, 2004) for *Waldsee*'s learners; and finally, we illuminate "in-place meanings of signs and discourses, and the meanings of our actions in and among those discourses in place" (Scollon & Scollon, 2003: 1) through a focus on two specific (types of) imported signs. By integrating insights from foundational work on intertextuality[3] (Bakhtin, 1986; Bauman & Briggs, 1990; Blommaert, 2013), we illustrate in these case studies how accessible, authentic texts in the village "scenery" (Paesani, 2018) can be seen as portals to understanding cultural practices and geopolitical-historical events.[4] We then close by considering how the language learning opportunities promoted by these signs are connected to the World Readiness Standards (the 5 C's) developed by the American Council on the Teaching of Foreign Languages (The National Standards Collaborative Board, 2015) and reflect on the implications of this study for language teachers who feature authentic signs in their own classrooms.

Background

Authentic signs (e.g., public street signs, advertising signs, commercial shop signs) have been examined over the past two decades by LL researchers in an effort to understand "what languages are prominent and valued in public and private spaces" along with the "social positioning of people who identify with particular languages" within these communities (Dagenais et al., 2009: 254). From the related perspective of geosemiotics (Scollon & Scollon, 2003: 3), any such "material object that indicates or refers to something other than itself" represents a point in time and space along a chain of discourses and actions (e.g., the discussions among communities and legislatures that lead to the design, production, and placement of an official notice) and affects future social actions undertaken "in and among those discourses in place" (Scollon & Scollon, 2003: 1). Given the light they shed on "societies, people, the economy, policy, class, identities" (Shohamy & Gorter, 2009: 2–3) and because "[s]igns lead us to practices, and practices lead us to people" (Blommaert 2013: 5), these small authentic texts can serve both as sources of insight for researchers striving to better understand a community and as highly productive sites of engagement for learners outside traditional classrooms (Malinowski, 2010, 2015, 2018).

The emphases of LL research have evolved as studies shift in focus from the relative prominence and value of certain languages to a broader investigation of signs as indexing the nature and change of community practices. Backhaus (2007) used a highly quantitative approach calculating the relative prominence of languages on signs to draw conclusions about language use and perceived value within an urban neighborhood; more recent studies have followed Blommaert (2013), who studied historical developments and people–sign interactions in order to "understand … how [signs] can inform us about social structure" (p. 55). Within this broader trend of a greater reliance on qualitative inquiry, LL studies have tended to expand the scope of the (a) items and (b) geographic areas under investigation, while differing in terms of (c) the role of interactions between and across signs and people; (d) signs' potential functions; (e) whether the LL in question is described as a snapshot in time or traced across a continuum in space *and* time; and (f) the degree of familiarity of the researcher to the landscape being examined, among other factors.

Early LL research typically restricted its focus to outdoor municipal and business signs in public spaces (Landry & Bourhis, 1997). Early studies also focused on urban spaces that were accessible to the public; most of these counted only outdoor signs, although some (e.g., Ben–Rafael et al. 2006; Shohamy et al., 2010) included public-facing signs visible inside public buildings. For feasibility's sake, researchers on urban linguistic landscapes typically counted all signs within an arbitrarily chosen geographic region. Blommaert (2013), remaining within the context of urban research, defined signs based on their purpose and accessibility rather than their location, expanding his scope to "publicly visible bits of written language: billboards, road and safety signs, shop signs, graffiti and all sorts of other inscriptions in the public space, both professional produced and grassroots" (p. 1). Later studies, including those of indoor "schoolscapes," moved more intentionally inside buildings to include classroom and hallway signs that constitute students' learning environments (Gorter & Cenoz, 2015; Pakarinen & Björklund, 2018; Savela, 2018).

All LL studies of which we are aware introduce qualitative distinctions of some kind among signs. Even Backhaus's (2007) early highly quantitative inventory not only noted the language of each sign but also considered its manufacturer, installer, and intended audience, as well as implications for a neighborhood's development that could be inferred from the sign. Later LL studies moved beyond categorizing the language of given signs to include function and authorship (Gorter & Cenoz, 2015).

A central insight of more qualitative LL research holds that signs participate in dialogue with each other and with their audiences; in interpreting a sign, a reader draws not only on the text of the sign itself but on their experience with other such signs and on shared cultural understandings that govern the interpretation of public texts, a key connection to the intertextual perspective referenced above. Bringing humans as sign-interpreters into LL research helps us to move beyond simple facts related to the intersection of languages and placement of signs. As exemplified by Cenoz and Gorter (2008), signs have a host of potential functions: "Street signs function to identify a place by name, placards inform the reader of the significance of the objects to which they are attached, graffiti are examples of transgressive discourse and other signs give indications to regulate actions and movements" (pp. 275–6). They may label the spaces in which they are installed or mandate, regulate, or encourage behavior among their readership (Dressler, 2015; Gorter & Cenoz, 2015). Signs in educational spaces are often didactic in nature (Hanauer, 2009). Even signs that appear fairly straightforward—e.g., place names, labels, opening hours—may also have symbolic functions. The very presence or relative prominence of a particular language (especially a minority language) can imply the relative value placed on that language by the local community (Cenoz & Gorter, 2008; Landry & Bourhis, 1997).

LL research today continues to explore the explanatory potential of signs broadly defined (including a greater range of mobile and mutable texts), and many LL researchers have called for an expansion of the field into additional sites of interaction (Van Mensel et al., 2016), particularly in educational contexts (Dagenais et al., 2009). In this study, we apply the LL lens to a new context and explore the value of the ethnographic approach favored by more recent research.

Methods

In what follows, we characterize *Waldsee* more fully, describe how we delineated our geographic research space, provide our definition of a "sign," and characterize the process we undertook as participant-observers over the course of six weeks at *Waldsee*.

Sociolinguistic Context: *Waldsee* German Language Village

Waldsee's thirty-five buildings and additional outside spaces (including sports fields, outdoor cafés, parks, nature trails, campfire circles, outdoor stages, and beach) spread across a 46-acre tract of land on a lake in northern Minnesota (USA) (see the website for Figure 1.3: Aerial map of *Waldsee*). From the moment the learners arrive on the first day, they acquire a new "identity" that they will be enacting as they "live the language." They arrive at the border of the "new" country, show their "passports," and go through customs. They choose a new name, find the new "city" (cabin) they will be living in, and open a bank account; they are surrounded by German language, music, and signs.

The physical setting and the participants come together to create a kaleidoscopic *playworld* (Hamilton & Cohen, 2004) that nourishes a wide range of learning activities through which learners can learn and use the target language in situationally appropriate ways, ranging from dealing with a problem in the store to representing a political party's views during a debate. Villagers interact with a range of different villagers and instructors throughout the day's events—whether during wake-up routines in their cabins, breakfast with different groups of friends, large-group singing sessions, small language groups, soccer games, stained glass-making activities, nature hikes, and collaborating to write for the village blog. At any given time at *Waldsee*, there are approximately 180 learners and 60 counselors/instructors on site, and they engage with each other in a range of combinations for a variety of purposes within the *playworld* environment.

Some readers may notice a possible paradox in this characterization: as part of the construction of a *playworld*, we highlight the importance of authentic objects and surroundings as well as participants' authentic practices related to real-world, needs-based communication. This paradox can be resolved if one keeps in mind the following point: the *playworld* is the dominant conceptual frame; in its service, authentic materials (including physical signs) are useful to participants as they try out authentic (real-world) communicative practices (and try on new identities, as Bruner [1990] suggests) within that world. It should also be clear from previous and subsequent descriptions of village activities that *Waldsee*'s goal is *not* to recreate everyday life in a German-speaking village. Each day offers any given resident a broader range of activities than most individuals undertake in a "normal" day, since the participant can select from among options related to the worlds of camp, school, and/or life abroad (for additional information, see Hamilton, Crane, & Bartoshesky, 2005).

Geographic Area Explored

Given the hybrid nature of the *Waldsee* environment, we followed practices of both urban landscape and schoolscape investigators in designating the physical dimensions of our research area. Following most studies within urban areas, we included signs displayed outside as well as any that would be visible (e.g., through windows and doors) to an observer standing outside (i.e., in Blommaert's [2013] terms, all signs that were "publicly available from the sidewalk" [p. 62]). In keeping with schoolscape studies (e.g., Savela, 2018), we also inventoried signs displayed inside buildings that we consider public spaces (e.g., that are used by all or most residents and are open to visitors, such as the dining hall, the health office, and the stores, in contrast to spaces that are used by only a subset of residents [i.e., classrooms and residential cabins]). Given *Waldsee*'s relatively modest geographic size in contrast to cities at the center of many LL studies, we had no need to sample an arbitrarily selected subsection of the environment and were able to count every sign in public view.

Defining What Counts as a "Sign"

With limited exceptions (e.g., Scollon & Scollon, 2003), the earliest LL studies adopted a somewhat restricted definition of what constitutes a sign, typically counting texts produced by municipal or commercial actors (Landry & Bourhis, 1997) and excluding "items without text, such as pictures, emblems, logos, and pictograms" (Backhaus, 2007: 66). Later studies expanded the scope to include less permanent fixtures; Itagi and Singh (2002) included newspapers, visiting cards, and other print media in their study, and Savela (2018) suggests an even more expansive definition of signs that would include text displayed on T-shirts, walls (e.g., graffiti), and skin (e.g., tattoos).

Given our specific motivation to understand the decentralized nature of education as practiced within the *Waldsee* village, we decided to catalogue every instance of a discrete handwritten or printed text that had been installed (more or less permanently) or posted (more or less temporarily) in public spaces. We included signs that featured nonlinguistic symbols/icons as well as language (e.g., pedestrian-only signs that showed images of people walking), since many of these signs were produced in German-speaking countries and had been specifically procured, shipped, and installed on the *Waldsee* site to enhance the *playworld* environment there. We also expanded our scope to include movable signs if those signs typically remained in one place on the site (e.g., labels on wheeled recycling bins that were regularly stationed outside certain buildings). To make it feasible to inventory the entire linguistic landscape, we excluded highly movable signs in the form of residents' name badges (though other research has investigated this topic; see, e.g., Hanson, 2012) or Euro coins, as well as signs that were installed or written on the floor or ground.

Cataloguing of Signs

In line with Blommaert's (2013) call for "slow ethnographic monitoring" vs. "hit-and-run ethnography" within LL research, we used our "longitudinal exposure and presence" (p. 114) as long-term summer residents of *Waldsee* to inform our examination of its linguistic landscape. We have participated in the *Waldsee* community for decades (first author twenty-two years; second author forty-seven years) in a variety of roles, beginning as child learners and working later as counselors, language instructors, and program directors. Over a six-week period during July and August 2019, we canvassed the site multiple times individually and together, photographing every sign that was visible from a public space as characterized above, and using our background knowledge as a guide to categorize each sign. Following Dressler (2015), who claims that "sign-making practices can be better understood by seeking out the sign makers or those who understand their decision-making" (p. 131), we took an extensive tour around all public areas of *Waldsee* with the camp director, a longtime staff member and former camp participant who has directed the camp since 1981.

As we added each sign to our inventory, we noted information related to its history, including who had made the decision to procure or produce it, who had installed it, and why. These discussions allowed us to maintain an awareness of the role of each sign in relation to shifts in the linguistic landscape over time. We then noted the language of each sign (German, English, bilingual German and English, languages other than German and English, or symbol/icon only) and finally assigned each sign a primary function.[5] We generated our list of functions through an iterative process; we assigned each sign a preliminary function or functions as we added it to the inventory and then combined or eliminated overlapping or marginal functions as category boundaries emerged. We identified the following functions as most relevant to the *Waldsee* linguistic landscape (photos of each of the example signs listed below can be viewed in the online photo gallery):

Labeling: Signs identifying/naming the space they index (e.g., a sign reading *Fußballplatz* [soccer field] at the edge of the soccer field; see website for Figure 1.4: recycling bins and Figure 1.5: drawer labels).

Informing: Signs that provide information about a particular space or appliance (see website for Figure 1.6: a sign on the door of the health center reading *Wo sind die Krankenschwestern?* [Where are the nurses?] and listing times of day when they can be found; and Figure 1.7: price labels in the camp store).

Directing: Signs that mandate, encourage, regulate, or forbid certain behavior (e.g., *Schuhe bitte HIER lassen* [Please leave shoes HERE] in the front entry of a public building; see website for Figure 1.8: *ZIEHEN* [PULL] on a door handle and Figure 1.9: a warning sign near the door to the sauna).

Indexing community: Signs installed to invoke the feeling of membership in a broader community, including the nexus of *Waldsee*'s summer participants, alumni, and donors; Concordia Language Villages as a whole; and German speakers worldwide (see website for Figure 1.10: *Albert Hohmann Turmuhr: In Anerkennung der vielen Beträge der Familie Hohmann, Waldsee, Juni 1986* [Albert Hohmann Clock Tower: In recognition of the many contributions of the Hohmann family, *Waldsee*, June 1986] and Figure 1.11: a villager-created poster encouraging fellow students to pick up trash).

Decorating: Signs that decorate public spaces (see website for Figure 1.12: panels adorning a central stone fountain painted by villagers as part of an elective course and Figure 1.13: photos of "word art" purchased in Germany).

Teaching: Signs used as reference material in order to support residents in successfully navigating an interaction in their second language (see website for

Figure 1.14: a sign reading *Wieviel kostet ... ?* [How much does ... cost?] that hangs above one of two cash registers in the café, Figures 1.15 and 1.16: signs in the dining listing example phrases for requesting food, and Figure 1.17: signposts featuring questions of the day that underpin the *Waldsee* curriculum).

Lending an air of cultural authenticity: Signs produced in German-speaking countries (realia) that were intentionally purchased, imported, and installed to enhance residents' impression of inhabiting a German village (see website for Figure 1.18: a sign on an official yellow German mailbox reading *Eilsendungen bitte bei den Postämtern einliefern* [Please send out urgent mailings at the post office], Figure 1.19: a parking sign reading *Nur für Besucher* [Visitors only], and Figure 1.20: a bus stop sign).

For the purposes of this study, we designated a single primary function for each sign. This process can be subjective; some signs can be construed as fulfilling multiple functions depending on the situation. Indeed, the function of any sign may vary depending on the individual viewing it; to illustrate, Cenoz and Gorter (2008) characterize a sign in Spain's Basque country that lists fish names in both Spanish and Basque. They point out that, although the basic function of the sign is to provide information, for a learner of Basque the text could also provide a learning opportunity. We drew on our experience participating in the *Waldsee* community in order to assign each sign's primary function, based on our understanding of how readers typically engage with these signs.

The Sign Inventory

As indicated in Table 1.1, as a result of our sign cataloguing process, we identified 722 public-oriented signs on the *Waldsee* site, 221 (30.6 percent) that were visible outdoors and 503 (69.7 percent) that were visible within the indoor public spaces. Of these, 74 percent contained text in German only (with or without an associated image); 12 percent contained text in English only; 6 percent contained a mix of German and English; 7 percent contained only symbols/icons; and less than 1 percent contained languages other than German or English. The ratio of German to English signs outdoors (6.61:1) and indoors (5.89:1) is relatively stable, indicating the villagers can interact with signs displaying the same relative frequency of their first and second languages, no matter where they go within the village.

When conducting LL research, it can be tempting to draw conclusions based on the numbers/percentages of signs featuring a particular language found in a given area. Such raw quantitative analyses, however, can obscure the fact that "signs occur in non-random ways in public space" (Blommaert, 2013: 41) and participate in different discourses. Based on our ethnographic perspective, we know that many of the English signs are intended to be used by members of the maintenance staff who, as nonresidents, do not participate in the daily programming (e.g., our inventory includes outdoor signs warning of hazardous voltage and buried cables, as well as indoor labels with instructions on operating air conditioners and thermostats). Several English signs relate to health and safety regulations (e.g., red exit signs, fire extinguisher instructions) and would remain in the background for most participants in most situations; treating these signs in the same way as signs used by residents would undoubtedly lead to misinformed conclusions. With the goal of "making the move from counting languages to understanding how they can inform us about social structure" (Blommaert 2013: 55), we shifted our focus to understanding the relationship between each sign's language and its primary function as a critical next step.

We therefore considered the language of each sign not in isolation, but in combination with the signs' primary function. As shown in Table 1.1, German appears on the majority of signs irrespective of function (with the exception of informing signs), but certain functional categories include a higher proportion of German than others. The overwhelming majority of teaching signs feature German (99.23 percent), as one might expect from signs installed in order to foster language acquisition. German is only slightly less ubiquitous on signs promoting community (92.03 percent); some of these signs include English-language dedications to English-speaking donors. On the lower end of the continuum, only 46.51 percent of directing signs contain only German, while 36.05 percent feature English; as we discuss in the following section, readers engaging with many of these signs do so while participating in a discourse in which English is expected or necessary. Interestingly, 26.22 percent of informing signs contain both German and English. On further investigation, we realized that this category contains a large number of labels on drawers and cabinets in one of the public kitchen spaces (e.g., "Löffel/Spoons," "Tassen/Mugs"). This type of bilingual labeling rarely appears in any other space, and we therefore considered this high percentage something of an outlier, though it is noteworthy that German is given precedence even on signs that also feature English.[6]

As Table 1.1 indicates, different patterns of language prominence occur within different functional groups. Differentiating signs by function and applying our awareness of the signs' history allowed us to isolate patterns of language use that might have been obscured by simply counting languages across the entire site or by location.

Discourses within the "Semiotic Aggregate" of *Waldsee*

The frameworks pursued by Scollon and Scollon (2003) and Blommaert (2013) offer us a way to connect the granular quantitative findings displayed in Table 1.1 above to a nuanced understanding of the complex whole within the larger linguistic landscape of *Waldsee*. This complexity is portrayed by Blommaert (2013: 107) as being both "polycentric and multifiliar," comprising different threads that "simultaneously develop there, not in harmony or synchrony, but still within a broader logic of the system. (…) These different infrastructures are tailored towards the needs of the different groups

Table 1.1 Languages appearing in the *Waldsee* linguistic landscape

	Labeling		Informing		Directing		Indexing community		Decorating		Teaching		Lending air of authenticity		Total	
	Frequency count	%	Frequency count	%	Frequency count	%	Frequency count	%	Frequency count	%	Frequency count	%	Frequency count	%	Frequency count	%
German	44	72.13%	68	41.46%	40	46.51%	127	92.03%	73	91.25%	129	99.23%	55	88.52%	536	74.20%
English	15	24.59%	33	20.12%	31	36.05%	6	4.35%	3	3.75%	0	0.00%	0	0.00%	87	12.05%
Both	0	0.00%	43	26.22%	1	1.16%	1	0.72%	0	0.00%	0	0.00%	1	1.64%	46	6.37%
Other languages	0	0.00%	0	0.00%	0	0.00%	1	2.17%	0	0.00%	1	0.78%	2	1.64%	4	0.55%
Icons/images only	2	3.28%	20	12.20%	14	16.28%	3	2.17%	4	5.00%	0	0.00%	5	8.20%	48	6.65%
Total	61		164		86		138		80		130		63		722	

with their different needs and trajectories of residence and use; consequently, there are multiple, they form a polycentric whole."

Scollon and Scollon (2003: 175) understand this polycentric whole as a "semiotic aggregate" that is formed "at any moment" by a "huge range of discourses." In their examination of five urban street corners, Scollon and Scollon (2003) identified four discourses that are present in the same place "even if only as the background" (p. 200): (a) regulatory discourses: municipal, such as traffic signs and public notices that carry some regulatory "weight"; (b) infrastructural discourses: municipal, such as signs directed to employees who work with city water and power sources; (c) commercial discourses, such as signs that identify and advertise businesses; and (d) transgressive discourses, such as graffiti and other signs that are "in the 'wrong' place" (p. 146).

Building on this concept of "partly overlapping but nevertheless distinct discourses operating within the semiotic aggregate" (Scollon & Scollon, 2003: 185), we identified the following discourses that play themselves out in the *Waldsee* linguistic landscape. Signs related to each discourse can be understood as comprising separate networks that can be examined separately, even though a newcomer to *Waldsee* may not discern this systematicity and see instead what appears to be "a random display of semiotic resources" (Blommaert, 2013: 47). Given space constraints, each discourse is characterized only minimally below:

European village discourse: In this discourse, signs that have been imported from Europe are *unmarked* (that is, they are unsurprising to participants in this discourse), although they can be seen as technically "out of place" or "transgressive" (see Scollon & Scollon, 2003: 147) in relation to a typical town in the United States, where they have no legal status (e.g., German traffic signs; see website for Figure 1.21: a sign denoting a *Naturschutzgebiet* [nature reserve]) or geographic accuracy (e.g., in the case of signs showing that a specific German town is just a kilometer down the road; see website for Figure 1.22: a sign listing distances to hiking locations in Switzerland). The German language is foregrounded, though other languages, including English, can be seen as "realistic" elements of an urban landscape—e.g., the use of English within a German-language announcement for an upcoming slam poetry event—rather than being seen as an artifact of the English-speaking Minnesotan communities outside the borders of *Waldsee*.

Educational discourse: In this discourse, signs that provide specific aspects of German grammar and vocabulary, sample sentences related to the village curriculum, and information on relevant practices and products of German-speaking communities of practice are unmarked, even if they may be seen as "out of place" or "transgressive" (see, e.g., photo showing *Sprachzonen* [language zones] and *Wegweiser* [signposts] on the soccer field) in relation to a typical town or a school, where such signs are not typically found outside places designated for learning (e.g., classrooms and libraries). Teaching signs are typically relevant in this discourse, though authentic signs imported from German-speaking countries often play into it as well, as teachers may use them as portals to cultural practices that are valued in *Waldsee* just as in Europe (see the section on recycling bins below). The German language is overwhelmingly the preferred language, particularly in written form (as is the case with signs) and in spoken language in public situations (spoken English tends to be used only by the learners and in cases of health and safety by the staff).

Community discourse: In this discourse, signs that memorialize or make specific reference to the contributions or individuals within the larger community of practice are unmarked. Beyond these explicit connections, this community discourse is supported by signs that are designed and handcrafted by community members to enhance the aesthetics of the place as well as to convey and/or reinforce shared community values (e.g., in the areas of sustainability and social justice). The German language is the preferred language, although English is occasionally found in cases where, for example, the contributions of a non-German-speaking donor are recognized.

Health and safety discourse: In this discourse, signs that provide information and directions related to the health and safety of community members are unmarked. Informing and directing signs constitute the bulk of signs that contribute to this discourse. In contrast to the discourses characterized above, this discourse is supported by a larger number of signs that are bilingual in German and English (e.g., list of food allergens in the dining hall; see website for Figure 1.23: a sign listing safety rules on the beach); English only (e.g., how to use the fire extinguishers; warning signs on machinery; see website for Figure 1.24: how to call for help on a landline); or German with iconic images (e.g., how to determine the current location of the nursing staff).

Municipal discourse: In this discourse, signs that provide information and directions related to local city and county infrastructure systems, including underground cables and high voltage machinery, are highly unmarked within the context of the United States (so much so that they almost become invisible to many viewers). In contrast to the discourse types above, the signs undergirding this discourse are written only in English and, occasionally, accompanied by Spanish (in recognition of the ubiquity of Spanish in the United States). From the point of view of the European village discourse, then, these English signs—often enhanced by bright orange or yellow colors—can be seen as "out of place" or "transgressive" to the point where they attract heightened and unwelcome notice.

Authentic Signs as Potential Portals to Cultural Practices and Historical Context: Focus on Recycling Bins and Checkpoint Charlie Sign

Bolstered by our general understandings regarding how various types of signs help to enact several larger discourses within *Waldsee*, we now focus our attention on a specific subset of the signs in our inventory—those that were produced in and exported from Germany and have found a new home in *Waldsee*'s decentralized learning environment in northern Minnesota. What about these authentic signs allows them to be transformed from being simple, almost unremarkable, signs in one location to becoming a center of pedagogical interest in another? How might they be understood not as lifeless signs made of plastic or metal, but as portals to cultural practices and geopolitical–historical understandings on another continent?

In this final analytical section, we follow Blommaert (2013: 49) in "turn[ing] space into a genuinely ethnographic object, full of traces of human activity, interactions, relations, histories and anticipated futures" by shifting the study of linguistic landscapes from "a rather complex tool for performing a basic operation—counting languages—into a simple tool for performing analyses of complexity." We connect our understanding of each of these signs "as a trace of situated actions in the past and a template of future actions" (Blommaert 2013: 51) through the related perspective of intertextuality, in which Bakhtin (1986) claims that any given utterance (in our case, "sign") is not only related to preceding utterances but also anticipates possible responses.

Because these ready-made signs have been physically moved from one location to another, we can take advantage of insights by Bauman and Briggs (1990) that describe the process that a given text may undergo as it is *entextualized*, "lifted from its originating context (*decontextualization*) and inserted into a new setting where it is *recontextualized*" (Hodges, 2015: 43). When a viewer engages with this text in its new setting, the discourse it encounters is potentially "double-voiced" (Bakhtin, 1981), carrying with it both the meaning from its "originating" context (to the extent that the viewer is aware of this earlier meaning) and from its meaning in the current interaction.

It is this process that allows us to discern the pedagogical power of these signs. Depending on one's familiarity with practices in Germany of which a particular sign was a part, American viewers may not "hear" the "original" voice of the sign. As Blommaert (2013: 32) writes about viewers' expectations about relationships between signs and particular spaces,

> [w]hen signs are "in place", so to speak, habitual interpretations of such signs can be made, because the signs fit almost ecologically into their spatial surroundings. When they are "out of place", or "transgressive" in the terminology of the Scollons (Scollon & Wong Scollon 2003: 147), we need to perform additional interpretation work because a different kind of social signal has been given.

When these naïve viewers stand in front of an unexpected sign, they are primed to learn something new—and productive conversational partners can be those individuals who *are* familiar with the sign. It is this constellation of viewers with different backgrounds in front of a single sign that can lead to new cultural learning. The signs themselves represent integral parts of recurrent conversations that contribute to the practices unique to a community, and in studying these signs with the benefit of context gained by experience, "we can perform a reconstruction of the communication patterns for which such signs were manufactured. (…) *Signs lead us to practices, and practices lead us to people* [emphasis added]. (…) This sequence, from signs to practices to people, is the true analytical potential of linguistic landscaping" (Blommaert, 2013: 50).

We turn now to two case studies to illustrate these pedagogical insights as "an interplay—a complex interplay—of systemic and non-systemic features co-occurring within one sign" (Blommaert, 2013: 119), first exploring German recycling bins and then moving to a reproduction of a sign that was posted for decades at border crossing points in Berlin.

Recycling Bins

In the mid-2000s, *Waldsee* acquired a set of approximately eighty recycling bins manufactured in Germany (see Figure 1.25). The color-coded bins reflect the waste sorting practice in most German municipalities, with yellow bins accepting *Verkaufsverpackungen aus Metallen, Kunststoffen und Verbundstoffen* [commercial metal, plastic, and synthetic composites], green bins accepting *Altglas* [glass], blue bins accepting *Altpapier* [paper], and brown bins accepting *Restmüll* [other waste].

For visitors to *Waldsee* unfamiliar with German or German recycling practices, these signs might be "out of focus," interpreted (if at all) as part of the semiotic background (Scollon & Scollon, 2003). However, they play a more active role within the counselor–villager discourse, as counselors regularly call attention to the directive function of the recycling bin signs. Villagers are typically introduced to *Waldsee*'s waste sorting system early in a session; a villager's first evening on site often begins with an introduction to the dining hall, the nurse's station, and the recycling bins. This emphasis on proper recycling makes it easier to care for a site holding over 200 people; villagers participate in daily camp cleanup and are regularly reminded to dispose of their waste in the proper bin. However, our observations over several years suggest that these signs play additional roles in counselor–villager discourse. The choice to install these particular German-made recycling bins was not a random one; in an interview, the camp director stated that he intended the bins both to enhance a specific sense of place and to prompt conversations about the role of recycling and other sustainability-oriented practices in modern German life. While German recycling ordinances vary from region to region, the general practice of *Mülltrennung* [waste sorting] is universal in Germany; the recycling bins therefore also constitute elements that contribute to the *playworld* atmosphere and replicate signs that villagers might see in a German city. (When the recycling bins were first installed at *Waldsee*, the sight of four large color-coded bins outside the dining hall prompted a German staff member to remark, *Ich fühle mich wie zu Hause* [I feel at home].) These signs might fulfill a different function depending on context, either directing (when referenced during cleanup), teaching (if a counselor refers to the bins as part of a consciousness-raising exercise relating to sustainability), or lending an air of authenticity (when encountered by villagers in their day-to-day exploration of the site).

The bin labels have taken on these new functions in part as a result of their removal from their original context, an action that deserves closer reflection. A sign's meaning derives not only from its text and audience but also from its spatial relationships (Backhaus, 2007; Scollon & Scollon, 2003). As Joseph et al. (2001) point out, a particular metal sign "may count as a 'sign' from the moment of manufacture until long after it has been uprooted and consigned to a rubbish tip. But this usage is of no interest to the semiologist, who is concerned with the object only in so far as it functions semiotically, as a sign" (p. 209). The bin labels, like any other signs, "index[] a larger discourse whether of public transport regulation or underground drug trafficking" (Scollon & Scollon, 2003: 2); in this case, analogous bins installed in Germany derive meaning from an existing discourse surrounding sustainability practices. This original directive function, however, has been somewhat obscured

28 *Linguistic Landscapes Beyond the Language Classroom*

by their removal from a German municipality. In producing the bins now used by *Waldsee*, a municipal authority in Germany intended to direct consumer behavior in order to successfully reuse as much waste as possible; the message communicated by each bin to its audience (any German speaker) was clear: "put *these* things in me, and not any *other* things." The municipal authorities in Minnesota, however,

Figure 1.25 Recycling bins

follow different recycling procedures. Beltrami County, in which *Waldsee* is located, practices single-sort recycling and accepts mixed deliveries of paper, glass, and plastic bottles; the materials that villagers separate when interacting with the recycling bins' signs, then, are recombined at the waste processing facility. The recycling bins still convey the same message ("put *these* things in me") to the same audience (German speakers), but the action they mandate is no longer directed to any further purpose; the sign readers at *Waldsee* are not participating in a larger recycling system that requires their compliance. In this sense, the recycling bin signs have been removed from their original contexts and recontextualized (Bauman & Briggs, 1990) within the *playworld* environment of *Waldsee*.

Sie verlassen den amerikanischen Sektor ("You Are Leaving the American Sector")

In 1945 the four powers that defeated Nazi Germany each supervised a sector of the country's capital of Berlin until a peace agreement could be reached. That agreement came only in 1990, as the Cold War ended and divided Germany was united. During the intervening forty-five years the US army posted signs in English, French, and Russian (the languages of the four occupying powers) as well as in German, instructing people that they were "leaving the American sector" (see Figure 1.26) and entering a sector under the purview of another of the four powers. When the Berlin Wall was built in 1961, the sign took on an ironic twist, as it was now difficult to leave the American sector in West Berlin for the Soviet sector in East Berlin and almost impossible to leave the Soviet sector for the American sector. While the sign was posted at various locations along the American sector, perhaps the most iconic setting for the sign was at Checkpoint Charlie at the intersection of *Friedrichstraße*, *Zimmerstraße*, and *Mauerstraße* in the center of divided Berlin. The simple black-on-white sign is immediately recognizable to anyone who is familiar with Cold War history or has encountered its representations in popular culture, and versions of the sign have been sold for years throughout both the eastern and the western areas of what is now a unified city.

In the 1980s, the camp director purchased one of these replicas and later installed it at the entrance to the *Bahnhof* (train station) building, the first structure villagers pass through when they arrive. The sign matches the character of other arrival-day activities; on this day, *Waldsee* counselors follow a schedule designed to impress upon students that they are entering a simulated village community designed to foster language learning. Students present mock passports, submit to checks for contraband, and communicate regarding their lodgings, mirroring many of the interactions visitors to a new country might have at a border crossing. For those who notice it, the Checkpoint Charlie sign contributes to an already powerful impression that students at *Waldsee* are crossing a metaphorical border.

As in the case of the recycling bin labels discussed above, this sign has been removed from the context that gave it its referential meaning. It no longer reflects an external political reality; no location at *Waldsee* is legally outside the "American sector." The reproduction of the sign differs from the bin labels, however, in that it also conveys a different message from that of the original. The original sign delineated a political border, fulfilling one of the key functions Blommaert (2013) identified for signs: "Signs demarcate spaces, cutting them up in precisely circumscribed zones in which identities are being defined and enacted, forms of authority can be exerted, ownership and entitlement can be articulated" (p. 15). The original sign marked a stark division of the neighborhood into political zones and conveyed information immediately relevant to its readers at the time (who could be expected to bring additional background knowledge to their interaction with this sign). The copy's message is entirely metaphorical. The "speaker" of this text has quoted an existing sign in order to express an idea thematically similar to but practically different from the original: that visitors to *Waldsee* will be entering a constructed world qualitatively different from their home environment. In this sense, *Waldsee*'s Checkpoint Charlie sign represents an instance of *varidirectional* double-voicing (Morson & Emerson, 1990), where the meaning in the current situation is at odds with the original meaning. Visitors to *Waldsee* would interpret this sign based on their past experiences and knowledge (Scollon & Scollon, 2003). For some readers, the sign adds additional granular detail to the simulated experience of joining an authentic German village; on reading the sign, readers familiar with twentieth-century history might modulate their reaction to the *Waldsee* border crossing from the impression that "I'm moving metaphorically out of the U.S." to the feeling that "I'm moving metaphorically into Berlin." While it might be tempting to dismiss the plaque as a simple decoration, this sign (like the recycling bin labels and

Figure 1.26 Sign reading "You are leaving the American sector"

potentially an array of authentic signs available to classroom teachers; see the following section) can also serve as an occasion for consciousness-raising conversations that lead learners to a greater understanding of the context framing other German texts they might encounter.

Implications for Traditional World Language Classroom Teaching

The linguistic landscape at *Waldsee* may appear chaotic at first glance. An overview of the full inventory of signs yields a profusion of signs involved in overlapping discourses; visitors to *Waldsee* might participate in a few of those discourses, or several, or just one. A schoolscape also plays host to a variety of discourses, including not only the educational discourse of the language classroom but also the community discourse of the entire school. In this section, we draw on lessons learned in our study of the *Waldsee* LL to offer potential exploitations of the LL within a school or language classroom.

Signs can support teachers working within the framework of the ACTFL World Readiness Standards (The National Standards Collaborative Board, 2015) in a variety of ways.[7] Many classroom language teachers already make use of teaching signs in ways that support students in pursuing the goal of *Communication*, posting phrases that commonly occur within the classroom's educational discourse (e.g., "how does one say x?" in the target language).

Authentic signs can also help learners pursue the *Cultures* goal. Any sign crafted for one culturally/historically relevant purpose (such as the Checkpoint Charlie plaque) can find itself co-opted for use in another context; as Blommaert (2013) points out, "signs only become meaningful and deployable as signs because they have been moved in place, so to speak, as possible resources for specific communicative tasks. These processes are 'pre-textual' (Blommaert 2005: 77) and systemic: they long precede the synchronic deployment of signs, and they determine not single instances of use, but categories of use" (p. 118). At *Waldsee*, the recycling bin labels offer portals to understanding of cultural practices related to sustainability; teachers could reflect on similar school- or municipality-mandated activities in which their class takes part and consider using an authentic sign to reflect on how those practices are enacted in the countries of their target language. For example, some American schools encourage the posting of signs in every classroom reminding students to turn the lights off (Dressler, 2015); are there analogous signs reflecting the target culture that could be installed instead?

Even a seemingly innocuous sign can provide fodder for critical framing activities. In a reflection on short authentic texts that "hid[e] in plain sight" at *Waldsee*, Paesani (2018) provides the example of a two-cell, three-word *New Yorker* cartoon that despite its simplicity requires familiarity with several cultural tropes in order to be understood; she calls on language instructors to devote more attention to such texts to "serve as an alternative to the more conventional literary, cinematic, or information texts that language teachers often turn to for instructional use" (n.p.).

While classroom teachers do not have access to authentic environments afforded by *Waldsee*'s location, they can still import realia from German-speaking countries into their classrooms, from reproductions of directing signs (e.g., *Eingang* [entrance], traffic or street signs) to images of public art in a German-speaking city. Classroom teachers can lay the groundwork for new instructional activities by keeping in mind that they may have recontextualized these signs by the act of placing them in their classroom, just as *Waldsee*'s camp director did by importing German recycling bins. A teacher may post a "no bicycle parking" sign in their classroom as a means of decorating the room or providing a visual aid for vocabulary acquisition. The same sign, however, could serve as a starting point for discussions about public transit in Germany; in a German city such as Münster, for example, bicycle ridership is common enough that the municipal authorities must regulate bicycle parking in a way that would be irrelevant in the United States.

The fifth goal area, *Communities*, encourages students to use language "within and beyond the classroom to interact and collaborate in their community." A subset of the *Waldsee* signs indexing community includes signs produced by villagers that applaud praiseworthy behavior (e.g., a list of people who had cleaned up the most trash) or highlight fun aspects of the day (in recent years, in the form of a *Meme des Tages* [meme of the day]). Even in the absence of authentic texts, students and teachers can contribute to their own linguistic landscape with signs that assert the norms valued in that classroom; classroom teachers can reflect on the ways existing signs in their schoolscape already index the school community's values and encourage their students to use the target language to continue engaging in that discourse.

Conclusion

In his foundational work, Blommaert (2013) highlighted the critical two-way relationship between LL research and ethnographic fieldwork, where each enriches the other. As longtime summer residents of *Waldsee*, we found this insight to ring true again and again as we carried out our six-week participant observation on the site. Having walked the village paths and having viewed its signs literally thousands of times over the years, our specific focus during the cataloguing activity, our observations of the ways in which residents were engaging (or not) with these signs, and our related in-depth discussions with each other and the camp director brought out the "full descriptive and explanatory potential" of the LL perspective; "[i]n such an integrated exercise, signs in public space document complexity—they are visual items that tell the story of the space in which they can be found, and clarify its structure" (Blommaert, 2013: 16).

Our intense focus on each of the 722 physical signs in place on the *Waldsee* site helped us to discern not only the many functions they fulfill but also the ways in which they combine to support the highly varied discourses that play themselves out across the same 46 acres of land. Against the backdrop of extensive opportunities for spoken interpersonal communication that is the hallmark of *Waldsee*'s curriculum, this particular spotlight brought to the forefront of our attention the many very small texts that are literally "scattered everywhere and easily accessible for the staff to use for teaching language" (Paesani, 2018: n.p.). This process helped us to recognize that we can do even more in the future with these texts, that we can be more intentional about moving them from the scenery (where they help to evoke the feel of a German village) to a more systematic means of nurturing lively discussions about cultural practices and geopolitical–historical events. And by connecting our insights to the rich perspectives of intertextuality, we can understand how it is possible to begin with given texts related to recycling practices or to circumstances during a divided Germany as they appear in the "here and now" and to work our way through meaningful discussions back to uncover some of the texts' meanings in their original locations and times.

The importation of a variety of authentic signs from Europe to *Waldsee* may have been motivated partly by a desire to enhance its level of authenticity and partly to assist in an historic move away from the rented summer campsites that housed *Waldsee* from 1961 to 1982 to its current site that looks a great deal more like German village architecture. Over the course of *Waldsee*'s history, the curricular philosophy toward literacy has shifted quite dramatically, moving from a time in which written German in public spaces was restricted almost completely to signs that labeled buildings and to villagers' individual name tags to the present, where many types of texts are intentionally placed across the entire landscape far beyond the individual language classrooms: poetry plaques hang around tree trunks; posters containing grammar tables can be found near climbing walls, beaches, and campfires; and word lists containing food items adorn a large central bulletin board in the dining room. As illustrated in the case studies related to recycling bins and the Checkpoint Charlie sign, a next logical step in this process will be an even more systematic linking of individual signs with *Waldsee*'s myriad curricular units on cultural practices, so as to help learners thrive far beyond the classroom within this decentralized landscape of learning.

Notes

1   *Waldsee* was founded as a summer language program in 1961 and moved in 1982 to its present permanent location; each year since 1982 has witnessed growth in terms of additional buildings. For early historical perspective, see Friedrichsmeyer (1962).
2   The other thirteen languages represented in Concordia Language Village programming are Arabic, Chinese, Danish, Finnish, French, Italian, Japanese, Korean, Norwegian, Portuguese, Russian, Spanish, and Swedish. Additional information regarding these villages can be found at http://www.concordialanguage villages.org/.

3   For insights on different aspects of the interrelationship between intertextuality and linguistic landscapes see also Blommaert (2013: 28) and Scollon and Scollon (2003: 192–3).
4   See also Shohamy and Waksman (2009: 328) for a related discussion in which "students would use visible texts as 'tips of icebergs' to a deeper and more complex meaning which [is] embedded in histories, cultural relations, politics and humanistic relations."
5   Signs that included both text and symbols or icons were counted as instances of that language.
6   Bolstering this impression was a response from the directors of *Waldsee*'s summer and academic-year programs, who both indicated that they consider these labels to be inconsistent with the signage practices at *Waldsee* and intend to replace them.
7   The goals of these standards, also known as the 5 Cs, are Communication, Cultures, Connections, Comparisons, and Communities; they can be viewed here: https://www.actfl.org/publications/all/world-readiness-standards-learning-languages

References

Aiestaran, J., Cenoz, J., & Gorter, D. (2010). Multilingual cityscapes: Perceptions and preferences of the inhabitants of the city of Donostia–San Sebastian. In E. Shohamy, E. Ben-Rafael, & M. Barni (Eds.), *Linguistic Landscape in the City* (pp. 219–34). Bristol, UK: Multilingual Matters.

Backhaus, P. (2007). *Linguistic Landscapes. A Comparative Study of Urban Multilingualism in Tokyo*. Clevedon/Buffalo/Toronto: Multilingual Matters Ltd.

Bakhtin, M. (1981). *The Dialogic Imagination: Four Essays* (M. Holquist, Trans, C. Emerson, & M. Holquist, Eds.). Austin, TX: University of Texas Press.

Bakhtin, M. (1986). *Speech Genres and Other Late Essays* (Trans. V. W. McGee). Austin, TX: University of Texas Press.

Bauman, R., & Briggs, C. L. (1990). Poetics and performance as critical perspectives on language and social life. *Annual Review of Anthropology*, 19, 59–88.

Ben-Rafael, E., Shohamy, E., Amara, M., & Trumper-Hecht, N. (2006). Linguistic landscape as symbolic construction of the public space: The case of Israel. *International Journal of Multilingualism*, 3, 7–30.

Blommaert, J. (2005). *Discourse: A Critical Introduction*. Cambridge, UK: Cambridge University Press.

Blommaert, J. (2013). *Ethnography, Superdiversity, and Linguistic Landscapes: Chronicles of Complexity*. Bristol: Multilingual Matters.

Bruner, J. (1990). *Acts of Meaning*. Cambridge: Cambridge University Press.

Cenoz, J., & Gorter, D. (2008). The linguistic landscape as an additional source of input in second language acquisition. *IRAL*, 46, 267–87.

Clark, B., Wagner, J., Lindemalm, K., & Bendt, O. (2011). Språkskap: Supporting second language learning "In the Wild," presented at INCLUDE, London, April 18–20. 10.13140/RG.2.1.3564.8489.

Dagenais, D., Moore, D., Sabatier, C., Lamarre, P., & Armand, F. (2009). Linguistic landscape and language awareness. In E. Shohamy, & D. Gorter (Eds.), *Linguistic Landscape: Expanding the Scenery* (pp. 253–69). New York: Routledge.

Dressler, R. (2015). Sign*geist*: Promoting bilingualism through the linguistic landscape of school signage. *International Journal of Multilingualism*, 12, 128–45.
Friedrichsmeyer, E. M. (1962). The language camp, a different approach to elementary foreign language instruction. *The German Quarterly*, 35(3), 322–6.
Gorter, D. (2006). Further possibilities for linguistic landscape research. In D. Gorter (Ed.), *Linguistic Landscape: A New Approach to Multilingualism* (pp. 81–9). Clevedon, UK: Multilingual Matters.
Gorter, D. (2018). Linguistic landscapes and trends in the study of schoolscapes. *Linguistics and Education*, 44, 80–5.
Gorter, D., & Cenoz, J. (2015). Linguistic landscapes inside multilingual schools. In B. Spolsky, M. Tannenbaum, & O. Inbar (Eds.), *Challenges for Language Education and Policy: Making Space for People* (pp. 151–69). New York: Routledge Publishers.
Hamilton, H. E., & Cohen, A. D. (2004). Creating a playworld: Motivating learners to take chances in a second language. In J. Frodesen, & C. Holten (Eds.), *The Power of Context in Language Teaching and Learning* (pp. 237–47). Boston: Heinle.
Hamilton, H. E., Crane, C., & Bartoshesky, A. (2005). *Doing Foreign Language: Bringing Concordia Language Villages into Language Classrooms*. Upper Saddle River, NJ: Pearson/Merrill/Prentice Hall.
Hanauer, D. I. (2009). Science and the linguistic landscape: A genre analysis of representational wall space in a microbiology laboratory. In E. Shohamy & D. Gorter (Eds.), *Linguistic Landscape: Expanding the Scenery* (pp. 287–301). London: Routledge.
Hanson, M. (2012). A participatory inquiry into Japanese name use, language learning, and identity development. *University of Hawai'i Second Language Studies*, 30(2), 1–41.
Hodges, A. (2015). Intertextuality in discourse. In D. Tannen, H. E. Hamilton, & D. Schiffrin (Eds.), *Handbook of Discourse Analysis*, 2nd ed. (pp. 42–60). Oxford: John Wiley & Sons, Inc.
Itagi, N. H., & Singh, S. K. (Eds.). (2002). *Linguistic landscaping in India with particular reference to the new states: Proceedings of a seminar*. Mysore: Central Institute of Indian Languages and Mahatma Gandhi International Hindi University.
Joselit, J. W. (June 2019). Speaking Camp Hebrew: Jewish summer camps offer kids a unique linguistic landscape. *Tablet Magazine*. Retrieved from https://www.tabletmag.com/jewish-life-and-religion/286444/speaking-camp-hebrew.
Joseph, J. E., Love, N., & Taylor, T. J. (2001). *Landmarks in Linguistic Thought II. The Western Tradition in the Twentieth Century*. London: Routledge.
Landry, R., & Bourhis, R. Y. (1997). Linguistic landscape and ethnolinguistic vitality: An empirical study. *Journal of Language and Social Psychology*, 16(1), 23–49.
Malinowski, D. (2010). Showing seeing in the Korean linguistic cityscape. In E. Shohamy, E. Ben-Rafael, & M. Barni (Eds.), *Linguistic Landscape in the City* (pp. 199–215). Bristol, UK: Multilingual Matters.
Malinowski, D. (2015). Opening spaces of learning in the linguistic landscape. *Linguistic Landscape*, 1, 95–113.
Malinowski, D. (2018). Linguistic landscape. In A. Phakiti, P. De Costa, L. Plonsky, & S. Starfield (Eds.), *The Palgrave Handbook of Applied Linguistics Research Methodology* (pp. 869–85). London: Palgrave Macmillan.
Morson, G. S., & Emerson, C. (1990). *Mikhail Bakhtin: Creation of a Prosaics*. Palo Alto, CA: Stanford University Press.
The National Standards Collaborative Board. (2015). *World-Readiness Standards for Learning Languages*, 4th ed. Alexandria, VA: Author.

Paesani, K. (June 19, 2018). Bringing the everyday into the language classroom [Blog post]. Retrieved from http://www.concordialanguagevillages.org/blog/villages/bringing-the-everyday-into-the-language-classroom.

Pakarinen, S., & Björklund, S. (2018). Multiple language signage in linguistic landscapes and students' language practices: A case study from a language immersion setting. *Linguistics and Education*, 44, 4–11.

Savela, T. (2018). The advantages and disadvantages of quantitative methods in schoolscape research. *Linguistics and Education*, 44, 31–44.

Scollon, R., & Scollon, S. W. (2003). *Discourses in Place: Language in the Materials World*. London: Routledge.

Shohamy, E., & Ben–Rampton, E. (2015). Linguistic landscape: A new journal. *Linguistic Landscape*, 1, 1–5.

Shohamy, E., & Gorter, D. (2009). *Linguistic Landscape: Expanding the Scenery*. New York: Routledge.

Shohamy, E., Rafael, E. B., & Barni, M. (Eds.). (2010). *Linguistic Landscape in the City*. Bristol, UK: Multilingual Matters.

Shohamy, E., & Waksman, S. (2009). Linguistic landscape as an ecological arena: Modalities, meanings, negotiations, education. In E. Shohamy & D. Gorter (Eds.), *Linguistic Landscape: Expanding the Scenery* (pp. 313–31). London: Routledge.

Soukup, B. (2016). *English in the Linguistic Landscape of Vienna, Austria (ELLViA): Outline, Rationale, and Methodology of a Large-Scale Empirical Project on Language Choice on Public Signs from the Perspective of Sign-Readers*. Vienna English Working Papers, 25.

Van Mensel, L., Vandenbroucke, M., & Blackwood, R. (2016). Linguistic landscapes. In O. García, N. Flores, & M. Spotti (Eds.), *Oxford Handbook of Language and Society* (pp. 423–49). Oxford: Oxford University Press.

2

Unveiling Sign Languages in the Linguistic Landscape: Representations of Sign Languages in Nonsigning and Signing Milieux

Jami Fisher, Donna Jo Napoli, and Gene Mirus

Much of linguistic landscape studies (LLS) concerns the appearance and presence of languages. Yet absence of representation also tells a story, as in the case of sign languages. Since the signage examined in LLS (as in Gorter & Cenoz, 2017, for example) uses text, the issues about signage immediately frame the focus of LLS as not language per se. That is, text is not language, but only a reflection of language, just as a photograph is not a person, but only a reflection of a person. In a strict sense then, languages lacking a written form lack a linguistic landscape (LL) and are, thus, irrelevant to LLS. Such a conclusion is regrettable in that it precludes from consideration many of the world's languages and linguistic communities, with the result of impoverishing LLS.

The literature on LLs includes few to no mentions of sign languages in the LLs of deaf[1] and non-deaf spaces. This is simultaneously unsurprising and startling. On first consideration, it may seem logical that sign language LLs are unrepresented because sign languages have yet to establish codified, written forms; instead, they borrow the text of the ambient spoken language to translate for the purposes of written documentation. In the spirit of Shohamy (2015) and subsequent authors who have expanded the notion of LL, we challenge the assumption that languages in the LL are necessarily written; surely, technology and creativity afford the ability to project once-evanescent signs and sign languages into the LL in both frozen and animated forms. Now more than ever, sign languages in the LL are ripe for analysis. We argue for a broader notion of LLS, by showing benefits that arise from considering analogues of signage in natural sign languages. In turn, we embark on (perhaps) the first discussion of sign languages in the LL.

In our internal musings on the sociohistorical and sociolinguistic factors influencing sign languages' appearance—both regarding their presence where they were once absent and what form they take—in the LL, we have come to recognize that there are many avenues to explore and far too much to be said for this chapter. We center this foray on a sociohistorical contextualization and subsequent analysis, revealing educational, social, and cultural motivations behind the production and publicity of sign languages. We pay particular attention but are not limited to American Sign Language (ASL) and its representations in the United States with the understanding that varying contexts will have different takes on and presentations of their sign languages. Furthermore, our analysis attends to the sensibilities of deaf people and preliminarily explores the LLs that crop up around deaf people and communities.

We first provide an overview of the sociohistorical context inhibiting the regular and systematic analysis of sign languages in the LL. We briefly trace the evolution of this context, ending with our current social and linguistic landscape, one more amenable to emergence and proliferation of sign languages. Throughout, we provide examples of sign languages as the basis for educational exchange, though with varied underlying motivations. Ultimately, we explore examples of when sign languages in the linguistic landscape serve as educational tools for inhabitants of and visitors to specific contexts, with particular attention to sign language linguistic landscapes (SLLLs), or places in which sign languages are more prominent and spoken/written languages are in the minority. In all cases, we specify the sign language under discussion.

Theoretical Frameworks and Literature Review

Sign languages have yet to be explored as viable contributors to the linguistic landscapes surrounding the world's multifarious communities. Here, we take this modest first ameliorating step, keeping in mind Gorter's (2013) assertion that "[t]he study of linguistic landscapes aims to add another view to our knowledge about societal multilingualism by focusing on language choices, hierarchies of languages, contact-phenomena, regulations, and aspects of literacy" (p. 191). Indeed, LLs are "contextual constellations" (Ben-Rafael et al., 2006: 9) of the actors within a particular time and place and are emblematic of the complex sociocultural inner-workings of a given society.

Waksman and Shohamy (2010) and Shohamy and Waksman (2008) demonstrate what Shohamy (2015) later summarizes about LL studies: "[G]aining a deeper meaning of the site must include, in addition to the written texts, images and pictures, the geographical locations where it is placed, the history, politics and the practices of the people who attend the site" (p. 154). Closer study of sign languages in the LL is bound to reveal historical, social, cultural, and political forces behind their display (or lack thereof). To understand these forces' true impact on signing communities we must expand our definition of what counts as a contextual landscape; we must look at what others have heretofore overlooked: deaf spaces and geographies.

Gulliver and Kitzel (2015) explain that the documentation of human geography has broadened over the last few decades from being limited to ones that emerge from "embodied experience[s] of the environment and ongoing social interaction" (p. 2). They are focused on how geographical spaces change when deaf people are present:

> Deaf geographies describe how, by the simple expedient of living out their lives from within visual bodies, rather than hearing ones, Deaf people produce Deaf spaces. These Deaf spaces might be small and temporary, like the signing space that exists between some deaf friends who meet by chance in the street. They

might be large but temporary, like a regular deaf pub gathering. They might be small and more permanent, like the home of a deaf family, or as large and as permanent as a Deaf university. But they all have a number of things in common, and in common with hearing spaces … Deaf spaces exist in time … [They] harness a neutral physical world … [They] progressively shape the physical world ….[and] [they] leave traces in the mind.

(pp. 2–3)

These features also exist in what the authors call "hearing"[2] geographies: the hegemonic notion of social formations in space and time when we forget—or ignore—the fact that deaf people exist within and co-create these spaces. Deaf geographers are thus concerned with power dynamics between hearing and deaf people and their impact on what surrounding spaces look like.

Here we are interested in exploring deaf and non-deaf geographies' impact on how sign languages are represented in the LL. How do the "temporary" and "more permanent" spaces of deaf people impact (sign) language use and recognition in everyday society? What are the social forces that militate against or encourage the use of sign languages in these contexts? How does expanding the criteria for LLs to include the various media through which sign languages can be depicted help us better understand underlying social forces at play that influence (sign) language representation and use? Sociohistorical, sociolinguistic, and deaf geographical contextualization of sign languages will help us better understand the how, when, and why of sign language use in the LL as educational tool (or linguistic prop). Many contexts discussed occur in predominantly nonsigning settings, though some occur in sign-dominant milieux, what we herein call sign language linguistic landscapes (SLLLs). By studying sign languages in the LL and in SLLL, we can better understand the dynamics between signers and nonsigners, and among signers. Unveiling these dynamics will increase readers' awareness of them and thus be a modest step toward mitigating social forces that have minimized and marginalized sign languages and deaf people and inhibited deaf people's movement toward equality with hearing counterparts.

A Brief Historical Contextualization of Sign Languages

With the exception of the few sign languages used by shared signing communities (small communities with a relatively high percentage of deaf members so that both deaf and hearing use sign language; see Kusters [2014]), sign languages have historically been marginalized by hearing people in most, if not all, countries. It was not until 1960, when Stokoe, a hearing linguist from Gallaudet College,[3] argued that the signing used by deaf Americans at Gallaudet was a bona fide language with a grammar separate from the ambient spoken language, English (Stokoe, 1960). Before then and for years after, until fMRI studies proved that sign languages are processed in the same parts of the brain as spoken languages (see Campbell et al., 2008, for an overview), there were pervasive misconceptions that sign languages were asystematic gestures and not natural human languages and that deaf people should, instead of signing, be encouraged to communicate through speech, lipreading, reading, and writing of the ambient spoken language (Baynton, 1996). Such beliefs were determined and codified in educational policy without consultation of deaf people and implemented in schools for the deaf. Thus, sign languages were banned in most deaf schools, and deaf people were punished for communicating in sign, the language most natural and accessible to them (Lane, 1984). Such oralist policies existed in deaf schools in Europe and the United States for nearly a century—from 1880 until the 1970s, and in some cases, even later.

With sign languages broadly seen as illegitimate forms of communication, it comes as no surprise that the contexts in which sign languages could be used freely were few, exclusive to deaf people who learned stealthily through peers or immediate family members and a handful of hearing people sympathetic to the belief that signing is the natural language of deaf people. In the past (as recently as a few decades ago), it was rare to see deaf people signing in public; if they did, their signing space (the space in which their manual articulators would move) would be smaller than what would be typically produced in a deaf-majority setting. Evidence of sign languages permeating the broader LL of hearing people is thus minimal.

Over the years, the growing acceptance of sign languages' legitimacy has fueled general public interest in and desire to learn a sign language. For thousands of signing people in the United States, ASL is the most frequently used language (in addition to written English) and the preferred language for conversation, although exact figures are hard to come by for a variety of reasons (Mitchell et al., 2006; Murray 2019; Oros, 2015). ASL vies with French for the position of second most commonly studied language (after Spanish) in postsecondary settings (Looney & Lusin, 2018). Sign languages are taught and proliferate in popular culture in other countries as well, particularly in Western Europe.[4] Accordingly, sign languages have entered the LL with higher frequency and visibility than before. This burgeoning presence of sign languages in everyday (hearing) settings is, we hope, an indicator of social progress with respect to how signing communities and deaf people are viewed.

Sign Languages and the "Problem" of Written Form

The reasons for marginalization of sign languages are largely based on historical prejudice against deaf people and a deaf way of life, some of which persist today under various guises (Humphries et al. 2017; Lane, 1992). One somewhat linguistic reason is relevant to the present discussion: the lack of a writing system can bias people. A prevalent idea of the past is that true, mature, valuable languages have a literature— and by *literature*, people mean a body of text, even though orally transmitted literatures are more common globally (Prendergast, 2001)—and that oral narrative is the most important foundation for hearing cultures historically (Niles, 1999). That there might exist visual literatures that are treasure troves of deaf communities' cultures is unfathomable to many, though they proliferate (Bauman & Rose, 2006; Sutton-Spence & Kaneko, 2016). The idea behind this misconception is that writing is a higher form of language, perhaps because in the past writing belonged to those with socioeconomic power[5]; writing is taken as somehow closer to the truth, more reliable, than other forms of language. In fact, looking at the history of the writing systems for different languages can offer insights about the linguistic knowledge that users of the language had about it (Daniels, 2013). So the lack of a writing system for sign languages might lead people to the mistaken conclusion that sign languages are not bona fide human languages and have no linguistic structure to use as a scaffolding for a writing system.

The reality is that writing systems for sign languages have been devised, such as Stokoe notation (Stokoe, 1960), Sign Writing (Sutton,1995), HamNoSys (Prillwitz et al.,1989), and Si5S developed by Robert Augustus (Bauman & Murray, 2017; McCarty, 2004; Miller, 2001; Karpov, Kipyatkova, & Zelezny, 2016), and are currently being devised (Guimarães, Guardezi, & Fernandes, 2014). However, the complexities of dealing with the multiple spatial and articulatory factors involved yield systems that, so far, are hard to learn and unwieldy enough to make them impractical for daily use. But even if one could solve those problems, an intractable one posed by the nature of sign language lexicons remains. While spoken languages have a fixed/frozen lexicon and speakers coin new words only occasionally, sign languages have both a frozen and a productive lexicon (Brennan, 2001). The problems of trying to convey in a writing system these various articulation possibilities in time and space are mind-boggling and, most certainly, are due purely to the modality not to deficits of linguistic structure. Finally, modern technology has made videos and video communication widely available, so the pressing need of the past for a sign writing system has waned.

Sign Languages in the (Hearing) Linguistic Landscape

Despite the lack of a writing system, sign languages filter into the LL with frequency and visibility that correlates strongly with hearing society's recognition and acceptance of deaf people and their sign languages. The tokens of sign languages themselves also reflect the social position of sign languages and deaf people. The following is a discussion and analysis of various representations of sign languages in the LL. Many of these tokens exist through an educational transaction, though not all deliver a positive message about sign languages.

The majority of sign language examples in the LL involve fingerspelling. Some sign languages eschew fingerspelling in the lexicon, for example, Italian Sign Language (LIS) (Nicodemus et al., 2017), and some allow it readily, for example, ASL (Morford & MacFarlane, 2003). Though fingerspelling use in the LL has yet to be examined, we believe its popularity rests on two facts: fingerspelling facilitates comprehension for nonsigners and serves as a signal of a likely sign-dominant environment (SLLL, to be explored below). For nonsigners, fingerspelling becomes a gateway point to learning the connection between the two languages—sign and spoken. Depictions of fingerspelling are thus treated as if it is the writing system of the sign language. For signers, depictions of fingerspelling cue different social and linguistic connections than the ambient spoken language. They act as symbolic invitations to a milieu enriched by visual-gestural and tactile communication, one that, until recently, was almost wholly siloed to signing-only spaces.

Tokens of deaf peddlers[6] are early examples of fingerspelling and sign language crossover from typically deaf into predominantly hearing spaces. Superficially, these tokens—often in the form of cards displaying the ASL manual alphabet—play on the intention of educating hearing people about the ASL alphabet. Upon further examination, it is clear that deaf peddlers—and impostor deaf peddlers[7]—functioned under exploitative terms, characterizing deaf people as pitiable, unable to earn a legitimate living.

In fact, deaf people's lives were far more complex than these tokens suggested. If a deaf person was not in contact with accessible language (spoken or sign), the person was alinguistic, with deficits that followed from the lack of language. That person truly was pitiable and unable to earn a legitimate living at any job other than those an alinguistic beast could handle. If, instead, the deaf person used a sign language, then that person had a basis for learning a vocation. Peddling alphabet cards with the pretense of being unable to work was thus exploitative. Furthermore, the act of peddling reinforces stereotypes that deaf people are pitiable victims of social forces, effectively undermining efforts toward equality with hearing people. Thus, peddling was and is anathema within deaf community circles and as such has been campaigned against—officially and unofficially—within deaf communities (Robinson, 2012). Even still, some of the tokens of peddling are premised on active educational exchanges between deaf and hearing people, albeit ones that reinforce negative stereotypes.

Examination of the cards and other wares sold by deaf and impostor-deaf peddlers shows that many play to hearing sentiments of pity without educational motives nor sign language imagery on the card. One early twentieth-century example of a token from a deaf peddler uses only written text to exploit the deafness-as-impediment model (Figure 2.1a). Others more relevant to this discussion, however, use drawings and other images of signing to embellish the English text on the card. Figure 2.1c includes a drawing of a person signing THANK YOU[8] alongside the request for donation. Unlike Figures 2.1d and e, there is no explicit connection to the English text that would indicate this sign means, "Thank you," although "Thank you very much" is written to the left of the image. Still, it is an early example of ASL crossover into predominantly nonsigning, hearing communities and takes the opportunity to passively educate the nonsigner by using an ASL image.

Meanwhile, Figures 2.1d and e—images from a double-sided card—promote a more instructional approach, as it is billed as a "Deaf Education System card." Many more signs are included on this card, signs aimed to pique the curiosity of nonsigning hearing people enough to prompt a purchase (or donation). The explicit and consistent pairing of ASL signs and English translation serves as an invitation for nonsigners to enter a signing community, one that has historically been hidden away, overlooked, and ignored by nonsigners. This quid pro quo strategy for procuring financial gain plays on nonsigners' naïveté, curiosity, beneficence, and, perhaps, ignorance; the card contains incorrect information that nonsigners would not pick up on, thus suggesting that the deaf peddlers likely were more interested in earning money through this exchange rather than accuracy of the tokens.

Figure 2.1 Examples of deaf peddler cards

These cards show an interesting representation of ASL in the tokens of deaf peddling. Here peddlers don't rely on pity—though other peddlers certainly do—but instead market the exotic nature of their language to the nonsigning public. This strategy, however, does little to improve the subordinated position of deaf people in that it shifts its hook from pity to sign-language-as-exoticized-asset, thereby maintaining a superficial and objectified portrait of deaf people vis-à-vis the hearing majority.

For example, one of the most ubiquitous instances of sign languages in the LL is the ILY handshape on magnets, stickers, clothing, and so on (see Figure 2.1b, circa late twentieth century, early twenty-first century). Each letter is the first letter of a word in the sentence "I Love You"; thus this handshape originated in America. Though its ubiquity is off-putting to some deaf people, many use this sign in everyday conversation. The sign can be seen on trinkets and other paraphernalia sold by deaf people. Modern technology has invited the ILY symbol into the world of emojis; is used in texting between signers and others in the know.

Why this handshape is so appealing is easy to figure out. For one, hearing people feel comfortable using it because it seems like what scholars of gesture call an emblem (Matsumoto & Hwang, 2013)—a gesture that has gained a conventional meaning so that it can be used in isolation like a word or phrase or even a sentence. Examples of emblems recognized in many (but not all) places with the same meaning around the globe include the thumbs-up handshape and the obscene middle finger. Second, deaf people use ILY with many orientations of the palm and in many locations in space and even, sometimes, on both hands simultaneously. This variability comes across as flexibility, so hearing people are not afraid that they will make ILY incorrectly. Third, the message is positive, and who doesn't want to send a positive message? A quick internet search confirms that many companies make money selling paraphernalia with the ILY handshape.

Perhaps the very reasons why the ILY handshape spread with such abandon are the same reasons why there is disagreement among deaf communities as to whether this is a positive or negative development. If only signs that feel somehow familiar, cutesy, or cuddly to nonsigning people catch on rather than ones that challenge them to pay attention to articulatory details and nuances of signing, what does that mean about nonsigning people's appreciation of deaf ways of being? Use of the ILY handshape might reflect no depth or insight into sign languages or deaf experiences. So the spread of this handshape suggests a superficial dip of the toe into deaf spaces, rather than efforts toward a deeper understanding of cultural values of deaf people. Indeed, the common use of ILY may be a convenient and thoughtless appropriation. Or worse, exploitation. An eloquent video (Ladines, n.d.) points out that those who sell ILY paraphernalia can make great amounts of money quickly—such as at feminist rallies—but often they contribute none of their profit to deaf organizations. The ILY symbol has also been used by deaf peddlers (again, see Figure 2.1b); its ubiquity makes it a simple and easy image to use in tokens for sale.

Since the formal recognition of sign languages (1960), through the deaf civil rights movements (such as the Deaf President Now movement at Gallaudet in 1988), and now with the current explosion of popularity of sign languages among hearing people, sign language representations (in film, pop culture, universities, and advertising) have become increasingly apparent. Burgeoning interest among typically nonsigning people and communities gives rise to sign languages' spread into the LL.

Evidence of this popularity is visible in pop culture and beyond: deaf characters are showing up in films not specifically about deaf people. To the point: deaf characters and sign languages are proliferating in popular culture and ultimately in the LL because they are more visible and accepted than ever before. Depictions of sign language use as everyday phenomena give rise to the opportunity for them to appear in the LL. In the century before Stokoe, it would likely not have occurred to most nonsigners to include sign languages in depictions of a typical setting. Now they proliferate, and not only in SLLLs, perhaps as an attempt by producers/broadcasters to demonstrate their awareness of diversity and commitment to inclusivity.

One of the authors of this chapter observed a framed poster of the LIS alphabet as part of a staged photograph advertisement for an Italian bank located on a metro line in Rome, Italy (Figures 2.2a–c).

This advertisement does not concern being deaf nor does it appear to be marketing to deaf people. The tagline translates to "Does your story need more space? The solution is a BPER bank mortgage." In the corner of the full ad (Figure 2.2c), a framed poster of the LIS alphabet with small Roman letters next to each fingerspelled letter is part of the set. It is not prominent, nor completely presented. But it is there and its existence helps to change the narrative of what can be part of the everyday LL. Perhaps these people depicted are supposed to be deaf; perhaps not. Regardless, the image sends a message to signers and nonsigners alike that sign languages are part of everyday life.

Figure 2.2 Italian bank advertisement featuring the LIS alphabet

Language Use in the Sign Language Linguistic Landscape

We have discussed evidence of sign languages appearing in a typically nonsigning LL. But is there a difference between the LL of spoken/written languages and languages that are signed? Might it be that the LL is different in predominantly signing environments? As Gulliver and Fekete (2017) remind us, "Deaf users of sign languages inhabit a world that is different than their Hearing [sic] counterparts due to their uniquely visual method of communication" (p. 121) and "Knowing more about the Deaf community, as producers of uniquely Deaf spaces, provides a means of considering the production of space in visual terms as defined by the lived experiences of a linguistic minority group" (p. 121).[9] These deaf spaces—some temporary, some permanent—indeed look different from those not heavily populated with sign language users. As such, the surrounding LL—one that is sign dominant—also displays differently. Not surprisingly, in SLLLs, sign languages—both in digital and in static form—are prominent. They are featured with or without the written text of the ambient spoken language. We posit that depictions of sign languages can stand alone in SLLLs, whereas, with the exception of the ILY sign—which we argue above has become an emblem—they would not exist without the written form as mediation in the general, nonsigning LL.

What follows is a brief sketch of several contexts within the SLLL, including examples from the earliest documentation of sign language in video form to contemporary SLLLs and the linguistic output they produce. We note the circumstances and participants that construct these deaf geographies and connected SLLLs, and describe the deliberate and incidental educational opportunities that arise in these contexts. Like written language tokens in a nonsigning LL, meaning for sign language tokens is made in what Shohamy and Waksman (2008) call "interwoven 'discourses'"; "what is seen, what is heard, what is spoken, what is thought" all interface to construct what is displayed and perceived (p. 313). To members of signing communities, visibility of sign language in the SLLL might prompt feelings of pride, community inclusion, cultural connection, and inspiration. For nonsigners, these tokens are a reminder of the visual and tactile orientation of the people within the SLLL. For those aware that they are in a SLLL, they serve as a reminder to respect and follow the cultural mores of signing people. For others who are unaware of signing community values, they might prompt curiosity and inquiry into the meaning of the signs, why they are articulated in that manner, and what more they can learn about the people in the SLLL.

Before the advent of film, the memory and history of deaf people were passed down among deaf peers from generation to generation using ephemeral signs and stories. The use of static drawings to document and preserve signs for their own use and for posterity was limited (see Long [1908], for example). To communicate from afar, deaf people in the United States relied on reading and writing of English text. A printing association known as Little Paper Family (LPF) emerged at various state residential school communities and served as an information network for deaf students, alumni, and associated signing people.

Film technology revolutionized the way deaf people could document their languages and histories. Indeed, film and video are integral to the persistence of sign languages—through oralist periods and still today. Some of the earliest films in history were used for such documentation and are the first examples of the animated forms of sign languages in the SLLL. Meanwhile, it is only recently (Shohamy, 2015; Shohamy & Waksman, 2008; Troyer & Szabó, 2017) that this medium was considered a possible tool in surveying, capturing, constructing, and analyzing the LL. Even still, there has yet to be discussion of the use of film and video for documentation and analysis of sign languages in the LL.

From 1910 through 1921, the National Association of the Deaf (NAD) organized, funded, and promoted a film series to document and preserve what was known then as "the sign language" and what we now recognize as ASL (NAD, 1910–1921). These films had an explicit educational intention: to remind deaf communities of the contemporary threat of oralism to their language and people as well as to prompt them to preserve their language and culture for posterity. They featured multiple sign masters performing stories of various topics and in varying registers for the purpose of preserving the sign language under threat by oralist methodology. The films were signed, with no subtitles and no voice-overs, targeting only signing deaf community members.[10] They are a tribute to the expected persistence of sign languages and are symbols of resistance to oralism. They were circulated in milieux that were majority signing rather than speaking—deaf clubs and deaf schools—and were the first contributions to and documentation of SLLLs.

One of the most well-known films of the series, "The Preservation of Sign Language," is a "strong, uncompromising, and unflinching" (Padden, 2004: 246) sermon-like lecture, which has been archived in the Library of Congress for its literary, linguistic, and cultural importance (Veditz, 1913). In the film, Veditz, the then-seventh president of the NAD, reaches wide audiences of deaf people by invoking the spirit of Abbé de l'Épée, the French priest considered to be the father of signing deaf education. He reminds the American deaf audience of the threat of oralism by warning, "Our beautiful sign language is now beginning to show the results of [oralist] attempts … to banish signs from the schoolroom, from the churches, and from the earth" (Veditz, 1913, as translated by Carol Padden). Veditz ends his address to American deaf people in hopeful terms intended to prompt deaf people to remain steadfast against oralist methodology. He professes, "As long as we have deaf people on earth, we will have signs. It is my hope that we all will love and guard our beautiful sign language as the noblest gift God has given to deaf people" (Veditz, 1913, as translated by Carol Padden).

The new film medium was a boon to dissemination of deaf-centered messages in deaf people's native language. Deaf people seized on opportunities to document and reach their widely dispersed deaf audiences via film despite exorbitant cost. Since then, documentation of sign languages in visual media has proliferated exponentially and plays a significant role in shaping the SLLL.

The most obvious environment to house, produce, and contribute to the SLLL is Gallaudet University and its surrounding community. Located in Washington, DC, Gallaudet is the first and only liberal arts institution for deaf people in the world. It has been the academic center and cultural anchor of the American—and even global—deaf communities since 1864. Though Gallaudet is committed to bimodal-bilingual[11] education, a campus visit reveals the primacy of and universal reverence for ASL and other sign languages. The SLLL presents itself across campus and in the surrounding neighborhoods.

A visitor to Gallaudet's campus who walks through the James Lee Sorenson Language and Communication Center cannot help but notice how the architecture facilitates signing. Walkways open on one side to a ceiling-high atrium allowing people on different floors to communicate with each other; windows from floor to ceiling allow people inside and outside the building to see each other and communicate. Orientation toward sign language use presents itself in explicit and implicit ways in signage and displays. Around campus, video announcements are displayed in ASL on TV screens and signing is seen in academic and social forms.[12] Upon entering the ASL and Deaf Studies Department, a sign reads in English, "Sim-Com [prohibited]. Use one language at a time, *please*."[13] Such signage, though in English, sets the linguistic tone of the setting.

Sign language images feature prominently in and around campus, signaling the SLLL for instructional as well as symbolic ends (see website for Figure 2.3). All are emblematic of the sign-dominant context. Figures 2.3c and 2.3d feature the ASL alphabet along with corresponding Roman alphabet letters. Figure 2.3c was taken on a playground close to campus. Such signage is likely less common in contexts where there are few-to-no signing people, but integration of signing into the everyday play life of deaf and signing children should come as no surprise. Figure 2.3d, displayed at the Kellogg Hotel and Conference Center on Gallaudet's campus, has a similar intent: it signals the sign-dominant context while facilitating ASL fingerspelling access to nonsigners.

The new Gallaudet logo (seen in Figures 2.3a, 2.3b, and 2.3d) also underscores the signing context, albeit implicitly. It is visible on and off campus, expanding the SLLL beyond Gallaudet proper. The images in Figures 2.3a and 2.3b show the etymological relation between symbol, form, and meaning. The image contains two banners that read, "We are Gallaudet [woman signing GALLAUDET]" and "A Signing Community." Figure 2.3b shows a stylized formation of movement feature in the sign for GALLAUDET. Figure 2.3d shows the logo along with "Gallaudet University" printed on the bus that transports Gallaudet community members around town and beyond. The mediating image of the woman signing GALLAUDET is not there, but its symbolic representation is evident to signing people. These qualities make it is a quintessential symbol of the SLLL.

Crossover between SLLLs and Nonsigning LLs

Sign languages might prevail in SLLLs, but as mentioned earlier, there are times when sign language images and tokens crossover into the nonsigning LL. These situations are instructive, particularly for those new or naïve to sign languages. Areas with a significant contingent of signing deaf people tend to produce tokens from sign languages but with the intended audience of both signing and nonsigning people. Said contexts are ripe for educational exchange, and savvy deaf and hearing people are now seizing on these opportunities.

As Gulliver and Kitzel (2015) note, intersecting LL and SLLL sometimes occurs temporarily, in typically nonsigning contexts, as in the case of Sainsbury's food store in Bath, England, in July 2019. Here, a typically nonsigning locale converted into a sign-dominant context for a four-day event in recognition of the deaf employees and deaf customers. During this time, store employees learned basic British Sign Language (BSL) and the store was temporarily renamed Signsbury's, a signal that this context intended to be perceived as sign-language learning. Staff communicated with customers in BSL as well as verbally, and attending children who learned basic signs earned a snack as a reward. A signing-friendly context was facilitated by installation of multiple video screens around the store that depicted BSL signs for relevant foods. Nonsigning passers-by could learn the demonstrated signs while signers could see familiar images become further integrated into their community (Sainsbury's, 2019).

Such an effort is emblematic of the widening understanding and acceptance of deaf ways of being, including but not limited to sign language use. It is also economically shrewd:[14] popularity of sign languages makes them broadly marketable: signers and nonsigners are drawn in by these efforts to create temporary SLLLs and such events are opportunities to exponentially expand customer base.

Another example of the marketability of sign language linguistic crossover is the "signing" Starbucks near Gallaudet. This Starbucks integrates multiple principles of a sign-dominant context to appeal to signers and nonsigners:

- It employs only signing people.
- There is widespread depiction of sign language imagery made by deaf people.
- It has abundant, but carefully positioned, light to increase visibility.
- It has low counters to increase sign visibility between patrons and employees.
- There is no music to distract people with any amount of hearing access from the signing.
- It uses deaf-friendly interfaces for transactions: digital notepads and styluses to place orders.
- Finally, they seize on opportunities to directly and indirectly educate their nonsigner patrons.

One example of direct educational instruction is their "Sign of the Week" blackboard display, an example of which is in Figure 2.4. The center top shows hands signing COFFEE and the center right shows someone signing SUMMER. This display, changing weekly, features an ASL sign alongside its English translation. Figure 2.4a showing a Starbucks employee apron with S-T-A-R-B-U-C-K-S fingerspelled along with corresponding letters signals the primacy of sign language to the location. Figure 2.4c features the hard-to-come-by signing Starbucks mug, with a drawing of the ASL sign STARBUCKS, and written English on the inside that says, "Coffee brings us together." It is coveted by deaf people around the United States (and maybe the world) for its symbolic representation of a space where signing and being deaf are valued and privileged. Finally, Figures 2.4e and 2.4f feature both ASL fingerspelling and English signage (separately), overtly reminding each customer and passerby that this is a signing-friendly store and sign-dominant context.

Interestingly, the S-T-A-R-B-U-C-K-S fingerspelling on the storefront and umbrella have no Roman alphabet translations as linguistic mediation for nonsigners, indicators that this space—unlike most—is one where signing is privileged and typical barriers that deaf people face are eliminated. The STARBUCKS mug, the apron, and, of course, the wall display that declares, "This store is dedicated to people united by sign language and Deaf culture," are additional reminders of the linguistic dominance subversion.

Sign language tokens broaden and make portable the potential for deaf geographic spaces. For example, the Starbucks mug is intended to be purchased and brought out into the world beyond the established signing space of that store. Once the mugs leave that space, the potential contexts for display and viewing of the image are infinite with the potential to spread far beyond the SLLL. Another example of a mobile signing

Figure 2.4 Gallaudet Starbucks signage

token intended for public consumption can be found in T-shirts and swag produced by an Italian educational and advocacy organization in Rome, Italy, called Gruppo SILIS. They contracted with a company to produce wearable and otherwise publicly visible items[15] featuring LIS signs. Additionally, Buske, a German publishing house that produces language-learning calendars, recently introduced a German Sign Language (DGS) calendar[16] produced by linguists at the University of Göttingen. Inevitably, these images—designed and developed by signing people—filter into nonsigning spaces by virtue of the fact that signers and nonsigners come into contact frequently—whether they realize it or not. Through these commodified sign images, deaf geographies proliferate beyond their once-siloed contexts, emerging in fleeting and more permanent milieux.

As noted, these tokens are all intended for public consumption. When nonsigners encounter said tokens, the opportunity is ripe for educating nonsigners in the sign translations as well as the ways and values of signing people and deaf communities.

They are a conversation starter, or as Caldwell (2017) calls them, a "conscious speech act," a dialogic model, which in and of itself is an educational opportunity. A nonsigner might see someone wearing a T-shirt with the LIS sign, AMO ("I love"), printed on the front, and recognize that the image displays someone signing. They might then ask what the sign means, prompting a signing-centered discussion that could go in myriad directions, many likely educational.

Unlike many of the other crossover tokens from the past discussed above, none of these signing images contain translations of signs. While we have not yet done a methodical study of images found in the SLLL, it is fair to say that the lack of translation— intended for nonsigning consumption—is likely a key feature of linguistic tokens from the SLLL.

Conclusion

We have attempted to unveil LL representations of sign languages that have heretofore been hidden away, as though behind a veil that obscures something taboo, by the dominance of textual representations. The consistent broadening of what encompasses a LL paved the way for us to look at situations that elicit, engender, and literally shape sign languages' appearance in the LL. We have provided a historical overview of sign languages in context which, in turn, buttressed our presentation and analysis of how representations of sign languages in the LL have evolved from ones that bordered on apologetic to ones that unapologetically burst with pride in signing and being deaf. Within said representations, we examined the potential for educational exchanges that the sign language tokens produce vis-à-vis their contextual appearance and those who have the opportunity to interact with these tokens in their respective milieux. This overdue first foray into the SLLL is hardly all-encompassing; multiple avenues remain to be explored. Future research should document extensively what sign languages look like in the LL, SLLL, and what happens when signing and nonsigning communities interface and/or collide.

Notes

1   For years, it was convention to use lowercase "d" to indicate audiological status and uppercase "D" to indicate sociocultural connections to signing people. More recently, this convention has been seen as divisive (Fisher, Mirus, & Napoli, 2018; Woodward & Horejes, 2016). We thus use lowercase "d" for all references to deaf people except in quotations in which cited authors used uppercase "D."
2   Many of the dynamics in these spaces stem from inclusion of signing people (or nonsigning as the case may be) rather than from being audiologically deaf, though it can be argued that some features of deaf geographies come strictly from audiological status. See Sections IV and VI from Bauman and Murray (2014).
3   Gallaudet College, now known as Gallaudet University, is the only liberal arts institution in the world with the mission to educate deaf and hard-of-hearing individuals. The dominant language is ASL. It remained a signing institution

	throughout the domination of oralist philosophy in the late nineteenth and throughout most of the twentieth centuries.
4	There are many more countries in which sign languages are still seen as underdeveloped gesture systems, inferior to spoken languages. We would imagine that sign languages hardly emerge in the ambient LL in those countries.
5	Some would argue that it still does today; Clark and Ivanic (2013).
6	Deaf peddlers have existed for decades if not centuries in the United States and beyond. There is evidence of deaf vagrancy and peddling in America in the 1850s (Chamberlayne, 1859/2001), during the peak of manualist education before the 1880 Milan Congress edict to ban sign languages in deaf schools (Moores, 2010). Furthermore, deaf peddling still exists today, albeit far less frequently. For a relatively recent account of deaf peddling, see Buck (2000).
7	Some hearing people pose as deaf to more quickly and easily solicit money via peddling. William A. Rockefeller, father of famous oil baron, John. D. Rockefeller, was one. Robinson (2012) gives information on these cases and on deaf community responses to peddling with respect to their own quest for citizenship and equal status to hearing people.
8	Text written in small capital letters represents glossing of ASL signs into written English form. This is conventionally used when discussing signs in textual formats.
9	It is not our intention to exclude deafblind populations here. Gulliver and Kitzel (2015) and Gulliver and Fekete (2017) mention visual orientation as part of deaf geographies. Though not our task at hand here, we would argue that deaf and deafblind geographies are also constructed by the use or exclusion of tactile communication and whether or not those spaces are physically accessible to deafblind people.
10	Padden (2004) notes efforts to provide ASL-to-English interpreters at some of these gatherings, though it is not clear that Veditz's written translation was necessarily the copy read aloud since there is evidence of significant delay of dissemination of a written translation by Veditz.
11	One that includes ASL and written English.
12	Thanks to Greg Niedt for pointing out this observation.
13	The sign, which can be seen in the online image gallery, does not read "prohibited"; it has the ∅ symbol around *sim-com*. *Sim-com* is short for "simultaneous communication," which means signing and speaking simultaneously. This is frowned upon because it is not possible to use both ASL and English at the same time without compromising the structural presentation of one of the languages, more typically ASL.
14	We are not advocating for the commodification of sign languages without direct involvement of or benefit to sign language communities and deaf people themselves. Nor do we advocate for exploitation of deaf people in this process. See Fisher, Mirus, and Napoli (2019) for more information on the problematic nature of sign language appropriation. We are simply pointing out the economic argument that the popularity of sign languages makes them riper for commodification.
15	To view some of these tokens, see https://worthwearing.org/store/gruppo-silis
16	View their site, https://buske.de/sprachkalender/sprachkalender-der-deutschen-gebardensprache-2020.html

References

Bauman, H-D. L., & Murray, J. (Eds.). (2014). *Deaf Gain: Raising the Stakes for Human Diversity*. Minneapolis, MN, and London: University of Minnesota Press.

Bauman, H-D. L., & Murray, J. (2017). Sign languages. In O. García, N. Flores, & M. Spotti (Eds.), *The Oxford Handbook of Language and Society* (pp. 243–60). New York, and Oxford: Oxford University Press.

Bauman, H-D. L., & Rose, H. M. (Eds.). (2006). *Signing the Body Poetic: Essays on American Sign Language Literature*. Berkeley and Los Angeles: University of California Press.

Baynton, D. C. (1996). *Forbidden Signs: American Culture and the Campaign against Sign Language*. Chicago, IL: University of Chicago Press.

Ben-Rafael, E., Shohamy, E., Hasan Amara, M., & Trumper-Hecht, N. (2006). Linguistic landscape as symbolic construction of the public space: The case of Israel. *International Journal of Multilingualism*, 3(1), 7–30.

The Brainy Deaf Site. (n.d.). Deaf Peddlers. http://www.thebrainydeafsite.com/p20.html. Accessed July 9, 2019.

Brennan, M. (2001). Encoding and capturing productive morphology. *Sign Language & Linguistics* 4(1), 47–62.

Buck, D. S. (2000). *Deaf Peddler: Confessions of an Inside Man*. Washington, DC: Gallaudet University Press.

Caldwell, D. (2017). Printed t-shirts in the linguistic landscape. *Linguistic Landscape*, 3(2), 122–48.

Campbell, R., MacSweeney, M., & Waters, D. (2008). Sign language and the brain: A review. *The Journal of Deaf Studies and Deaf Education*, 13(1), 3–20.

Chamberlayne, H. M. (1859/2001). Vagrancy among deaf-mutes. In L. Bragg (Ed.), *Deaf World: A Historical Reader and Primary Sourcebook* (pp. 237–38). New York: New York University Press.

Clark, R., & Ivanic, R. (2013). *The Politics of Writing*. New York: Routledge.

Daniels, P. T. (2013). The history of writing as a history of linguistics. In K. Allan (Ed.), *The Oxford Handbook of the History of Linguistics* (pp. 53–69). Oxford: Oxford University Press.

DeafAdvocacy.org (n.d.) des.pdf https://7a46b124-a-2780ccf2-s-sites.googlegroups.com/a/deafadvocacy.org/orange-county-deaf-advocacy-center/free-sre/des.pdf?attachauth=ANoY7cpYU6LgvbHb-6iM2977gT-gjUpmoFewMMiHTwISYMIG_f5t0AJAihe3m5RAMRB9oKgl3myfNpIaKLFt8jaiIqS91WvSm5u7Ss3G9yF6dm7-ITFz4sYeQQlHgGW91HVuAFSzI_YvREcPvTcW-fEyurY6pVNeTkZeqQsAhKtmpKinbgrxjkKwNCtxR-s7VhIIUxQJ9ltjRDK-dkur0fT2XErqmFf5484-d_VKceiWGvQhTAy19YrJgv436OL81nASAW6zg2fA&attredirects=2 (accessed July 9, 2019).

Deafdigest. (n.d.). Deaf-pin-deaf-peddler-handmade. http://deafdigest.net/deaf-pin-deaf-peddler-handmade/ (accessed July 9, 2019).

Fisher, J., Mirus, G., & Napoli, D. J. (2018). Sticky: Taboo topics in deaf communities. In K. Allen (Ed.), *Oxford handbook of taboo words and language* (pp. 160–79). Oxford: Oxford University Press.

Fisher, J. N., Mirus, G., & Napoli, D. J. (2019). STICKY: Taboo topics in deaf communities. In K. Allen (Ed.), *The Oxford Handbook of Taboo Words and Language* (pp. 160–79). Oxford: University of Oxford Press.

Gorter, D. (2013). Linguistic landscapes in a multilingual world. *Annual Review of Applied Linguistics* 33, 190–212.

Gorter, D., & Cenoz, J. (2017). Linguistic landscape and multilingualism. In J. Cenoz, D. Gorter, & S. May (Eds.), *Language Awareness and Multilingualism*, 3rd ed. (pp. 233–45). Cham, Switzerland: Springer.

Guimarães, C., Guardezi, J. F., & Fernandes, S. (2014). Sign language writing acquisition— Technology for a writing system. In R. H. Sprague, Jr. (Ed.), *2014 47th Hawaii International Conference on System Sciences* (pp. 120–9). Los Alamitos, CA: IEEE.

Gulliver, M., & Fekete, E. (2017). Themed section: Deaf geographies—an emerging field. *Journal of Cultural Geography*, 34(2), 121–30.

Gulliver, M., & Kitzel, M.B. (2015). Deaf geographies. In G. Gertz, & P. Boudreault (Eds.), *The SAGE Deaf Studies Encyclopedia* (pp. 451–3). Washington, DC: Sage.

Humphries, T., Kushalnagar, P., Mathur, G., Napoli, D. J., Padden, C., Rathmann, C., & Smith, S. (2017). Discourses of prejudice in the professions: The case of sign languages. *Journal of Medical Ethics*, 43(9), 648–52.

Karpov, A., Kipyatkova, I., & Zelezny, M. (2016). Automatic technologies for processing spoken sign languages. *Procedia Computer Science*, 81, 201–7.

Kusters, A. (2014). Language ideologies in the shared signing community of Adamorobe. *Language in Society*, 43(2), 139–58.

Ladines, Mara. (n.d.) ASL history is cherished. Video. Retrieved from https://www.facebook.com/bymaraily/videos/10155179898463872/ (accessed July 12, 2019).

Lane, H. L. (1984). *When the Mind Hears: A History of the Deaf.* New York: Vintage.

Lane, H. L. (1992). *The Mask of Benevolence: Disabling the Deaf Community.* New York: Knopf.

Long, J. S. (1908). The sign language. A manual of signs. *American Annals of the Deaf*, 53(3), 230–49.

Looney, D., & Lusin, N. (2018). Enrollments in languages other than English in United States institutions of higher education, Summer 2016 and Fall 2016: Preliminary Report. *Modern Language Association*. New York: Modern Language Association. Retrieved from https://www.mla.org/content/download/83540/2197676/2016-Enrollments-Short-Report.pdf (accessed July 12, 2019).

Matsumoto, D., & Hwang, H. C. (2013). Emblematic gestures (emblems). *Journal of Nonverbal Behavior*, 37(1), 1–27.

McCarty, A. L. (2004). Notation systems for reading and writing sign language. *The Analysis of Verbal Behavior*, 20(1), 129–34.

Miller, C. (2001). Section I: Some reflections on the need for a common sign notation. *Sign Language & Linguistics*, 4(1), 11–28.

Mitchell, R. E., Young, T. A., Bachelda, B., & Karchmer, M. A. (2006). How many people use ASL in the United States? Why estimates need updating. *Sign Language Studies*, 6(3), 306–35.

Moores, D. F. (2010). Partners in progress: The 21st International Congress on Education of the Deaf and the repudiation of the 1880 Congress of Milan. *American Annals of the Deaf*, 155(3), 309–10.

Morford, J. P., & MacFarlane. J. (2003). Frequency characteristics of American Sign Language. *Sign Language Studies*, 3(2), 213–25.

Murray, J. J. (2019). American Sign Language legislation in the USA. In M. De Meulder, J. J. Murray, & R. L. McKee (Eds.), *The Legal Recognition of Sign Languages: Advocacy and Outcomes around the World* (pp. 119–28). Bristol: Multilingual Matters.

NAD. (1910–21). George W. Veditz Collection. Film collection. Retrieved from http://libguides.gallaudet.edu/c.php?g=773917&p=5553210 (accessed July 9, 2019).
Nicodemus, B., Swabey, L., Leeson, L., Napier, J., Petitta, G., & Taylor, M. M. (2017). A cross-linguistic analysis of fingerspelling production by sign language interpreters. *Sign Language Studies*, 17(2), 143–71.
Niles, J. D. (1999). *Homo Narrans: The Poetics and Anthropology of Oral Literature*. Philadelphia, PA: University of Pennsylvania Press.
Oros, C. (2015). Research journal: Estimates of ASL users. Retrieved from https://eportfolios.macaulay.cuny.edu/storytelling/2015/04/25/research-journal-estimates-of-asl-users/ (accessed July 12, 2019).
Padden, C. A. (2004). Translating Veditz. *Sign Language Studies*, 4(3), 244–60.
Prendergast, C. (2001). Negotiating world literature. *New Left Review*, 8(8), 100–22.
Prillwitz, S., Leven, R., Zienert, H., Hanke, T., & Henning, J. (1989). *HamNoSys Version 2.0. Hamburg Notation System for Sign Languages: An Introductory Guide*. Hamburg: Signum.
Robinson, O. E. (2012). *The Deaf Do Not Beg: Making the Case for Citizenship, 1880–1956* (Unpublished doctoral dissertation). Columbus, OH: The Ohio State University.
Sainsbury's. (2019). Welcome to Signsbury's … Sainsbury's unveils UK's first signing store. Retrieved from https://www.about.sainsburys.co.uk/news/latest-news/2019/18-07-2019-signsburys-150-days-of-community (accessed July 9, 2019).
Shohamy, E. (2015). LL research as expanding language and language policy. *Linguistic Landscape*, 1(1), 152–71.
Shohamy, E., & Waksman, S. (2008). Linguistic landscape as an ecological arena: Modalities, meanings, negotiations, education. In E. Shohamy, & D. Gorter (Eds.), *Linguistic Landscape: Expanding the Scenery* (pp. 353–71). Abingdon: Routledge.
Stokoe, W. (1960). Sign language structure: An outline of the visual communication systems of the American deaf. Studies in Linguistics. *Occasional Papers 8*. Buffalo, NY: Department of Anthropology and Linguistics, University of Buffalo (reprinted in 2005, *Journal of Deaf Studies and Deaf Education*, 10(1), 3–37).
Sutton, V. (1995). *Lessons in SignWriting*, La Jolla, CA. Retrieved from http://www.signwriting.org/archive/docs2/sw0116-Lessons-SignWriting.pdf (accessed July 9, 2019).
Sutton-Spence, R., & Kaneko, M. (2016). *Introducing Sign Language Literature: Folklore and Creativity*. London: Palgrave.
Troyer, R. A., & Szabó, T. P. (2017). Representation and videography in linguistic landscape studies. *Linguistic Landscape*, 3(1), 56–77.
Veditz, G. W. (1913). Preservation of the Sign Language. [Video]. Retrieved from https://www.loc.gov/item/mbrs01815816/. Translated into English by C. A. Padden. Retrieved from https://culturasurda.files.wordpress.com/2013/09/preservation-of-sign-language.pdf (accessed July 9, 2019).
Waksman, S., & Shohamy, E. (2010). Decorating the city of Tel Aviv- Jaffa for its centennial: Complementary narratives via linguistic landscape. In E. Shohamy, E. Ben-Rafael, & M. Barni (Eds.), *Linguistic Landscape in the City* (pp. 57–73). Clevedon: Multilingual Matters.
Woodward, J., & Horejes, T. (2016). Deaf/deaf: Origins and usage. In G. Gertz & P. Boudreault (Eds.), *The Sage Deaf Studies Encyclopedia* (pp. 285–7). Thousand Oaks, CA: Sage doi: 10.4135/9781483346489.n93

3

New Caledonia: A Semiotic Analysis of the Landscape as an Opportunity for Learning

Diane de Saint Léger and Kerry Mullan

Introduction

Political upheaval in New Caledonia in the 1980s culminated in the Matignon (1988) and the Noumea (1998) accords with France. In the preamble and Article 1 of the latter, considerable emphasis is placed on the notions of *rééquilibrage* ("rebalancing") and *destin commun* ("common destiny"). These terms circulate widely on all political sides, particularly in the context of the referenda on independence (the first of which was held in November 2018, and the second of which is due to be held in October 2020). These notions are linked with the acknowledgment that the colonization process resulted in the Indigenous Kanak people, their languages, and culture becoming institutionally invisible, depriving them of a legitimate collective identity over time. As a result of the Noumea accord, various programs were launched to protect and value Kanak cultural patrimony as one of the ways to address this unbalance. The primarily oral and immaterial dimensions of Kanak culture have led to a focus on toponymy in an attempt to reconnect the land and places of particular significance with their people (Chatelier, 2007), most noticeably through double signage used to name places in both French and a local language. The predominately rural Province Nord (Northern Province) has been rather active in this process. In the Province Sud (Southern Province), however, and in Noumea in particular, the materiality of change, and the notions of *rééquilibrage* and *destin commun* (including the visibility of Kanak languages), remain less apparent to the external observer (Fillol et al., 2017).

A number of educational and research visits to New Caledonia since 2013 led the authors to become interested in the linguistic and semiotic landscapes of the different regions they encountered and to design a related pedagogical activity for the French students enrolled in the 2019 study abroad program. The objective was to develop students' critical awareness of this complex environment and direct their attention toward important aspects of the cityscape.

This was the third iteration of this biennial program[1] run by the authors (two French teacher-researchers from two universities in Melbourne, Australia). The two-week intensive in-country part of the program followed twelve hours of preparatory lectures and workshops before departure. The aim of the program was to explore the historic, economic, political, and cultural aspects of this neighboring French territory. In-country, our stay was organized around three main locations:

- Days 1–6 on a university campus in Noumea
- Days 7–9 in a Northern Province Kanak community
- Days 10–11 in the touristic area of Noumea
- Days 12–14 on one of the Loyalty Islands
- Days 15–17 back in the same touristic area of Noumea.

While staying at the university campus in the first week, students attended their choice of eight hours of lectures (scheduled for local undergraduate students) on geography, society and history, as well as the Kanak languages and culture. For the duration of the seventeen-day program, they also participated in a large number of guided site visits in all locations, followed by regular debriefing sessions. No formal French language instruction took place, since this was not a language class in the traditional sense, but the entire program was undertaken in the target language. The instructors spoke only French with the students, beginning with the pre-departure selection interviews, which took place between nine and twelve months before departure, and all materials, seminars, in-country visits, and other interactions were conducted in French. The students also primarily spoke French to each other during the formal parts of the program. The student proficiency level in French ranged from low B2 to C1 on the CEFR (Common European Framework of Reference for Languages), which meant that they could engage in complex interactions in the target language without having to resort to English. Sixteen students participated in the tour, representing the enrollment cap for the program.

Our purpose for this study tour was to build on our previous observations of how Kanak and other communities' identities are represented by linguistic and semiotic material in the landscape (such as the symbolic location of administrative and cultural buildings and the positioning of various historical and commemorative monuments) and to demonstrate how such linguistic and semiotic landscapes can be used as a pedagogical tool (Rowland, 2013; Sayer, 2010). We wanted to create opportunities for our students to critically reflect on the signs and symbols they would see to enhance their understanding of the historical and sociopolitical context of their surroundings. Our study can therefore be said to operate at "the intersection of visual discourse, language and sociocultural aspects of spatial practices" (Jaworski & Thurlow, 2010: 1).

This chapter is divided into five sections. The first two sections outline the theoretical and analytical frameworks employed for the study. The third section describes the actual linguistic and semiotic landscape task given to the students and the methodology used for the analysis of the student diaries. This is followed by the results of our analysis of the students' observations and, finally, a discussion section that includes pedagogical implications and conclusion.

Theoretical Framework

Linguistic landscapes (LL) are no longer restricted to the oft-quoted definition by Landry and Bourhis (1997: 25): "[t]he language of public road signs, advertising billboards, street names, place names, commercial shop signs, and public signs on government buildings." To take into account a wider view of communication and representation, Shohamy (2015: 153–4) expanded this list to include non-language-related items such as "images, photos, sounds (soundscapes), movements, music, smells (smellscapes), graffiti, clothes, food, buildings, history, as well as people who are immersed and absorbed in spaces by interacting with LL in different ways." Even earlier than this, Jaworski and Thurlow (2010) had introduced the concept of "semiotic landscapes," which considers places as symbolic representations of social, cultural, and political values. More recently still, Pütz and Mundt (2019: 1) have claimed that LL can in fact be seen as a metaphor, which includes the whole set of "semiotic assemblages" (Pennycook, 2019).[2] This expanded notion of semiotic assemblages "allows for an understanding of how different trajectories of people, semiotic resources and objects meet at particular moments and places, and thus helps us to see the importance of things … and the significance of place alongside the meanings of linguistic resources" (Pennycook, 2017: 269). It "gives us a way to address the complexity of things that come together in the vibrant, changeable exchanges of everyday urban life" (Pennycook, 2017: 278).

Shohamy and Waksman (2009: 326–8) described LL as a "powerful tool for education" in the "need for students to be aware and *notice* the multiple layers of meanings displayed in the public space" (emphasis in original). However, given that Kanak culture (and history) is primarily oral and that we, the authors, were already aware of the general lack of visibility of Kanak languages, particularly in Noumea, we needed to widen our scope from a straightforward LL project per se. The above-mentioned concepts of semiotic assemblages and semiotic landscape provided a suitable backdrop against which it was possible to answer our research questions, which are divided into two parts.

Semiotic Landscape Research Questions

How does one account for a primarily oral culture in colonial settings, where written language is not traditionally a primary means to convey information or knowledge, or perform identity of some kind?

How is the public space in an urban setting such as Noumea materially marked as shared by different cultural groups who orient toward various identities in the age of globalization?

Learner Project Research Question

How can students learn to notice and derive meaning from their surroundings (people and place) and thus begin to understand the complexities of such places without falling into superficial stereotypes or exoticism?

This study was undertaken to address these specific research questions, within the context of a broader research project: the semiotic analysis of the landscape of Noumea. The primary focus of this chapter is to address the research question associated with the learner project.

Analytical Framework

In order to answer these questions, it was necessary to find an analytical approach from which we could design a manageable but meaningful project for our learners within the vast range of possibilities created by linguistic and semiotic landscapes.

For this, we used Scollon and Scollon's framework of geosemiotics, defined as "the study of the social meaning of the material placement of signs and discourses and of our actions in the material world" (2003: 2). The fundamental principles of geosemiotics are: indexicality (the context-dependency of signs), dialogicality (the interdependency of signs), and selection. Geosemiotics also identifies three broad systems of social semiotics that are interconnected at any sites of social action (Scollon & Scollon, 2003: 7–8):

- *Interaction order* (the way in which humans form social arrangements and produce social interactions among themselves)
- *Visual semiotics* (signs, images graphics, texts, photographs, billboards, etc., and the way they interact with one another to produce meaning)
- *Place semiotics* (built environment and the "natural" landscape)

This allowed us to match the aspects of semiotic landscape we considered the most manageable and pertinent for our students against the three elements of the framework as follows:

Interaction Order

- Layout and public use of the Place des Cocotiers, the main city square in Noumea where large numbers of people gather (see below)
- The use of language(s)
- Any other elements that seem to stand out

Visual Semiotics

- Location and types of flags (in general)
- The use of language(s)
- Any other elements that seem to stand out

Place Semiotics

- Streetscape: main arteries, name of streets (see the website for Figure 3.1), location of key buildings (institutional, political, cultural, educational, etc.) in relation to these; parks, squares, statues, and artifacts associated with these spaces; other natural features (position of trees, floral displays)
- The use of language(s)
- Any other elements that seem to stand out

This framework is based on the fact that most external observers typically gravitate toward the city center. The Place des Cocotiers (see website for Figure 3.2) has been unequivocally associated with the hub of city life since the early days of the establishment of Noumea in the mid to late 1800s and has until relatively recently been associated with the presence of white free settlers since the city was not open to convicts or the Melanesian population without special authorization (Hamelin, 2000). It is now the main city square, which continues to bear the marks of this narrative via the various memorials and monuments featured in and around the square.

The place is an aesthetically pleasing space for people to gather informally. It attracts people of various backgrounds and ages, from youth groups listening to music associated with the hip-hop culture, to passersby, schoolchildren, tourists, and locals having their lunch or resting, families, and older generations sitting in the shade. Numerous Melanesians of all ages and other groups use the space, which at first sight suggests strong cultural diversity. At the weekend, this space is also used for organized events such as flea markets, book fairs, music concerts, and so on. A number of museums and other places of interest are located nearby and the Place des Cocotiers itself is a tourist destination attracting, among others, large numbers of cruise ship passengers just for the day. The place is discreetly but continuously policed, with a police station "hub" located at the center of the square, recently replacing the tourist information office, which has been relocated to the waterfront, to better cater for the needs of cruise ship passengers.

Aspects of semiotic landscape can be approached from a conceptual and experiential perspective (looking at maps, photos, and online information during pre-departure seminars or on-site observation). We decided to integrate the task to on site observations as is described below.

The Linguistic and Semiotic Landscape Task

The linguistic and semiotic landscape task presented to the students was embedded in an existing reflective journal task (worth 30 percent of the total assessment for the subject)[3] with specific criteria around recording their critical reflections, questions, experiences, and observations while in-country. Students were asked to write between six and eight entries of at least 300 words each for these journals, although many wrote much more.

At the end of our first full day in Noumea (following a visit to the market, the supermarket, and an orientation tour around the city on the local tourist train that included passing through the Place des Cocotiers), we held our first debriefing session with the students. The aim of this session was to follow Rowland's suggestion that students would benefit from explicit instruction about certain features of linguistic landscapes before embarking on a project (2013: 503). We asked them about their first impressions, what they had noticed so far, what stood out for them in particular, and encouraged them to formulate hypotheses about these observations. There were already a number of interesting reflections and discussions, which helped guide the session.

To avoid information overload in a completely new and semiotically complex environment and to situate this ethnographic type of task within their reflective journals, students were then asked to select one of the following five key areas of focus, to pay particular attention to them when around the Place des Cocotiers, and to incorporate their observations into their journals. The following questions were suggested to the students to orient their noticing:

1. Language/s: which language/s? In what form? Where? Who for? Objective?
2. Flags and associated buildings: what flag/s? Where? What for? Placement in relation to building/each other.
3. Public landmarks and monuments (squares, statues, memorials, public art, fountains, commemorative plaques, etc.): What type? Where? What for? Who for (e.g., tourists, locals, particular communities)?
4. Signs of cultural diversity (people, shops, signs, languages, anything): Where? What type of signs? What for? Who for?
5. Layout and public use of the Place de Cocotiers: who uses the space? What for? Which language/s? Which monuments are associated with the space? Surrounding street names and landmarks.

Methodology

Eight student journals were selected for analysis: four journals from the 2019 cohort and, by way of comparison with a group that did not undertake the semiotic landscape task, four from the 2017 cohort. All eight journals received grades of 80–85 percent to ensure comparability and a certain level of student reflection.

Coding was carried out in several stages: first, we examined a total of 303 passages from fifty-six entries in the eight journals to identify examples of students' noticing and reflection. We then employed descriptive coding (Saldaña, 2015) to determine the range of topics covered. Thematic analysis was then undertaken to sort the examples into specific category headings according to themes. These were further divided into semiotic and non-semiotic observations and mapped against the levels of reflective writing outlined in Appendix 1 (i.e., descriptive writing, descriptive reflection, and critical writing).[4] At each stage, the coding and the analysis were carried out independently by the authors before comparing and discussing the examples.

In what follows, data drawn from both cohorts of student travel diaries are scrutinized to establish if and to what extent the 2019 students drew on the various elements of the semiotic landscape task to scaffold learning and generate further insights about people and place in this Pacific territory, as opposed to the 2017 cohort where no such an approach was adopted. An overview of the findings is presented first. Salient student reflection associated with the above-mentioned domains is then explored and discussed. Limitations as well as pedagogical implications are highlighted in the concluding remarks of the chapter.

Results

Overview

Overall, students from both cohorts focused on a range of similar topics such as food, the built and natural landscape, people, the impact of colonization, the tertiary educational setting, and established parallels and contrasts between New Caledonia and Australia.

Many drew on past travelling experiences to compare and contrast people and places with the new space they were discovering: Australia, but also France and other territories known to students that had gone through similar processes of colonization. As their knowledge of New Caledonia developed, they also started to compare and contrast the various sites they visited, slowly shifting toward a more local or emic understanding of the role (social, political, cultural, etc.) of particular places and people.

If the various themes and categories covered were overall similar, the focus of the reflection was different. The 2017 students took on a more historical perspective whereas the 2019 group concentrated more on contemporary realities (and the colonial processes that have led to it). This divergence is to be associated with the focus we chose on the two iterations of the trip, since the 2017 groups was led in conjunction with two historian colleagues, whereas in 2019 our focus was on local institutions. This difference in emphasis therefore seems to have influenced student reflection in important ways. While on one level this may seem logical (not the least because the journal was assessed), it also stresses the saliency of the decisions academics make as tour leaders in the learning process, particularly in the context of a study tour where many other experiences and encounters (i.e., uncontrolled variables) are available to students. In other words, the perspective adopted encouraged students to reflect and look at this new geopolitical space with a particular lens, directing their attention toward a range of salient parameters among the many other parameters that were available to them.

The Five Focus Areas

In this exercise in meaning making, our 2019 focus, then, was to encourage students to use the built and natural landscapes, the semiotics of the city, to make sense of what they could see, hear, smell, and feel, to avoid clichés and delve deeper into their own lived understanding of people and place.

Overall, the 2019 students tried to achieve this through two means: they focused more on people as social groups and they paid more attention to small details in their surroundings. Referring back to the five focus areas, this mainly translated with students paying particular attention to cultural diversity and the way it was materialized in the urban landscape, and the dynamic interaction of people and place, as manifested in the Place des Cocotiers as well as other places in the city and the territory. The visual semiotics associated with flags was noticed by some but no students specifically focused on public landmarks and monuments to infer meaning or gain greater insights on the narrative of places. Language was a central concern in the sense that as language learners they were keen to develop their knowledge and skill in French, but also in the vernacular languages they encountered, some of them drawing up lists of vocabulary in Drehu[5] for instance. However, none commented on the lack of material realization of those languages in the built landscape. In other words, students mainly picked up on semiotic items that were part of their immediate surroundings or that were mediated by the presence/absence of particular groups. In this complex, sensory-laden, and multilayered urban landscape, absences (or, according to Macalister, 2010, "silence"), it seems, were more difficult to notice.

Place des Cocotiers and Other Spaces (Interaction Order and Place Semiotics)

In 2017, the Place des Cocotiers (see Figure 3.1) was described as a "community space" (2017#1DW1-S2[6]) where "children play" (2017#1DW1-S3), and the flea market that the group attended on the first day (a Sunday), as well as the gym apparatus equipment on the beach front, were referred to as signs of "happiness," "community spirit" and "pleasant lifestyle" (2017#1DW1-S1). In 2019, however, students more readily picked up on the segregation that seemed to exist between people and place and that they linked with wealth disparity. For instance, upon a small tourist train tour that both groups undertook, students in the 2019 cohort readily commented on the "two worlds" that seemed to exist alongside one another (2019#2DR2.2-S1; 2019#1DR2.1-S3). The observation of people in relation to the space they occupied went beyond the contrast they could see between the city center materialized by the Place des Cocotiers and the strong presence of Melanesian people, and the more chic and touristic sector of *Anse Vata* mainly vested by white people. This kind of noticing followed through for the whole duration of the trip, and across a range of settings, from a broad geographical and administrative perspective, where wealth disparity between the north and south of the main island became quite apparent to students (2019#9 DR2.2-S1), and within the microcosm of the university classroom, where local students seemed to "self-organise" into ethnic groups (2019#3 DR2.1-S2). If place was conceived of mainly as a social space, the incidence of the natural landscape in fragmenting or bringing communities together was also picked up on by students. The mountain chain in the north that divides the east and west coasts and the cluster of islands associated with the Grande Terre (main island) led students to wonder about the efficiency of a single political and administrative system that the population lived under (2019#4 CR-S3) and the extent to which the geographical fragmentation of this geopolitical space impacted culture (2019#7 CR-S1).

In the 2017 data, two comments may be associated with the relationship of people and place. A student attending a Nengone class, a language spoken in an island off the coast of the Grande Terre, noticed the exclusive presence of Wallisian and Melanesian students in the tutorial (2017#4DR2.1-S2), while another student visiting a decommissioned building covered in graffiti (Figures 3.3 and 3.4) noted her satisfaction to see a public space associated with Kanak youth culture (2017#1DR2.1-S1). This theme, however, was not picked up again in these students' diaries, and these important insights felt more akin to passing remarks than based on a principled and ongoing reflection on people and place.

A Semiotic Analysis of New Caledonia 65

Figures 3.3 and 3.4 Street art photographed in 2015, *Fédération des oeuvres laïques* (FOL), Nouméa

Cultural Diversity (Interaction Order and Visual Semiotics)

If both groups commented on cultural diversity, the strong focus on people and place in 2019 enabled students to quite quickly develop a more layered and multidimensional understanding of diversity. For instance, using aspects of the learner task suggested to them to help identify signs of cultural diversity (i.e., people, shops, signs, languages, anything: Where? What type of signs? What for? Who for?), the multicultural dimension of the Place des Cocotiers was unpacked by one student who examined the type of food sold, the products found in shops, the languages heard, the presence of tourists and of Kanak people and the presence of Melanesian public art (2019#2DR2.2-S4). Cultural diversity was also picked up by students visiting the local market (Figure 3.5).

Clear connections between stall location (indoor or outdoor), type of products sold, stall holders and currencies displayed were made. The selling of vegetables was associated with Melanesian and Vietnamese groups, whereas the French-related products (i.e., sausages, cheese, honey, etc.) were associated with *Caldoche* (local French) stall holders (2019#2DR2.1-S2). Tourist goods with prices displayed in both Australian dollars and Pacific francs (2019#1DR2.2-S3) were observed at outside stalls for Australian cruise ship passengers stopping over for a few hours, whereas local market goers shopped inside the market hall, where prices were marked in Pacific francs only. Without perhaps yet grasping the significance and implications of their noticing, the students were observing what Pennycook and Otsuji refer to as

Figure 3.5 Local market, Noumea

"particular assemblages of material and semiotic resources as customers, goods and languages assemble" (2017: 435). In their study of two Bangladeshi shops in Tokyo and Sydney, the authors describe how "artefacts come together in particular assemblages that result from the histories of migration, the spatial and economic organization of suburbs, local economies, the layout of shops and the goods they have for sale, and the trajectories of people who come to these shops for the various goods on offer" (Pennycook & Otsuji 2017: 446).[7]

In contrast, the 2017 cohort drew on aspects of the built landscape to pinpoint similarities with France that the configuration of supermarkets and associated products exemplified (2017#1DW1-S3, #1DW1-S4) and commented on the French influence more broadly (2017#9DR2.1-S2). They also used buildings to draw on the missionary narrative (see website for Figure 3.6), commented on the presence and role of the church (2017#7DW1-S4, 2017#4DW1-S2, 2017#5 DR2.1-S1) and discussed the urban impact of colonialism in town planning and colonial architecture (2017#5DR2.1-S4).

Figure 3.6 Église du Sacré-Cœur, Bourail (available online)

Students also drew on other places of worship and memorials such as the mosque and the First World War New Zealand cemetery to gain some insights into the cultural complexity of the place (2017#3DR2.1-S2) and on the difficult colonial history associated with the territory (tomb of Jean-Marie Tjibaou in Tiendanite; 2017#7 DR2.1-S4, 2017#4 DW1-S2). The built environment was therefore an important trigger that guided student noticing in 2017 and seems to have combined well with the historical perspective adopted on the occasion of that tour. Student remarks tended to be more confined to basic levels of reflection, however, suggesting that the absence of focus on the dynamic relation between people and place limited the students' ability to infer meaning beyond descriptive levels and they failed to problematize new knowledge adequately.

Indeed, such comments fell short of acknowledging the multilayered cultural diversity in the urban landscape that reflects the various needs and orientation of users and showed a less refined and nuanced understanding of place than the 2019 cohort. In many ways, the lens adopted in 2017 was very much a top-down rather than a bottom-up approach. Both approaches are legitimate and indeed complementary, but the bottom-up approach favored in 2019 drew student attention away from the prevalent and clearly apparent French narrative that permeates numerous domains (linguistic, cultural, political, administrative, etc.) to focus on local-level narratives. This, in turn, helped students further their understanding of the sociocultural complexity of the terrain.

Flags and Symbols (Visual Semiotics)

Flags and associated buildings (see website for Figure 3.7) were not a domain that generated many comments in the 2019 data—nor in fact in the 2017 data, where there is no mention of it at all—despite lecturers explicitly commenting on it on both occasions. Since both the French and the Kanaky flags fly on top of every town hall and institutional building, students perhaps felt there was not much to discuss once this was acknowledged, despite the fact that marked variation in the ordering and presence/absence of flags can be seen in the whole territory and despite ongoing controversies over the place and use of the Aboriginal flag in Australia, for example, who can reproduce, who can use it, and when it can be used.[8] Although widely acknowledged by all students from both cohorts during the tour, the ubiquitous presence of the Kanaky flag in Northern Province, placed along the roads on poles, trees, houses, roadside stalls, and so on, was only acknowledged by one student who saw the flag as a daily reminder of the independence struggle in the region and the entering into separatist land (2019#3 DR2.2-S3).

Figure 3.7 European Union, French, and Kanaky flags on the *Centre de formation en alternance* (i.e., TAFE school) (available online)

French National Day (Interaction Order and Place Semiotics)

The highly symbolic and charged French National day and associated parade that took place in Noumea on 14 July and to which our delegation was invited generated many comments with the 2019 group (the 2017 group left before that date). On this occasion, the full suite of the French Republican symbols was on display and the French local reserve troops paraded down the main street. The student focus continued to be on people and they readily noted the proportionally low number of Melanesians in the crowd, as well as in the parade, and the unusually high influx of white people in the city center for the occasion (2019#6 DR 2.2-S4, 2019#9 DR2.1-S2, 2019#6 DR2.1-S3, 2019#8 DR2.2-S1). The whole event was described as a "cut and paste" of the parade taking place in France on the Champs Elysées and suggested a striking lack of inclusiveness that some also compared with Australia Day.[9] The whole event led one student to comment that she now fully comprehended the impact of colonization on the various groups of people on the land and what the waving of the French flag meant in this part of the globe (2019#6CR-S4).

Language

As discussed briefly above, the focus on language mainly consisted in vocabulary lists drawn up in both French and local languages as students learnt new words of interest to them. One student noticed that signs at the Tjibaou cultural center[10] were in French, English and Japanese (2019#4DW1-S2) but failed to notice that no signs were in local languages and no visual representation of any of the twenty-eight local Kanak languages were readily visible. Similarly, no student commented on this silence in the context of the city center (see website for Figure 3.8) or on the fact that the toponymy in the Province Nord was rendered in both French and local language, as opposed to (what they saw of) the Province Sud, where places were only signposted in French.

Figure 3.8 Fontaine Céleste, Places des Cocotiers, Noumea (available online)

The clear discrepancy between the oral mode of interaction where a range of local languages are being heard and the written language used in public space was not problematized. One student, however, noticed that while in Lifou, one of the

Loyalty Islands off the coast of the Grande Terre, a local student was tattooed in Drehu, the local language, and that the importance of the language for that student was greater than for the university students she had met on campus in Noumea who seemed to be more Franco and Euro-centered because of the associated advantages (2019#6DR2.2-S3).

Although not framed in terms of language, but in terms of the relationship with land and orientation toward their own culture, the various stakes associated with rural and urban communities were also picked up on by students. They could see the tension between the Melanesian cultural heritage that is unequivocally present in rural contexts and the realities of the twenty-first century that the Kanak youth, urban or otherwise, may wish to orient to. This insight was then problematized in light of the independence movement (2019#4CR-S4).

Discussion, Pedagogical Implications and Conclusion

Overall, it is fair to say that both cohorts developed important insights into the complexity of the territory during their stay and that the students' good mastery of the French language was critical in the learning process because of the direct access to people and places that it enabled. The noticeably different perspectives adopted by each cohort that broadly echoed the perspective adopted in the course (historical in 2017 and political sciences in 2019) are also noteworthy because they framed the student reflection in important ways.

In light of this, the more overtly critical approach adopted by the 2019 cohort and the emphasis placed on geosemiotics seem to have better equipped students toward the development of independent and critical thinking by focusing on the dynamics of people and place. Indeed, rather than relying on the declarative knowledge of others, as students seem to have done more frequently in 2017, the relatively simple framework based on careful observation helped the 2019 students pick up on important facets of this complex landscape. This bottom-up approach is more akin to ethnographic modes of inquiry and combined well with the objectives and design of the tour where numerous opportunities were offered to students to interact with local populations in a range of places and settings. Importantly, this approach also seemed to have steered students away from the traps of essentialism, whereby particular groups might have been labelled or associated with particular values without questioning assumptions any further. The above-mentioned insight gained by one student over the cultural complexities that Kanak youth have to face in light of the realities of the twenty-first century, where both decolonization and globalization processes are at play, is a case in point, as is this same student's realization of her naïve assumption that Melanesian communities were not motivated by capitalist gains (2019#5CR-S4).

The task embedded in Scollon and Scollon's (2003) geosemiotics framework seems to have also fostered noticing in a broader range of domains than that displayed in 2017. It included for instance the evolving place and role of women in Melanesian communities and the variation in practice of the *coutume* (a traditional form of greeting based on the recognition of entering the land associated with a particular clan), both domains that were not discussed by students in 2017.

The framework also enhanced the breadth and depth of reflection of students as the range of themes evoked at DR2.2 and CR levels seem to suggest: in 2017 students focused on the impact of colonialism and contemplated the various stakes associated with independence, together with the various issues associated with tourism. Parallels and differences with Australia were also drawn in relation to history, the indigenous population, and the mining industry. In 2019, in addition to these themes, students discussed the place and role of the strong centralized French education system in sustaining the colonial process; they observed variation in cultural practices and gender role distribution, as discussed above; and they pondered over the role of the geographical features and the type of setting in shaping people and politics. Most importantly (unlike some instances in the 2017 cohort), despite the incompleteness of some of their insights, none made incorrect assumptions based on stereotypical views or inappropriate projections. Although difficult to know to what extent the semiotic landscape task was directly responsible for this difference, what we saw in the 2017 cohort was a more top-down received form of knowledge than in 2019.

Indeed, despite the fact that the 2019 students did not always "know" what to do with the information gathered (that which was categorized at DW or DR2.1 levels), or how to immediately infer meaning from their observations, reflective writing acted like a repository of thoughts, ideas, and observations, like pieces of a puzzle that include narratives mediated not only by an intermediary person (a tour guide, the lecturers, students met on campus and so on) but also by astute personal observations that could be modified or revised as their journey of discovery unfolded. This dynamic form of learning and meaning-making is in our view central to any programs concerned with the development of students' critical thinking in the context of a study tour, and the framework derived from geosemiotics was an important means to achieve this.

The lack of extensive engagement with the linguistic landscape and the semiotics of public landmarks indicate that more formal training is required for students to learn to *notice* in the sense meant by Shohamy and Waksman (2009). This process could start well before arriving on-site, looking at the city map and noticing various features that seem to stand out (e.g., street names, buildings, or places of interest that index a particular narrative) with the objective of developing hypotheses over the potential meaning of salient features that could be verified once on-site. This approach could encourage learners to be critically engaged from the outset to sharpen their observational skills as they familiarize themselves with the new space. This step is often undertaken by tour leaders instead, who are typically in charge of guiding participants to places of interest, thus lessening opportunities for noticing. We strongly believe that in the context of a tour where the development of learners' critical awareness is central, such a step—where safe and practical—needs to be taken by students instead, so that they can develop an awareness of place as a concept situated in a particular time and geopolitical space.

The analysis for this study was based on eight student diaries that best represented what was deemed a good level of achievement in terms of breadth and depth of reflection as indicated by the student grade. The focus was therefore not on "outstanding" students who demonstrated a very high level of critical awareness and insights on the occasion of both tours, nor those who only partially adequately addressed the requirement of the task. For a more complete picture, however, it would be necessary to analyze all thirty-two student diaries.

It is also important to acknowledge that in addition to the assessment guidelines, student reflection was motivated by personal and subjective preferences and the many conversations students had among themselves. The learning recorded in the journal represents therefore only a partial snapshot of the students' experience and understanding of people and place. We cannot be absolutely sure that students did not notice something just because they did not mention it in their diaries. Provisions should also be made for the fact that the recurrence of particular themes in the data may also be due to the collective, informal form of scaffolding generated by the group.

This chapter aimed to show how linguistic and semiotic landscapes can be used for educational purposes, in particular for the development of students' critical thinking and to enhance their understanding of a nearby territory with a specific sociopolitical context. Despite the recent increase in linguistic and semiotic landscape pedagogical projects for students, New Caledonia and the Pacific have featured in very few of these to date, and it is to be hoped that this pilot study might inspire further research and student projects in the region.

Acknowledgments

The authors would like to acknowledge the New Colombo Plan 2019 mobility funding that the students received from the Australian government to participate in this study abroad program.

Appendix 1

Levels of reflective writing (adapted from Hatton & Smith, 1995 except where indicated)
  Level 1—descriptive writing (code: DW1)
  No evidence of reflection is shown: the student describes what they see, hear, experience without any attempt to interpret, analyze, or "unpack" what they have chosen to report on.
  Note: This level of writing is legitimate and expected since students are engaged in writing a sort of travel diary. Descriptive writing should not however be the main kind of writing. This was clearly stated in the task description and repeatedly explained to students in pre-departure seminars and during the trip.
  Level 2—descriptive reflection (code: DR2.1 and DR2.2, see below)
  Not only a description of events but some attempt to provide a reason or justification for events or actions, although still in a reporting or descriptive way.
  Students typically draw on prior knowledge (what they have learned about the place) and link this knowledge with what they see, hear, experience, etc. This can manifest on two levels:

Level 2.1 Reflection is based generally on one perspective/factor as rationale. *(code: DR2.1)*

Level 2.2 Reflection is based on the recognition of multiple factors and perspectives. *(code: DR2.2)*

Reflection takes a concept and considers it in relation to personal experiences. This level is legitimate in the sense that it recycles what was discussed and learned in pre-departure seminars and formal and informal discussions held with various local actors (students on campus, artists met, local personalities, tour guides, etc.). It is a means to recycle learning, put it into context, and apply it to lived realities. There is however no attempt to critically challenge or question that learning or to take it further and apply it to new contexts.

Level 3—critical reflection: challenging students' beliefs and expectations (code: CR)

Students notice patterns, behavior, practice, elements of the (built) landscape to infer knowledge and/or further their understanding of a particular phenomenon. They are able to articulate why this noticing is significant to their learning and understanding of people and place.

The student "[d]emonstrates an awareness that actions and events are not only located in, and explicable by, reference to multiple perspectives but are located in, and influenced by multiple historical, and socio-political contexts" (Smith, 1992 cited in Hatton & Smith, 1995, : 49).[11]

Students involved in critical reflection do most or all of the following (adapted from Ash & Clayton, 2004: 146):

- Make statements of fact that are accurate, supported with evidence. (Accuracy)
- Address the complexity of the problem, answer important question(s) that are raised, avoid oversimplifying when making connections. (Depth)
- Give meaningful consideration to alternative points of view, interpretations. (Breadth)
- Demonstrate a line of reasoning that is logical. Draw conclusions that follow clearly from it. (Logic)

Notes

1. See also de Saint-Léger and Mullan (2018).
2. Although Pennycook cautions against adding ever more semiotic items to LL inventories (2019: 77).
3. Other assessment includes oral presentations undertaken before departure or in-country (30 percent) and a research project on our return (40 percent).
4. Many students included photographs and hand-drawn images in their diaries to support their observations. For the purposes of this study they are considered as *Level 1—descriptive writing* (DW1).
5. The language spoken on the island of Lifou.
6. Coding indicates cohort year, journal entry number, level of reflection, and student code name (S1, S2, S3, or S4). For instance, (2017#1DW1-S2) indicates that it is from

the 2017 cohort, diary entry number 1 produced by student 2 and that the reflection level corresponds to descriptive writing. See Appendix 1 for more information on the levels of reflective writing.
7   For other research into the linguistic landscape of small shops and markets, see Blackledge, Creese, & Hu (2016), Hua, Otsuji, & Pennycook (2017).
8   The Aboriginal flag is a copyright work owned by the artist who created it in 1971, Luritja man Harold Thomas. (Cf. https://aiatsis.gov.au/explore/articles/aboriginal-flag, accessed December 28, 2019.)
9   Twenty-sixth of January is celebrated as the day Australia was founded. In contrast, it is also referred to as "Invasion Day," and in recent years there has been a growing movement to Change the Date. (Cf. https://australianstogether.org.au/discover/australian-history/australia-day/, accessed December 28, 2019.)
10 The center was built as part of the Matignon Agreement and aims to promote Kanak culture.
11 The actual reference is not listed in Hatton and Smith (1995), and a database search did not uncover Smith (1992).

References

Ash, S., & Clayton, P. (2004). The articulated learning: An approach to guided reflection and assessment. *Innovative Higher Education*, 29(2),137–54.

Blackledge, A., & Creese, A. (2019). *Voices of a City Market: An Ethnography*. Bristol: Multilingual Matters.

Blackledge, A., Creese, A., & Hu, R. (2016). The structure of everyday narrative in a city market: An ethnopoetics approach. *Journal of sociolinguistics*, 20(5), 654–76.

Chatelier, J. (2007). La révision toponymique (et cartographique) en Nouvelle-Calédonie (1983–1993). *Journal de la Société des Océanistes*, 125, 295–310.

De Saint-Léger, D., & Mullan, K. (2018). A short-term study abroad program: An intensive linguistic and cultural experience on a neighboring Pacific island. In C. Sanz & A. Morales-Front (Eds.), *The Routledge Handbook of Study Abroad Research and Practice* (pp. 293–307). London: Routledge.

Fillol, V., Colombel-Teuira, C., Geneix-Rabault, S., & Vandeputte-Tavo, L. (2017). Les langues dans la ville de Nouméa: sociolinguistique urbaine et interdisciplinarité. Pour une recherche à visée sociale en contexte postcolonial. *SOCLES*, 10, 101–17.

Hamelin, C. (2000). Les gens de Nouméa. Mutations et permanences en milieu urbain. In A. Bensa & I. Leblic (Eds.), *En pays kanak: Ethnologie, linguistique, archéologie, histoire de la Nouvelle Calédonie* (pp. 339–54). Paris: Éditions de la Maison des sciences de l'homme.

Hatton, N., & Smith, D. (1995). Reflection in teacher education: Towards definition and implementation. *Teaching and Teacher Education*, 11(1), 33–49.

Hua, Z., Otsuji, E., & Pennycook, A. (2017) Multilingual, multisensory and multimodal repertoires in corner shops, streets and markets: Introduction, *Social Semiotics*, 27(4), 383–93.

Jaworski, A., & Thurlow, C. (2010). *Semiotic Landscapes: Language, Image, Space*. London and New York: Continuum.

Landry, R., & Bourhis, R. Y. (1997). Linguistic landscape and ethnolinguistic vitality: An empirical study. *Journal of Language and Social Psychology*, 16(1), 23–49.

Macalister, J. (2010). Emerging voices or linguistic silence?: Examining a New Zealand linguistic landscape. *Multilingua—Journal of Cross-Cultural and Interlanguage Communication*, 29(1), 55–75.

Pennycook, A. (2017). Translanguaging and semiotic assemblages. *International Journal of Multilingualism*, 14(3), 269–82.

Pennycook, A. (2019). Linguistic landscapes and semiotic assemblages. In M. Pütz, & N. Mundt (Eds.), *Expanding the Linguistic landscape: Linguistic Diversity, Multimodality and the Use of Space as a Semiotic Resource* (pp. 75–88). Bristol: Multilingual Matters.

Pennycook, A., & Otsuji, E. (2017). Fish, phone cards and semiotic assemblages in two Bangladeshi shops in Sydney and Tokyo, *Social Semiotics*, 27(4), 434–50.

Pütz, M., & Mundt, N. (2019). Multilingualism, multimodality and methodology: Linguistic landscape research in the context of assemblages, ideologies and (In)visibility: An introduction. In M. Pütz & N. Mundt (Eds.), *Expanding the Linguistic Landscape: Linguistic Diversity, Multimodality and the Use of Space as a Semiotic Resource* (pp. 1–22). Bristol: Multilingual Matters.

Rowland, L. (2013). The pedagogical benefits of a linguistic landscape project in Japan. *International Journal of Bilingual Education and Bilingualism*, 16(4), 494–505.

Saldaña, J. (2015). *The Coding Manual for Qualitative Researchers*, 2nd ed. London: Sage.

Sayer, P. (2010). Using the linguistic landscape as a pedagogical resource. *ELT Journal*, 64(2), 143–54.

Scollon, R., & Scollon, S. W. (2003). *Discourse in Place: Language in the Material World*. London/New York: Routledge.

Shohamy, E. (2015). LL research as expanding language and language policy. *Linguistic Landscape*, 1(1/2), 152–71.

Shohamy, E., & Waksman, S. (2009). Linguistic landscape as an ecological arena: Modalities, meanings, negotiations, education. In E. Shohamy & D. Gorter (Eds.), *Linguistic Landscape: Expanding the Scenery* (pp. 313–31). New York: Routledge.

Part Two

Structured Spaces Becoming Classrooms

4

The Linguistic Landscape of Public Health Institutions in Tanzania

Paschal Mdukula

Introduction

Linguistic tokens that constitute what is popularly known as linguistic landscape (LL) are everywhere in our public spaces in modern cities and public health institutions in particular—thus one cannot walk through a road or a street for 0.5 km in a city or an institution without encountering them. These linguistic tokens have become an integral part of the cities' built environment that manifest the representation of written language(s) on the public space ranging from a tiny handwritten piece of paper expressing a note of welcome to a huge advertising billboard put up in a public space (Gorter, 2006). Their presence indicates to an individual in which linguistic culture he/she is navigating, which languages are spoken therein, which languages are accepted in that space, and which languages he/she is supposed to know so as to be able to navigate well in such a public space.

One can appreciate the same when visiting public health institutions in Tanzania—where different visual linguistic signs put up around the hospital compounds welcome, direct, inform, warn, instruct, educate the hospital clients and the hospital community in general. In the context of the health facility where people visit for medical services, there are many elements that can help people visiting the hospital to be comfortable and feel welcomed though they are sick or accompanying their relatives or friends. These include the healthcare provider's sense of caring and most importantly the language they encounter and read on the LL of the facility they are visiting because public signs are the most visible and appealing linguistic objects in the public space of the hospital that are meant to disseminate important information to the hospital clients and make their hospital life easy. In fact, public signs are the first elements any conscious hospital client is likely to encounter before getting to the information desk for more instructions because they speak on their own. They are normally used to direct hospital clients to their destinations in the hospital context. In addition, not all hospital clients can get access to health, administrative, regulatory, and client's rights information contained in books or brochures but can access the same through scattered public signs in the hospital environment.

The current study adopts the concept of LL (with slight modifications) as treated by Landry and Bourhis (1997) in which LL will mean 'a field of study that deals with analysis of language on signs in the public space. These signs are linguistic objects as marked by the use of written language in the public space such as road signs, advertising billboards, place names, commercial shop signs, and public signs on public and private buildings which combine to give shape of the linguistic landscape of a given institution or territory'.

The motivation for this modification is meant to accommodate some useful theoretical constructs that were not included in the previous definition such as institutions. With this modification, the current study extends the scope of area of study for linguistic landscape studies that LL can also deal with a single specific institution and other fields like healthcare rather than dealing with commercial spaces, classrooms (educational settings) in an urban agglomeration as it has been always the case in many LL studies. Commenting on the features and expectations borne by LL, Garvin (2011: 13) claims that

> LL is dynamic and multi-layered, constantly changing to represent the values, needs, resources, institutions, restrictions, contestations, cultures, languages, and dreams of its multiple authors who are positioned and actively positioning themselves within a geographical space.

Literature shows that language use and practice in healthcare delivery systems is one of the important aspects that play a great role in assisting access to information, provision of therapy, curative drugs, administrative information as well as general information that promotes public health to clients attending the health facilities (Martinéz, 2014; Schuster, 2012; Schuster, Elroy, & Elmakais, 2016). While there are many studies on LL addressing language practice and language management in public spaces such as education and language policy (Clemente, Andrade, & Martins, 2012; Shohamy, 2015; Spolsky, 2009), commercial and economic centers (Bwenge, 2009; Claus, 2002; Singhasiri, 2013), language prevalence and attitude (Wamalwa, Adika, & Kevogo, 2013), urban multilingualism (Backhaus, 2005; Gorter, 2006; Ranga, 2012), the LL literature focusing on social domains such as healthcare seem to be inadequate and for Tanzanian context it is even nonexistent. Due to this inadequacy, this chapter aims at exploring more on LL in a healthcare field in Tanzania so as to explain the nature of LL in this public space and show how it influences access to information in the studied public hospitals in Tanzania. It is anticipated that the lack of language access leads to failure of hospital clients to access the information necessary to make an informed health decision while navigating in the health environment like a hospital, and then it is very likely that the person's health and the services rendered will be compromised or become inadequate. It is a fact that although language is spoken and heard, it is also equally represented and displayed through signs for informational or symbolic purposes in the public space. The use of written language in the public space is essentially the main focus of linguistic landscape studies in which it is used to fulfill either information or symbolic functions in the public space (Backhaus, 2007; Ben-Rafael et al., 2006; Gorter, 2013; Landry & Bourhis, 1997). The language(s) displayed in the hospital's public space are important in enabling access to information that matters to clients as they navigate through the hospital's space. This in turn educates and helps them to make informed decisions about their health plans, healthcare services, rules, rights, and responsibilities to observe while navigating the hospital environment.

General Sociolinguistic Situation of Tanzania

Tanzania is a home to many languages used by people to share and meet their communicative needs in different formal and informal domains. The exact number of languages spoken in Tanzania is not clear though many scholars quote 120+ as the approximate number of the languages spoken in the country. The most recent survey of linguistic situation in Tanzania estimates the number of languages spoken in Tanzania to be 150 (Languages of Tanzania, 2009). The surveyed 150 languages across the country are mostly spoken rather than written because majority of speakers of these languages are not conversant when it comes to reading or writing their Ethnic Community Languages (ECLs). Among the surveyed languages, Kiswahili was noted to be the dominant language compared to others with more than 90 percent of speakers (Languages of Tanzania, 2009). Mazrui and Alamin (1998) positively argue that Kiswahili managed to occupy a dominant position in a plural society in postcolonial Tanzania simply because it was seen as a solution to ethnic linguistic diversity at the time and was associated with political integration and freedom from the nails of colonial languages. They further argue that Kiswahili received its place in the national policy in East Africa and Tanzania in particular because it was a *"preponderant"* language—an indigenous language that is very widespread as a second language but whose native speakers are not numerous enough to exert political threat.

The other group of languages spoken in Tanzania falls under category of foreign languages. Languages like English and French are spoken by a small number of speakers in Tanzania, and in recent times we encounter the emergence of Chinese language in the linguistic landscape of Tanzania—a situation that proves the dynamics of language contact. In terms of use, the three language groups can be said to fulfill both instrumental and symbolic functions at different levels and space (Ben-Rafael et al., 2006; Landry & Bourhis, 1997). Kiswahili is mainly used as an official language of administration in various government organs such as parliament, in press, as medium of instruction in primary schools, inter- and intra-communication within Tanzanian communities, window for economic opportunities, sign of modernity, identity for Tanzanians, and national unity (Lusekelo, 2019).

Similarly, English is mainly used in the education system as a language of instruction, especially in secondary schools and higher learning institutions. It is also used in parliament for documentation purposes, used as a symbol of modernity, used for communication with the outside world in different matters like signing of trade contracts, and also used in the high court as an official language (Biswalo, 2010; Petzell, 2012; Tibategeza, 2009). On the other hand, ECLs are spoken in specific areas where their speakers live and they are mainly used for local communication and ethnic identity (Petzell, 2012). In fact, they are confined around the homes and informal settings within their communities, mostly in rural areas. They are not acknowledged even in policy documents such as National Health Policy (URT, 2007) and Educational Policy (URT, 1995) and are not represented in the linguistic landscape of the country.

Generally, the linguistic situation of Tanzania essentially consists of a triglossic situation, which follows a three-language model by Bamgbose (1991) as quoted in Petzell (2012: 9). Based on this model, there is Kiswahili, English (and other languages in the group of foreign languages), and ECLs—Kiswahili being the dominant language spoken by almost 90 percent of Tanzanians (Qorro, 2009; Rubagumya, 1990). This means, the majority of Tanzanians (90 percent) share Kiswahili as their common language than any other language being used side by side for informal and formal communication at home and on official gatherings such as political rallies, religious matters, administration, education, and media. The question is, to what extent is the language of the majority (Kiswahili) represented in the public signs that are found in the linguistic landscape of public hospitals in Tanzania?

Conceptualizing Linguistic Landscape

Constructing the Public Space in the LL in Tanzania

According to Landry and Bourhis (1997) and Ben-Rafael et al. (2006), linguistic landscape encompasses the visibility of languages on objects that mark the public space. These linguistic objects constitute road signs, names of sites such as streets, buildings, and institutions, as well as advertising billboards on commercial centers in the cityscape. In the context of this study they include medical forms by health insurance agencies, signs put on windows and doors for direction purposes, signs on billboards for education purposes, signs in different public spaces at the hospital compounds for both administrative and educational purposes. These linguistic objects are issued to the public space either by public authorities such as government agencies or individuals, associations or firms acting independently without restrictions or intervention from the state (Backhaus, 2009). The public authorities normally act under the control of legal limits of local and central policies (Ben-Rafael et al., 2006). Spolsky and Cooper (1991), Spolsky (2009), and Landry and Bourhis (1997) demonstrate that the signs available in the public space function as information markers or symbolic markers—communicating the relative power and status of linguistic community groups in a given boundary. Informational marker function deals with how public signs are used to disseminate information to the general public such as indexing, warning, instructing, prohibiting, promoting, educating, or simply the use of signs for instrumental purposes. In other words, this is a communicative function of public signs in the public space. Because of symbolic influence attached to language by the dominant group, it is not a startling thing to find only one language represented highly in the linguistic landscape of a public space. In this regard, therefore, public space is constructed by competing social, political, and ideological forces, which are brought to practice through LL.

Linguistic Landscape Actors in Public Hospitals in Tanzania

Understanding the linguistic landscape of a place means understanding the key actors who make the linguistic landscape flourish in a given space. It also means understanding the scenes where society's public life takes place, their attitude, and beliefs. In this regard, therefore, what is seen in the linguistic landscape is a function of various actors as they interact and express their sense of values in the public space. For a linguistic landscape to exist and take shape, there must be agents or actors that are closely involved in the creation, advancing and shaping it. Their participation takes different roles, such as creating the LL signs through writing the texts and putting up the signs in different public spaces and identifying themselves with the language used on the signs. The current chapter adopted the categorization of these actors by Backhaus (2007) and Gorter (2006) who categorized them as top-down actors and bottom-up actors.

(i) Top-Down Actors

These are bodies working on behalf of the government. For the context of this study, they include medical insurers and medical supporting agencies such as NHIF and Abbot Fund, medical institutes such as MOI and JKCI, medical bodies such as Medical Society of Tanganyika (MST), Midwives Association, and the hospitals' management and staff. These bodies at different times create and post signs that are meant to provide instructions, warnings, or disseminate health-related information and other regulatory information to the general public as can be appreciated in the public hospitals' linguistic landscape; hence they act as agents of linguistic landscape development (Backhaus, 2009; Ben-Rafael et al., 2006) in their areas of operation. However, their production and placement of signs differ significantly among these groups due to power relations they hold in a hospital context. Commenting on differences between top-down and bottom-up items in relation to language policy, Ben-Rafael et al. (2006: 10) argue that

distinguishing top-down and bottom-up flows of LL elements, that is, between LL elements used and exhibited by institutional agencies which in one way or another act under the control of local or central policies, and those utilized by individual, associative or corporative actors who enjoy autonomy of action within legal limits. The main difference between these two wide categories of LL elements resides in the fact that the former are expected to reflect a general commitment to the dominant culture while the latter are designed much more freely according to individual strategies.

According to Ben-Rafael et al. (2006) and Gorter (2006), the official language policy is normally reflected on top-down items than bottom-up items. However, we should emphasize here that language being a fluid entity in the public space cannot be easily controlled by top-down-bottom-up agencies because this is seen, in some context, as individual's freedom in using language (Backhaus, 2009).

(ii) Bottom-Up Actors

These are individuals or private companies who are not controlled or regulated by any governmental agencies (Backhaus, 2009; Gorter, 2006). In most cases, these actors do not operate within established legal limits of language policy. A good example of how bottom-up actors operate is through use of graffiti in the street and walls of buildings. In fact, linguistic landscape actors differ from one setting to another. For example, bottom-up actors have no official logo of identity, unlike top-down actors who act within legal limits and have to follow some specifications for writing and posting the signs (Backhaus, 2007). For the context of this study, bottom-up actors were clients from outside the hospitals such as patients and family members, catering companies, mobile communication vendors, security guards, and janitors.

Characteristics of Language on Public Signs

The language on signs is different from the one used in spoken language. Backhaus (2005: 21) identifies the following unique characteristics with regard to language of public signs.

(i) It lacks a recognizable emitter; thus it is not easy to identify the specific writer on the sign.
(ii) It lacks a specified target group; thus the language on signs has unknown readership. That is why it is said that access to a public sign is free to everyone.
(iii) The sign reader has no immediate means of responding to the transmitted message on the sign.
(iv) It has indexical qualities, which make it different from letters, memos, books, and newspaper.
(v) It functions independently of its emplacement.
(vi) It can be permanent or temporal depending on the context and use.

The Role of Signs in Public Health Facilities

Signs have become a common feature of our today's modern society in which there is massive generation of signs every day in the public space (El-Busaidy, 2014). Health facilities like other public domains cannot function without public signs as these serve different roles to the community in which the facility is located; hence communication in whatever way would be inconceivable without the use of signs in big health facilities. These roles include:

(i) Source of Information

Public signs play an important role in delivering information to the public. One main function of linguistic landscape signs in the public space is that they act as an informational marker or educational marker (Akindele, 2011; Backhaus, 2007). This means that public signs are an alternative way of conveying information to the public through visual language, as it could be very difficult to depend on verbal means every time they need to understand something in the public space of the hospital. With informative public signs, people can go without asking anybody around for information about areas of services, medication, therapies, hours of operation; warnings, regulations, and location of buildings are easily accessible through public signs.

(ii) *Introduce People to New Things at the Health Facility*

Public signs introduce people to new things that they would otherwise not know without these signs (Martínez, 2014). At the hospital there are many things such as instructions, warnings, prohibitions, and rules posted every day, which cannot be introduced to people verbally every time, but the sign fulfills this function. Therefore, information on public signs help people make sense of which world they are and sense about events, services available, instructions to follow and the things to pay attention to (Schuster et al., 2016).

(iii) *Public Signs Help People Make an Informed Decision While at the Facility*

Signs are said to be a means of disseminating information of interest to the general public. That means, people can make a number of decisions about their health and service they receive based on what they interpret across the signs because signs carry meaning depending on the context they are placed. On the other hand, signs help people to create awareness on how to behave and do while in the public hospital spaces or other domains. This means that the decisions made by hospital clients in the hospital contexts sometimes are partly the function of the interpretation of the signs they come across in the public space (Martinéz, 2014).

(iv) *Public Signs Are Educational Tools in Promotion of Public Health and Social Service*

The best way to enhance and promote public health is through use of billboard signs, public notices, and warnings about health behavior that influence good public health (Martinéz, 2014). Also, in a public space like a hospital, there are a lot of hazardous materials such as solid and fluid wastes, chemicals, and radiations that can affect human beings, so the one way to put people on alert on those harmful materials is through use of public signs. The method has been so successful in promotion of products and services in the business industry (El-Busaidy, 2014; Siau, 2003). Through these public signs on billboards, notice boards, or warning signs, awareness and information about contracting diseases like cholera, malaria, dengue, Ebola, Zika, and HIV/AIDS can be easily disseminated to hospital clients and the general public. Commenting on the role of signs in the public space of the hospital, Schuster et al. (2016: 23) substantiate that

[h]ospital signage is a critical element in the patients' and visitors understanding of directions, instructions, and warnings in the facility. In multilingual environments, organizations need to make sure that the information is accessible in the languages of the people who consume their services.

However, this was not the trend in most of the visited hospitals as most of the signs were signed in English—the language known to few in the country. Martinéz (2014) in her study observed that for signs to be effective in meeting the objective of educating the public, a common language understood by the most encountered group should be adapted on signage. This was further substantiated during the interview as can be noted in the excerpt below:

[S]igning by use of language that is used by the majority or the mostly encountered group in the public space of the hospital particularly on signboards is the best policy that can help many to have access to the information on signs. So if you ask me to suggest, I will suggest Kiswahili because it is the only language used by majority of Tanzanians who are served here.

Methodology

Research Design

This study adopted a mixed approach in which both quantitative and qualitative approaches were brought into operation in order to unleash all the angles of the problem under investigation. Mixed approach normally falls under the pragmatic paradigm focusing on facilitating human problem-solving (Pansiri, 2005: 15), with an assumption that using or adopting only one methodological approach in data collection and analysis may fail to unleash all the angles of the problem under investigation (Miller & Cameron, 2011). The main feature for mixed method approach is its ability to bring together the best qualities from both quantitative and qualitative approaches.

The study was conducted in three referral hospitals where their linguistic landscapes were investigated. These hospitals include Muhimbili National Hospital in Dar es Salaam (MNH), Bugando Medical Centre (BMC) in Mwanza, and Ligula hospital in Mtwara. Bugando is found in the lake zone in Tanzania serving as a referral hospital for five regions while Ligula is found in the southern part of Tanzania, serving three regions. The three hospitals were selected based on their location and coverage and one key criterion to be included in the sample was to be a referral hospital its zone.

Survey Items, Sampling, and Sample Size

In order to collect optimal LL signs (photographic data) at the hospital, the following strategy was used during sampling and getting the sample size. Firstly, the researcher visited the hospital's public spaces and photographed the signs in the specified areas of activity by using a digital camera in the hospital compounds. Secondly, the researcher

Table 4.1 Summary of interview respondents' profile

Area of activity	Outpatient	Family members	Doctors	Nurses	Admins
MNH	4	3	3	3	2
Ligula	2	2	2	3	2
Bugando	2	2	2	3	2
Ministry of Health	1	-	-	-	-
Total	9	7	7	9	6

used observational guide questions such as the following: what language was most preferred on linguistic sign? What is the sign about/what information does the sign communicate—educational, administration, etc.? A total of 225 public signs were collected from these areas of activity in the three hospitals during a field survey. These were signs that met the established criterion to be included in the sample as unit of analysis. The current study adopted a definition of sign by Backhaus (2006: 55) who defines a sign to mean "any piece of written text within a spatially definable frame which gives information or instruction [...], including anything from handwritten stickers to huge billboards." Therefore, criteria for a sign to be included in a sample for analysis were: it had to be in a definable frame and accompanied with a text. This means a sign without a text was not considered to constitute the sample.

Similarly, in order to collect optimal primary data from human respondents, a sizable sample of thirty eight (38) respondents was involved. These were sampled from different groups of respondents such as hospital staff (doctors, nurses, and administrative staff), hospital clients (family members and outpatients), and representatives from the Ministry of Health. The aim was to get across all the key linguistic landscape actors in the surveyed hospitals and the Ministry of Health in Tanzania (see Table 4.1).

The involvement of human respondents was important in order to provide supporting evidence from peoples' experience on LL practice at the hospital, because these are key actors in the LL of the hospitals. They live the effects realized from language use on public signs in these public spaces.

Sampling Procedure and Data Collection and Analysis

The study employed a non-probability sampling procedure. Since the study involved two different variables of data (human subjects and public signs scattered in various parts of the hospitals), two techniques were used to obtain data from these sources: purposive sampling technique and convenient sampling technique. Purposive sampling technique was used to collect data in the specified areas of activity of the hospital in which data were in the form of public signs/photographs and a section of human respondents such as hospital staff (administrators) and representatives from the Ministry of Health. Data in these sampling procedures were collected through observation (photographical data) and interviews from human respondents. During observation sessions, the following signs were collected from the identified areas of activity: signs communicating education on health promotion; signs communicating education on social welfare information; signs communicating administrative information such as hours of operation, insurance carriers, clinic rules; and signs communicating education on regulatory discourses such as prohibitions and warnings.

The primary data collected and analyzed from the field survey involved audio tape-recorded data and field notes, which were subsequently transcribed, with a focus on content of their ideas and less attention on discourse features, before being sorted out into various themes. The interviews were conducted mainly in Kiswahili and English. Another form of data analyzed was digital photographs or simply public signs from the LL in selected areas of activity at the selected hospitals. Photographed public signs from areas of activity were analyzed quantitatively through use of SPSS version 24 and qualitatively so as to understand their nature and patterns as well as their implications on access to information in the provision of healthcare services. On the other hand, qualitative data from human respondents were analyzed through thematic approach.

Findings on the LL in Selected Public Hospitals in Tanzania

Signs Based on LL Actors from the Three Public Hospitals

In a research that was conducted in three public hospitals, namely Muhimbili National Hospital in Dar es Salaam, Ligula referral hospital in Mtwara, and Bugando referral hospital in Mwanza in the lake zone, it was revealed that top-down signs were mostly represented in the LL than bottom-up actors in which 96.4 percent of the signs analyzed were top-down signs and only 3.6 percent of the signs analyzed were bottom-up signs. Top-down signs came from designated locations such as on top of buildings, on walls of buildings, or special signboards with a hospital logo in various parts of the hospital. This suggests that the public space in the three public hospitals is highly controlled space by hospital management, in which not everyone can place their signs without permission by the hospital management. Table 4.2 demonstrates this.

Language Choice and Preference on Signs

In the three surveyed hospitals, it was revealed that the public space of these public hospitals is dominated by three languages, namely English for large percent, followed

Table 4.2 Linguistic landscape actors

Linguistic landscape actors	Sign frequency	Valid percentage
Top-down	217	96.4
Bottom-up	8	3.6
Total	225	100.00

by Kiswahili, and to small percent there was presence of Chinese, especially at Muhimbili National Hospital. The reason for presence of Chinese in a predominantly Kiswahili user space was said to have been due to the construction industry; both the materials and experts who built some of the buildings at MNH were Chinese; hence their signage was left in this public space. Top-down actors chose English as their default language for signage in the LL as the research findings indicated that more than 33 percent of the signs used English as their language of preference and bottom-up actors chose Kiswahili as their default language in signing the public space. Table 4.3 below demonstrates this preference.

The language choice and preference are further portrayed by the following signs in Figures 4.1 and 4.2.

The photo in Figure 4.1 is a sign that indicates the presence of Emergency building, a building that every hospital client seeking medical attention has to pass

Table 4.3 Language preference on top-down vs. bottom-up signs

Language on signs	Top-down signs	Frequency %	Bottom-up signs	Frequency %
Kiswahili	60	26.6	3	1.3
English	75	33.3	-	-
Kiswahili-English	21	13.7	-	-
English-Kiswahili	31	9.4	-	-
Kiswahili-Chinese	1	0.5	-	-
Chinese-English	5	2.3	-	-
Code switching	24	10.7	5	2.2
Total	**217**	**96.5**	**8**	**3.5**

Figure 4.1 Top-down sign indicating administrative information

by at Muhimbili. The language used on the sign above is exclusively English without a translation, which in Kiswahili could read as follows:

(1) Emergency Medicine Department—*Jengo la huduma za Dharura*
    On the other hand, in Figure 4.2 (see website for Figure 4.2) is a sign that shows some basic do's and don'ts for every client and even hospital staff to observe when navigating the hospital's public space. The sign is placed very near to the main entrance gate at MNH being so conspicuous that can be seen by all passers-by in private cars and those walking on foot. The contents in sign 2 are exclusively in Kiswahili language without a translation but it could be translated as follows:
(2) Usipige honi (*Do not sound your horn*)
    - Usipaki gari hovyo (*Do not park your car*)
    - Usivute sigara (*Do not smoke cigarettes*)
    - Usitupe takataka hovyo (*Do not litter carelessly*)

The nature of signs in Figures 4.1 and 4.2 suggests that they cannot be put up in the hospital's public space by a hospital client or any other person from the bottom-up category as they carry authority, and in fact violation of the contents in Figure 4.2 bears a penalty for defaulters. The pertinent question was whether the presumed readers visiting the hospital are able to follow and access such information in that language, especially those who are not Kiswahili proficient or not English proficient, and whether this language pattern(s) fulfils the main function of communicating educative information to the hospital's clients and hospital community in general. This question was answered by hospital clients who were involved in the interview. Majority noted that they were unable to access the educational information signed through English as one respondent hinted during an interview in the excerpt below:

> *I think the hospital's LL to large extent is not user friendly because most of public signboards are in English and many of them have no even a translation while the presumed readers here are predominantly Kiswahili speakers. So, I think there is a need to improve the LL, especially on notice boards and signs that give directions and educational information for health promotion.*

A close examination on the results from the table shows further that among the two dominant languages in monolingual pattern, English is relatively more visible compared to Kiswahili but observation on bilingual signs shows a minor difference, in that there are more signs translated from Kiswahili to English than vice versa. The general picture suggests that, among the three identified languages in the LL of the studied hospitals, English enjoys more access on the public space than Kiswahili and Chinese in terms of content coverage, dominance, presence, visibility, and font size as can be seen in the sign in Figure 4.3 (see website for Figure 4.3).

The sign in Figure 4.3 is an educative sign exclusively written in English, which suggests that the intended audience is only those who can read and understand English. This sign was very popular in the three hospitals with very important message.

However, the extent to which the sign was accessible to majority of clients in these hospitals was questionable as many reported to lack the proficiency in the language used.

Linguistic Signs Based on Language Functions in the Hospital Contexts

Since the presence of different signs at the studied hospitals is meant to provide educational information to the hospital clients and other readers on the entire hospital community, the following educational informational functions of LL were categorized from the data:

(i) *Signs communicating administrative information such as hours of operation in various units at the hospital, insurance carriers, modes of payment, location of buildings, offices, and other general information.*
During the field survey, it was observed that most of the signs, about 176 out of 225, were signs communicating administrative information. This was equal to 78.2 percent of the total signs in the surveyed areas of activities. The information on signs was geared to educate the hospital client(s) identify easily different areas of activity at the hospital without being compelled to ask security guards, receptionists, or hospital staff. It was also meant to educate visitors to make an informed decision on number of things while at the hospital. Figure 4.4 below shows an example of these signs, where monolingual English or Kiswahili was predominant.

(ii) *Signs communicating education on health and social welfare information such as blood donation and keeping the hospital environment clean by not littering carelessly.*
The field observation revealed a good number of signs that were designated for providing health information, promotion of public health, and social welfare of the community. As we are aware that peoples' public health is a priority of any

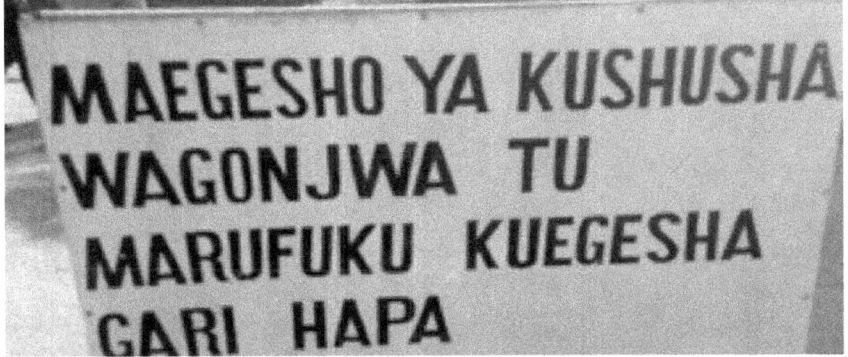

Figure 4.4 Monolingual Kiswahili sign communicating administrative information

government and its institutions, health promotion about taking care of one's health toward communicable and non-communicable diseases, blood donation to save other people's lives, and so forth were easily displayed through public signs. This suggests that the government and its health institutions are much concerned and they take the issue of public health information seriously. During the field survey, it was revealed that 22 signs out of 225 analyzed signs, equal to 9.7 percent, were about health education or promotion and social welfare. These signs used English and Kiswahili exclusively and some were translated into English-Kiswahili and Kiswahili-English. Only seven used English alone, equal to 31.8 percent, and only eight with Kiswahili alone, equal to 36.4 percent. Signs translated from Kiswahili into English were only five, equal to 22.7 percent, and those translated from English-Kiswahili were two, equal to 9.1 percent. The importance of educational signs in the LL of public hospitals was also noted by respondents in interview below.

Depending on hospital staff to get instructions and educational information might not be enough or effective; hence, presence of public signs complement the effort done by hospital management in educating and alerting the public visiting the hospital on issues that matter to their health and stay at the facility.

(iii) *Signs educating clients on their rights and responsibilities such as paying service fee, and not taking or offering bribe.*

Rights and responsibilities are supposed to be clear and accessible in the public space where everyone can follow or make use of them without depending on asking from the hospital management. From the field research, it was revealed that there were only four (4) out of 225 signs educating hospital clients on their rights and responsibilities. This is equal to 1.7 percent of all the signs collected and analyzed. However, the signs in this category were all written in Kiswahili language, suggesting that their readership was only accessible to those who are Kiswahili proficient as can be seen in one of the signs (Figure 4.5) at MNH communicating rights and responsibilities to the hospital community not to give bribe for exchange of service that is supposed to be offered freely.

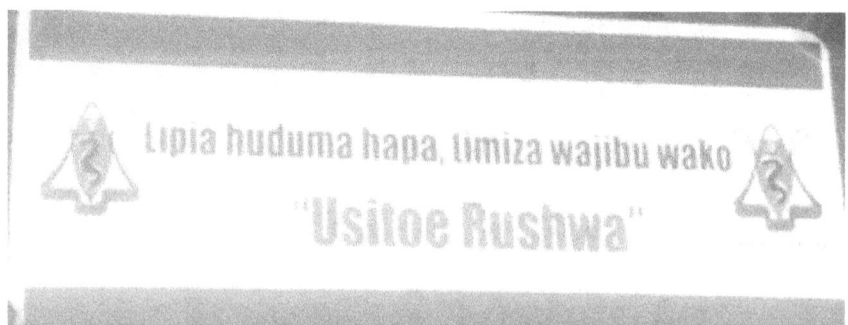

Figure 4.5 Monolingual Kiswahili sign communicating client's responsibilities

(iv) *Signs communicating regulatory discourses such as prohibitions and warnings on things to avoid, issues about policies and clinical rules, safety and emergency measures as can be seen in Figure 4.6 (see website).*

Only 23 out of 225 signs providing education on regulatory information were only 23 out of 225, equal to 10.2 percent of the total signs. Among them, 30.4 percent (7 signs) were Kiswahili only and signs with English only were also seven (7), equal to 30.4 percent, while those with Kiswahili-English were two (2), equal to 8.7 percent, and signs with English-Kiswahili were five (5), equal to 21.7 percent, and those with Chinese-English were two (2), equal to 8.7 percent. This sign was photographed at Ligula hospital in Mtwara, and although it gives very vital information to the hospital clients, its readership and accessibility are limited to only a few—those who are English proficient. Respondents through interview also noted:

> *Majority of hospital clients struggle to understand the regulatory information provided through English signs while navigating in the hospitals' public spaces. But if the language was clear, I think everyone would be happy because s/he will be able to read in the language s/he knows well.*

The above response suggests that the use of monolingual English on signs leaves many without an alternative to understand what is meant on these signs while attending hospital.

Furthermore, during an interview with some respondents on the role of language functions in the public spaces of the selected hospitals, it was revealed that all had a positive perception on educational role played by LL although the nature of the language that was predominantly used caused some communication challenges as others failed to understand what were meant by the signs.

> *[T]he presence of various billboards and signs in the hospitals' public space help many of us to understand various matters at the hospital which could be very difficult without them as we could entirely depend on asking nurses and other hospital assistants who are also busy attending other issues.*

Generally, the categories of language functions pointed above were meant to identify clearly the nature of language used to present the educational information in the public space of public hospitals in Tanzania and whether hospital clients have access to those information in the language they are proficient. More discussion and implication of these findings are given in the next section.

Discussion

The research findings in this chapter have indicated that public signs are integral part of the LL in health facilities. Thus, their presence, role, and use in the public space of health institutions refute the long-held perception that LL confines itself mostly to language classroom and other spaces such as education and language policy (Clemente, Andrade, & Martins, 2012; Shohamy, 2015; Spolsky, 2009), commercial and economic centers (Bwenge, 2009; Claus, 2002; Singhasiri, 2013), urban multilingualism (Backhaus, 2005; Ranga, 2012) but not healthcare field.

Generally, the findings have showed that English, and not Kiswahili, is predominantly represented on linguistic landscape signs in the researched public hospitals, in which monolingual English was dominantly represented on signs for about 80 percent and Kiswahili, which is the language of the majority, was represented for only 20 percent. The finding contravenes the Swahilisation policy in public offices introduced by the government in a special circular of 1974 (URT, 1974). The circular, among other things, insisted on the use of Kiswahili—which is a national language—in all public signs and offices so as to enhance effective communication to clients who are the majority. This was a smart realization that Kiswahili, and not English, could accommodate many Tanzanians for about 95 percent (Rubagumya, 1997). However, the situation at the ground is quite different from what envisaged in the circular. Observation on language pattern used in the LL of these hospitals showed that the role of signs to be used as a medium of education to hospital clients is somehow hindered by use of certain language patterns.

It should be noted further that the literacy level in English among common Tanzanians attending these hospitals is very low as it was observed by UNESCO (2013) and Mkumbo (2014). Readership of signs depends much on literacy of the presumed readers. Regardless of the importance of information on the signs, if they are not accessible to the target audience then that information becomes useless. Looking at this linguistic repertoire suggests that the key target for this linguistic landscape is left out as they cannot access the information packed in these signs; hence the target audience cannot benefit from the educational information provided through English language. Nevertheless, the linguistic repertoire presented in these hospital's public spaces suggests that all hospital clients are conversant in the English language—something that is not quite true. This finding goes contrary to the model that was suggested by Backhaus (2007) and Spolsky (2009) who substantiated that signage in the public space should consider the presumed reader(s) of those signs to whether they can read and understand the information presented on the sign.

Similarly, the presence of these signs in the public space presents a challenge to the general public even if they might not complain; hence it affects the efforts of promotion of public health. This result is in line with the finding by Martinéz (2014) in the United States who investigated the language access in the LL of a medical facility in a predominantly Spanish-speaking community and found out that majority were unable to benefit from the services provided in monolingual English.

The issue of language on signs is critical element in the field of LL and particularly in public space of medical facilities as substantiated by Schuster et al. (2016: 23) in their study, noting that "hospital signage is a critical element in the patients' and visitors' understanding of directions, instructions and warnings in the facility. In multilingual environments organizations need to make sure that the information is accessible in the languages of the people who consume their services." Speaking to outpatients in all the hospitals represented in this study, they all agreed that the use of language on signs, which is not the language of the majority, has a negative implication on their access to different services and educational information while attending hospital facility. The literature shows that language use and practice in healthcare delivery systems is one of the important aspects that play a great role in assisting access to educational information, provision of therapy, curative drugs, administrative information as well as general information that promotes public health to clients attending the health facilities especially when such language is the language that is understood by the mostly encountered group in the hospital space (Martinéz, 2014; Mdukula, 2018; Schuster, 2012; Schuster, Elroy, & Elmakais, 2016).

Conclusion

This chapter has shed light on application of linguistic landscape beyond language classroom. Thus, expanding the scenery of LL can best enlighten a number of educational issues in the field of healthcare. However, to realize this role, the language aspect on signs has to be well checked. Through this chapter it has been revealed that the general linguistic landscape in public hospitals in Tanzania is dominated by English language, which enjoys the three-stage model of a sign as was proposed by Backhaus (2007): *presence*—that English is more visible and prominent in the LL, *autonomy*—that in most cases it is presented alone on a sign (monolingual), and *dominance*—that the language covers a large part of the content on the sign, especially on bilingual signs. The dominance of one language pattern, however, denies access to key information and services to some of target audiences—a situation leading to the role of LL in provision of education to the general public to fall short, to some extent. The research findings have further showed that both English and Kiswahili are significant languages in enabling access to educational and administrative information and that they are all needed in the public space of the hospital due to presence of clients with diverse linguistic needs for which majority of them in these public hospitals fall in either of the two language groups—Kiswahili, English, or both.

References

Akindele, O. (2011). Linguistic landscapes as public communication: A study of public signage in Gaborone Botswana. *International Journal of Linguistics*, 3, 1–11.

Backhaus, P. (2005). Signs of multilingualism in Tokyo: A linguistic landscape approach. Unpublished PhD thesis, University of Duisburg-Essen, Tokyo.

Backhaus, P. (2006). Multilingualism in Tokyo: A look into the linguistic landscape. *International Journal of Multilingualism*, 1, 52–66.

Backhaus, P. (2007). *Linguistic Landscapes. A Comparative Study of Urban Multilingualism in Tokyo*. Clevedon-Toronto: Multilingual Matters Ltd.

Backhaus, P. (2009). Rules and regulations in linguistic landscaping: A comparative perspective. In E. Shohamy & D. Gorter (Eds.), *Linguistic Landscape: Expanding the Scenery*. New York: Routledge.

Bamgbose, A. (2011). African languages today: The challenge of and prospects for empowerment under globalisation. In E. G. Bokamba, R. K. Shosted, & B. T. Ayalew (Eds.), *Selected Proceedings of the 40th Annual Conference on African Linguistics*. Somerville: Cascadilla proceedings project.

Barni, M., & Bagna, C. (2010). Linguistic landscape and language vitality. In E. Shohamy, E. Ben-Rafael, & M. Barni (Eds.), *Linguistic Landscape in the City*. Bristol: Multilingual Matters.

Ben-Rafael, E., Shohamy, E., Amara, M. H., & Trumper-Hecht, N. (2006). Linguistic landscape as symbolic construction of the public space: The case of Israel. *International Journal of Multilingualism*, 3(1), 7–30.

Ben Said, S. (2010). Street signage in Tunisia: Reconciling multilingualism, Arabization, and vernacularization. *Journal of the American Society of Geo-linguistics*, 36, 33–45.

Biswalo, T. (2010). Policy processes in relation to language in Tanzania: Examining shifts in language policy. Unpublished PhD dissertation, University of Illinois.

Braun, V., & Clarke, V. (2006). Using thematic analysis in psychology. *Qualitative Research in Psychology*, 3, 1–41.

Bwenge, C. (2009). Language choice in Dar es Salaam's billboards. In F. Mc Laughlin (Ed.), *The Languages of Urban Africa* (pp. 152–77). New York: Continuum International Publishing Group.

Bwenge, C. (2012). Business signs in Dar es Salaam: A sociolinguistic perspective. *Language in African Performing and Visual Arts*, 1, 48–59.

Claus, R. J. (2002). The value of signs for your business. *Signline*, 38: 1–8.

Clemente, M., Andrade, A. I., & Martins, F. (2012). Learning to read the world, learning to look at the linguistic landscape: A primary school study. In C. Hélot, M. Barni, R. Janssens, & C. Bagna (Eds.), *Linguistic landscapes, multilingualism, and social change* (pp. 267–85). Frankfurt, Germany: Peter Lang.

Creswell, J. W. (2003). *Research Design: A Qualitative, Quantitative and Mixed Method Approaches*, 2nd ed. London: Sage.

El-Busaidy, N. A. (2014). Public perceptions towards billboard advertising in Tanzania. Unpublished Master of Business Administration dissertation, Open University of Tanzania.

Garvin, R. T. (2011). Emotional responses to the linguistic landscape in Memphis, Tennessee: Visual perceptions of public spaces in transition. Unpublished PhD thesis, Indiana University of Pennsylvania.

Gorter, D. (2006). Introduction: The study of the linguistic landscape as a new approach to multilingualism. *International Journal of Multilingualism*, 3(1), 1–6.

Gorter, D. (2013). Linguistic landscapes in a multilingual world. *Annual Review of Applied Linguistics*, 33, 190–212.

Landry, R., & Bourhis, R. (1997). Linguistic landscape and ethno-linguistic vitality: An empirical study. *Journal of Language and Social Psychology*, 16(1), 23–49.

Languages of Tanzania Project (LOT). (2009). *Atlasi ya lugha za Tanzania*. Dar es Salaam: Mradi wa Lugha za Tanzania, Chuo Kikuu cha Dar es Salaam.

Lusekelo, A. (2019). The linguistic situation in Orkesumet, an urban area in Simanjiro District of Tanzania. *UJAH*, 20.(1). doi:10.4314/ujah.v20i1.2.

Martínez, G. A. (2014). Vital signs: A photo voice assessment of the linguistic landscape in Spanish in healthcare facilities along the U.S-Mexico border. *The Journal of Communication and Health*, 1, 1–21.

Mazrui, A. A., & Alamin, M. (1998). *The Power of Babel: Language and Governance in the African Experience*. Oxford: James Currey.

Mdukula, P. C. (2018). The Linguistic Landscape of Public Health Institutions in Tanzania: The case of Muhimbili National Hospital. Unpublished Doctoral Thesis in Linguistics, University of Dar es Salaam.

Miller, P. J., & Cameron, R. (2011). Mixed method research designs: A case study of their adoption in a doctor of business administration program, *International journal of multiple research approaches*, 5 (3), 387–402.

Mkumbo, K. (March 2014). Kingereza tunakipenda lakini hatutaki kujifunza (We love English but we are not ready to learn). *Raia Mwema*, Toleo Namba 3415.

Muaka, L. (2014). Language use in advertisements as a reflection of speakers' language habits. In E. Z. Zsiga, O. T. Boyer, & R. Kramer (Eds.), *Languages in Africa: Multilingualism, Language Policy, and Education* (pp. 137–57). Washington, DC: Georgetown University Press.

Muhimbili National Hospital (MNH). (2015). *Customer Service Charter*, 2nd ed. Dar es Salaam. Muhimbili National Hospital.

National Bureau of Statistics (NBS). (2012). *Population and Housing Census: Population Distribution by Administrative Units; Key Findings*. Dar es Salaam: Government Printer.

Pansiri, J. (2005). Pragmatism: A methodological approach to researching strategic alliances in tourism. *Journal of Tourism and Hospitality Planning & Development*, 2(3), 191–206.

Pennycook, A. (2011). Spatial narrations: Graff capes and city souls. In A. Jaworski & C. Thurlow (Eds.), *Semiotic Landscapes: Language, Image, and Space* (pp. 137–50). Seattle, USA

Petzell, M. (2012). The linguistic situation in Tanzania. *Modernaspråk*, 1, 136–44.

Qorro, M. S. (2009). Parent's and policy maker's insistence on foreign languages as media of education in Africa: Restricting access to quality education—for whose benefit? *Languages and Education in Africa: A Comparative and Transdisciplinary Discussion*, 4, 57–82.

Ranga, A. (2012). Linguistic landscape and language attitude: A case on Jimma Oromo. *International Journal of Sociology and Anthropology*, 4(7), 218–25.

Rubagumya, C. M. (1990). Language in Tanzania. In C. M. Rubagumya (Ed.), *Language in Education in Africa: A Tanzanian Perspective*. Clevedon, UK: Multilingual Matters Inc.

Rubagumya, C. M. (1997). Disconnecting education: Language as a determinant of quality of education in Tanzania. *Journal of Linguistics and Language in Education*, 3, 81–95.

Schuster, M. (2012). Language accessibility of signage in public settings—a case study of a healthcare service. *SALALS*, 30(3), 311–24.

Schuster, M., Elroy, I., & Elmakais, I. (2016). We are lost: Measuring the accessibility of signage in public general hospitals, *Lang Policy*, 16, 23–38.

Shohamy, E. (2015). Linguistic landscape research as expanding language and language policy. *Linguistic Landscape*, 1(1/2), 152–71.

Siau, K. S. (2003). Building customer trust in mobile commerce. *Communications of the ACM*, 46(4), 91–4.

Singhasiri, W. (2013). Linguistic landscape in the state railway station of Thailand: The analysis of the use of language. Official conference proceeding for the European conference on language learning. King Mongkut's University of Technology Thonburi, Thailand.

Spolsky, B. (2009). Prolegomena to a sociolinguistic theory of public signage. In E. Shohamy & D. Gorter (Eds.), *Linguistic Landscape: Expanding the Scenery*. New York: Routledge.

Spolsky, B., & Cooper, R. L. (1991). *The languages of Jerusalem*. Oxford: Oxford University Press.

Tibategeza, E. R. (2009). Language-in-education planning in Tanzania: A sociolinguistic analysis. Unpublished PhD thesis, University of the Free State, Bloemfontein.

UNESCO. (2013). *Adult and Youth Literacy: National, Regional, and Global Trends, 1985–2015*. Paris: UNESCO Institute for Statistics.

United Republic of Tanzania (URT). (1974). *Government Circular No.1 on Use of Kiswahili in Public Offices*. Dar es Salaam: Government printer.

United Republic of Tanzania (URT). (1995). *Education and Training Policy. Ministry of Education and Culture*. Dar es Salaam: Government Printer.

United Republic of Tanzania (URT). (2007). *National Health Policy*. Ministry of Health and Social Welfare, Dar es Salaam: Government Printer.

Wamalwa, E. W., Adika, S., & Kevogo, A. U. (2013). Multilingualism and language attitudes: Students' perceptions towards Kiswahili in Mtwara Region in Tanzania. *Journal of Research on Humanities and Social Sciences*, 3, 12.

Yang, C. (2014). Shifting agency in shaping linguistic landscape: Evidence from Dar es Salaam, Tanzania. *The Sociolinguistic Journal of Korea*, 22(2), 45–64. doi:10.14353/sjk.2014.22.2.45.

5

Information, Education, and Language Policy in the Linguistic Landscape of an International Airport in New Zealand

Una Cunningham and Jeanette King

The study of linguistic landscapes initially centered on public signage in multilingual environments (Landry & Bourhis, 1997; Spolsky & Cooper, 1991). The many studies in this field have examined both signage produced by public authorities ("informative signs," Spolsky, 2009) and privately produced advertising signs. Cenoz and Gorter (2006) connected the linguistic landscape of public spaces to the official language policy of the setting. Alongside these studies there have been many studies on the purposes and information in linguistic landscapes associated with semi-public environments, including the classroom environment. In a recent article, Gorter (2018) offers an overview of schoolscape research and points out that signage can have a pedagogical application and also be relevant for language learning. Aiestaran, Cenoz, and Gorter (2010) found that signs in schools are related to the teaching of subject content and language, but also intercultural awareness, establishing behavioral rules, as well as practical or commercial information.

This chapter expands the study of multilingual signs in (semi-)public places by examining signs in an airport. Since the 1970s as airports worldwide have increasingly become private companies, there has been a move toward commercial branding of the airport as a destination (Castro & Lohmann, 2014). Airports are on the one hand semi-public spaces but as they are increasingly administered by private companies the larger airports have a strong branding and commercial focus. The most recent example of this is the opening in April 2019 of Changi Airport's Jewel shopping mall, which is a landside attraction (Jameson, 2019).

Spolsky (2009: 34) outlines eight major types of sign distinguished by Spolsky and Cooper (1991):

1. Street signs
2. Advertising signs
3. Warning notices and prohibitions
4. Building names
5. Informative signs (directions, hours of opening)

6. Commemorative plaques
7. Objects (postbox, police call box)
8. Grafitti

In this chapter we describe signs in an airport setting, which, according to the taxonomy above, are informative, but also have an element of educational or sociocultural purpose. By educational, we mean that there is an attempt to facilitate learning. We therefore extend the notion of an "educational" purpose of multilingual signs from the classroom into this public/private environment.

The Setting

New Zealand is a nation of 4.9 million people located in the South Pacific. Māori, the indigenous inhabitants, comprise 15 percent of the population. In addition to British migrants who settled from the mid-nineteenth century onward, there has been increasing migration in recent years from Asian countries such that New Zealand, or more particularly, the largest city Auckland, is defined as "superdiverse" (Royal Society of New Zealand, 2013) due to the large number of languages and people who were born overseas. Geographically the country consists of two main islands, prosaically named the North and South Islands. While historically, meat and dairy exports have been the main export earners, in 2016 tourism became the largest export industry in terms of foreign exchange earning (Bradley, 2017).

Because New Zealand is an island nation that shares no land borders with other countries, 99 percent of visitors arrive by air (Tsui & Henderson, 2018). The two largest airports by passenger volume are Auckland International Airport (at the northern end of the North Island) and Christchurch International Airport (located in the middle of the South Island) with Auckland handling 71.4 percent of international arrivals in 2016 and Christchurch handling 14.3 percent (Tsui & Henderson, 2018: 256). The top nationality for international arrivals into New Zealand is Australia with 1.5 million visitor arrivals, followed by China (just under 500,000) (Stats NZ, 2018). These two countries account for half of international visitor arrivals. Among the top eight nationalities 74 percent are from English-speaking countries (Australia, the United States, the UK and Canada). The other four nationalities imply four different languages: Chinese (Mandarin), German, Japanese, and Korean (Tsui & Henderson, 2018: 256). At Christchurch Airport we found signs in Chinese, Japanese, and Korean. Signs in German were absent, reflecting possibly the expectation that German tourists know at least some English. Our interview with the airport services manager confirms this: "So it's that idea that culturally again trying to avoid putting a myriad of languages on some signage. Just say 'OK we'll go with the English, the Mandarin, Japanese and Korean', we hoped we'd covered the vast majority of our demographic."

Internationally, smaller-sized airports (those with 5 to 14.99 million passengers per year), such as both the Christchurch and Auckland Airports, typically market themselves by linking themselves with tourism-related content (Castro & Lohmann, 2014: 9). Since 2008, Auckland Airport has incorporated a strong Māori focus with a carved wooden gateway through which all international arrivals enter (Auckland Airport, 2008: 2). Auckland Airport describes itself as the "gateway to New Zealand" and has recently upgraded its international departures area to incorporate Māori design elements throughout the facility (Paranihi, 2019). In contrast, Christchurch is a main entry point for tourists who are visiting attractions in the southern part of the South Island (notably Queenstown and Milford Sound). Consequently Christchurch Airport sees itself as the "gateway to the South Island" and brands itself as such (Christchurch Airport, 2016: 4). Thus the visual imagery in the airport has a different focus to that evident in Auckland. Internal walls in Christchurch Airport display large photographs, which highlight attractions based on natural features, such as glacier hiking, cruises on the fjords of Fiordland, or bungee jumping from bridges over river gorges. While these attractions may sometimes be operated by Māori tribes or organizations, the imagery does not particularly reflect Māori culture. Both Auckland and Christchurch Airports play an important role in the tourism sector by not only providing connections to the main tourist destinations and attractions but also distributing information to tourism providers about how to optimize their operations for the international market (see, e.g., Christchurch Airport, 2016).

As with most airports there are several areas through which international arrivals transition on arrival at Christchurch Airport. These areas are termed "airside" as they are controlled areas, which are only accessible to passengers and authorized staff. These areas are listed below in the order in which they are encountered by an international arrival:

1. Airbridge and connecting corridors
2. Duty free
3. Immigration
4. Baggage collection
5. Customs
6. Exit to meeting area, "landside"

For a visual example of this layout, see, for example, Auckland Airport, (2008: 3). Those who regularly travel internationally by air will know from experience that movement through these sectors is sequential and designed to maximize throughput and minimize confusion and frustration (Blow, 2013).

Education in the Airport

Airports can be characterized as spaces where diverse groups of people come into the same space. Many of them are first-time visitors in the space; others are locals who regularly depart from and arrive at the airport. Many will be fully proficient speakers and readers of the majority language; others may have little or no knowledge of that language. Some will need directions to the standard functions of airports (baggage claim, passport/immigration, transit, check-in, etc.); others are at the airport for other reasons, e.g., to meet a returning family member. The information needs of these groups are different, and they have different levels of knowledge and experience of the environment within and outside the airport and the expectations of the people they will come into contact with there. Supplying these groups with the information they require in a way that is accessible is a fundamental function of airports.

This chapter is structured according to the discursive frames (Coupland & Garret, 2010) or objects of education that we have identified. Each of these uses a particular set of linguistic choices, which Coupland and Garret (2010) associate with the cultural and symbolic values that are intentionally or unintentionally activated by language choice in a particular context. The activated symbolic values are, of course, unlikely to be the same for the senders, the intended readers, and other incidental readers. In this way, biosecurity information is focused on Asian languages (Chinese, Japanese, and Korean) alongside English; Chinese and Korean are prominent in behavioral information; tourist information is generally in English, and airport branding information uses Chinese and Māori to drive home specific points. While the Ministry for Primary Industries (2018: 10, cited in Sherring, 2019) identified a relative lack of signage in other languages as an issue, in 2016 this study did find signs giving directions in Chinese, Korean, and Japanese at Christchurch Airport.

A particular educational need in the case of entry to New Zealand is the matter of biosecurity in that many elsewhere innocuous items are strictly regulated. Sherring (2019) describes the efforts put into changing the behavior of international travelers to comply with biosecurity regulations. Airport signage is an important part of this effort. New Zealand's biosecurity program adopts the VADE model (Voluntary, Assisted, Directed, and Enforced) of encouraging compliance, starting with information intended to encourage travelers to follow the rules voluntarily, moving through nudging to more explicit directions and finally to enforcement. One of the reasons passengers in 2017 gave as a barrier to complying was lack of information in their native language (Sherring, 2019). Chinese visitors were found to be most influenced by disposal bins and signage at airports. There is an assumption that New Zealand residents and citizens, including those who are themselves migrants from China, will be more aware of and willing to comply with biosecurity restrictions, so information is aimed at visitors.

Another potential need for the education of travelers is in cases where they are assumed to have different, and in the local context, unacceptable, behavior. Matters such as the appropriate use of toilet facilities and prohibition against smoking and other behavior are often held to be a problem for visitors from some other countries.

Helping newly arrived travelers to learn about New Zealand in general and the local area in particular is a further aspect of education in the airport. Once visitors have actually arrived at their destination airport, local and national tourism interests will want them to experience as much as possible with a view to encouraging return visits. In addition, visitors who come for business purposes can be encouraged to visit tourist destinations while in the vicinity. New Zealand is a long way from anywhere else, and many visitors are aware of its reputation of having an unspoiled nature and the opportunity for a wide variety of outdoor activities. They may be less familiar with other destinations and activities in New Zealand, and this kind of tourist information may increase visitors' spending in the region.

The final kind of education provided by airports that we will consider here has to do with the airport's branding—the image they want to portray. Part of this has to do with corporate responsibility. Christchurch Airport is a company jointly owned by Christchurch City Council (75 percent) and the NZ government (25 percent). Any kind of participation in official drives of various kinds, such as the airport's engagement in Chinese language week, can cast the airport in a favorable light, and these activities will be more or less prominently presented depending on the level of engagement from the airport. Similarly, government policy on various matters may be part of the airport branding, with associated educational activities and materials reflecting the airport's interpretation of the issue at hand. In this chapter we will consider aspects of New Zealand's policy of self-identification as a bicultural nation (Hayward, 2012). We note that in the wider New Zealand context, the use of Māori words and expressions without italicization or glosses in text that is otherwise written in English is increasingly recognized as being an unmarked, integral part of New Zealand English (Macalister, 2006). The official government website notes that "whether you're a visitor to NZ or you live here, it's important to be aware of Māori customs and how to interact in Māori culture" (New Zealand Government, 2019).

Airport Signage

Airport signage has an important role in perceived service quality. Signs and symbols (airport décor) are part of passengers' expectations of the servicescape of an airport (Fodness & Murray, 2007). Fewings (2001) mentions some airports that are particularly difficult to navigate and, as passenger numbers increase, the pressure to provide efficient signage to support passenger wayfinding first to check in and subsequently to the departure gate, via security, immigration, and shops. There are several principles at play in the design and placement of airport signage. Firstly, signage should be clear and unambiguous. Secondly, the signage should be at the point of need in time and space. Thirdly, the reader should immediately be able to see from the form of the sign if it is intended to communicate directions, identify a location, or reassure the reader that they are still going the right way (Fewings, 2001).

Gibbs (2014) found that passengers of all ages in New Zealand prefer to navigate terminals by being guided by static signs rather than asking airport staff or using digital tools. This means that static signs are given a good deal of attention by passengers. The choice of which languages and other elements to use on the signs, and how they are placed, is carefully thought out and not accidental.

Analysis

In early September 2016 the authors, along with some graduate students, arranged to visit Christchurch Airport. The group underwent induction and was signed in to allow admittance to airside facilities. The group was guided in a terminal walk through the domestic airside facilities, back to landside, then in to the airside international departure and arrival areas. We were able to take as many photos as we wished as we walked around. Our tour was arranged at a time when there were no international arrivals so we were able to move through those areas and take photos without disrupting passenger movements.

Subsequently the first author interviewed an airport services manager at the airport and in particular discussed a set of the images that the group had taken. The following analysis incorporates images and information from the visit and subsequent interview. It is particularly important to note that some of the images and signage we observed at that time have since changed. Within this context, we want to look in particular at two languages, Māori and Chinese. These languages were selected because they are both prominent at the airport but used for very different reasons. A number of signs and displays, including interactive screens, and TV/display screens, as well as badges worn by ground staff, were chosen for each language. This broader conception of signage is in line with Sebba's (2010) "mobile texts," which include texts such as banknotes, stamps, and bus tickets, which are rarely recognized as texts. These signs and displays were analyzed both inductively and deductively from the perspective of Aristotle's rhetorical triangle (logos—the text itself, pathos—the emotional appeal with its expected effect on the implied reader, and ethos—the character or intention of the implied speaker) as interpreted by Kinneavy (1980), with consideration of the relationship between the sender, receiver, and purpose of a sign, to reveal the intentionality and effect of the captured signs and displays. In addition, we consider the use of position order and size of text in different languages.

Burke's (1969) extension of this triangle to a pentad—agent (who?), action (what?), scene (when and why?), purpose (why?), and agency (how?)—is also useful here. The interview data and other material are then brought to bear on the analysis of each of the signs, and emergent themes are identified and later discussed in the context of the educative function of the sign. We consider the origin of each sign or display and its purpose in a potential macro (national), meso (airport), or micro (individual) level in our analysis. Bell's (1984) "audience design" theory is also useful here. Audience design describes how speakers adapt their styles in response to who the audience is. Because signs are designed to be read, they are styled to deliver their messages to the intended audience (Juffermans, 2012).

In the following sections we examine a range of signage at Christchurch Airport that relate to wayfinding, behavior modification, language promotion, biosecurity, tourism, and the role of Māori in the linguistic landscape. In these sections we consider signs that have an element of Chinese language and those that we perceive as being intended for or particularly relevant to (among others) Chinese visitors, followed by signs that contain Māori language elements.

Wayfinding

The sign in Figure 5.1 is representative of a large number of navigational signs placed hanging from the ceiling throughout the airport (see website for Figure 5.1). It has a number of linguistic and other semiotic elements. There are three wayfinding destinations on the sign: "Baggage Reclaim," "Exit," and "Domestic Departure Gates 3–14." Arrows point in the direction visitors are to take. Pictograms illustrate "Baggage Reclaim" and "Departure," and these have Chinese, Japanese, and Korean translations in smaller text under the large English-language words. There is no translation or icon on this sign of the word *Exit*. The sign is black with white lettering and the only other color is the yellow background of the "Departure" icon. This kind of sign and its accompanying pictograms are subject to considerable design constrictions to be maximally readable, intelligible, and comprehensible to as many people as possible (Gupta, 2008).

The sender of the sign is the airport on a meso level, and the decision of which languages to include on the sign would have been made at that level. Similarly, the relative size and order of the languages are not accidental and reflect what Scollon and Scollon (2003: 120) call "a system of preference." Chinese, Japanese, and Korean are the languages other than English spoken by most visitors arriving at the airport (Christchurch Airport, 2016). The decision not to accompany the important word *Exit* with translations and an icon is less easy to understand. The exact design of each sign may well be made by an individual employee, and the placement of the sign relevant to other signage may have made this information less important. In addition, international travelers may well recognize the English word *Exit*.

The sign has multiple implied receivers. Visiting and local passengers and other airport visitors who are literate in one or more of the languages of the sign are several such groups (Gupta, 2008). Still others will be able to understand the icons and arrows to find the Baggage Reclaim and the Departure area (Tan & Said, 2015). As well as those who are able to read the sign, it is visible to those who cannot read all of the languages on the sign. If such a person notices the presence of other languages on the sign, this gives information about the presented linguistic policy of the place and about what languages (and by extension, their speakers) are ostensibly valued and welcomed there. Since many people in the airport are not literate in Asian languages, and the font used for these languages is relatively small, they may not even notice the presence of these languages on the sign (Pakarinen & Björklund, 2018), but to those who see them, the message is clear. The purpose of the sign is therefore for navigational assistance for those who can read it or interpret the icon and as an indication of which languages are prioritized by the airport. It is in this respect notable that there is no presence of the Māori language on the sign or on any other informational sign. The interview with the airport services manager confirmed that Māori is not included in informational signs as all Māori speakers are also English speakers, unlike speakers of other languages involved in this chapter. The potential interpretation of this as deprioritizing the Māori language is contrasted by the use of Māori on other displays as described in the "Places to See" and "Māori Linguistic Landscape" sections below.

No Spitting

The sign on the left of Figure 5.2 is in Chinese and Korean only. It has a large icon with a crossed-over picture of a person with drops of liquid apparently coming from the mouth. The message underneath the icon reads "No spitting anywhere" in Chinese and "No spitting" in Korean. The sender is, according to the information at the foot of the sign, the airport itself. The choice of languages is of interest here, as both Japanese and the main airport language, English, are absent from the sign. The implicit recipients are clearly literate in Chinese and Korean. Just as in the case of the navigational signs considered above, the choice of which languages to include is a way of directing the attention of those who can read the languages (Bell, 1984), but also perhaps a way of diverting the attention of those who are not being addressed. The lack of a message in English can make the sign inconspicuous to those who cannot read it. This could be a way of attempting to be discreet and avoid explicit racial profiling. In contrast, there was a report of a sign urging Chinese people not to spit, published just five days before the interview (Miller, 2016), which was mentioned by our interviewee: "I did see actually a newspaper report come out recently. I think it was the NZ Herald talking about a swimming pool where there was a sign that said 'Chinese people, do not spit', in English."

The presence of the "no spitting" sign immediately outside the terminal building was reminiscent of the reported publishing a few years ago of guidelines for Chinese tourists abroad (Guilford, 2013) and an associated fake news story (Hoaxbuster, 2013) about a nonexistent Chinese language sign outside the Louvre in Paris, forbidding those who could read it to defecate in public (Guilford, 2013). Unfortunately, this fake news was picked up and spread by other mainstream media (Le Figaro, August 22, 2013). Our surprise at seeing this "no spitting" sign at the airport may have been behind the fact that after the interview on subsequent visits to the airport we noticed that this sign had been removed from its place outside the terminal building.

Figure 5.2 From left: "no spitting" sign in Chinese and Korean outside terminal; sign outside terminal for Chinese Language Week; staff buttons for Chinese Language Week, Christchurch International Airport, September 2016.

Chinese Language Week

Chinese Language Week was celebrated the week after our visit, and this was observed at the airport in the presence of temporary signs outside the terminal building (center photo, Figure 5.2) and also by buttons worn by airport ground staff (right-hand photo, Figure 5.2). Not only is the fact that Chinese Language Week is upcoming mentioned on the signs, there is also a greeting in Mandarin, written in both simplified Chinese characters and in Pinyin. On another part of the sign, in a smaller font, the translation into English is given as well as instructions for the pronunciation of the greeting by English speakers.

The sender of the message, according to the sign, is New Zealand Chinese Language Week, which, according to the website linked on the sign (www.nzclw.com), is a registered Charitable Trust with the support of a number of key names in New Zealand, the Chinese Ambassador and the Race Relations Commissioner. The airport display was "supported by Christchurch Airport." Notably, the 2019 event is "endorsed by the Asia New Zealand Foundation, New Zealand China Friendship Society, New Zealand China Council, New Zealand National Commission for UNESCO, Immigration NZ, Tourism NZ, Education New Zealand, our major universities, Confucius Institutes and local body councils," and features a video endorsement from the prime minister, Jacinda Ardern. The intended message can perhaps be best understood in the words of our interviewee, the airport services manager:

> [The sign] is a placement. We wanted to be proactive because the Chinese market is very important to the airport and the local economy, and is growing. We've recently attracted far more Chinese passengers—we have China Southern now, [and] China Airlines from Taiwan coming in. So, that just fits in with our general promotional market and engagement with the Chinese market. It's an opportunity to celebrate that connection, that partnership, and the welcoming of more Chinese visitors. And in conjunction with that we also have the staff wearing badges and even little buttons. It was great. We had all the staff learning key Mandarin phrases, even if it was just "hello".

When we asked who the signs were intended for, the answer was "the travelling public." Of course, this travelling public comprises both locally resident Chinese speakers and Chinese-speaking visitors who may be interested to see that English speakers are encouraged to learn a Chinese greeting, as well as non-Chinese speakers who may be interested in learning Chinese greetings. The covert message then would be that the Chinese language and by extension its speakers are valued.

The week of our visit was actually Tongan Language Week (September 4–10, 2016), but we saw no information or recognition of that. There are no direct flights from Tonga to the airport, which may be an explanation. When asked about this lack of Tongan Language Week signage in the interview, our interviewee reported that there was not an explicit policy about which language weeks to observe, but that the Chinese market was important to the airport. We do not have data about whether for example Māori language week is celebrated at the airport, or which other holidays and the like are observed.

Biosecurity

New Zealand is geographically fairly isolated from other parts of the world and this necessitates keeping out invasive species, parasites, and diseases that might affect people, animals, or plants, including farmed crops. The Ministry of Primary Industries monitors the borders, making sure that incoming international passengers have correctly filled in their biosecurity declaration cards. These are available in a number of languages. As passengers approach the biosecurity control area at the customs checkpoint they are exposed to an array of information. The message that is repeated in signage, regardless of the language used, is "Declare, dispose or pay the fine." This information is available in a multilingual sign placed above a baggage carousel and a Chinese-only sign indicating the "price" of attempting to bring in prohibited food items. English-speaking passengers are told that an illicit apple will cost them 400 NZD, while Japanese passengers are told that a jar of honey will cost them the equivalent amount in yen. Similarly, food items that Korean (root ginger, garlic, and ginseng) and Chinese speakers (medicinal plants) may wish to bring into New Zealand have price tags in the relevant currencies. In another display (left-hand photo, Figure 5.3) it is the Chinese speakers who are expected to be drawn to the photos of garlic, ginger, and ginseng. The center photo in Figure 5.3 is one of the strategically placed "amnesty bins" where forbidden items can be deposited without penalty. The text on this bin ("Please dispose here; declare, dispose or pay the fine of 400 NZD") is entirely in Chinese, while other bins in the area have text in English (right-hand photo, Figure 5.3). The sender

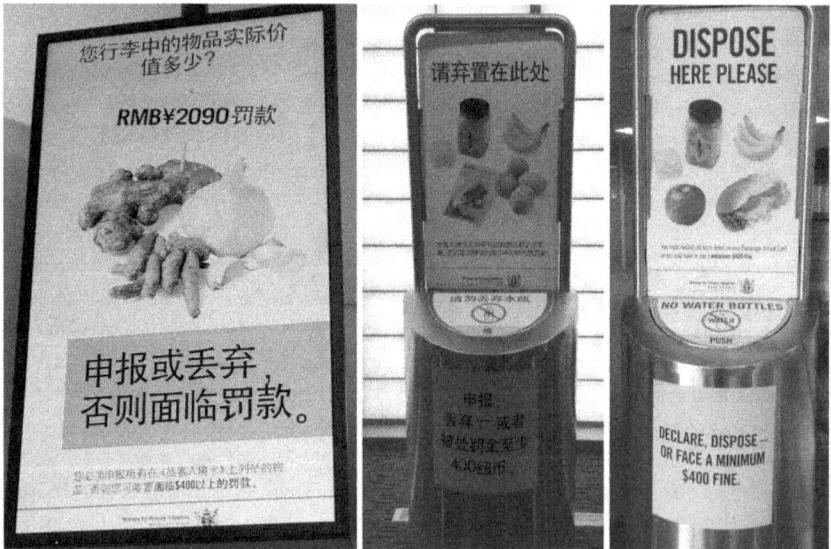

Figure 5.3 Chinese biosecurity sign before customs, Chinese biosecurity amnesty bin, English biosecurity amnesty bin, Chinese biosecurity sign before customs, Christchurch International Airport, September 2016.

here is in all cases the Ministry for Primary Industries, while the intended recipients are all travelers, both local and visitors.

As mentioned above, the aim of this signage is to encourage compliance with New Zealand's biosecurity rules, through Voluntary, Assisted, Directed, and Enforced means. The point of this and other information is presumably to assist the traveler to comply voluntarily. The teaching that is going on is about which items are prohibited and that declaration will not be penalized. The recurring message "declare, dispose or pay the fine" is a matter of directing the traveler, apparently giving a choice, while the mention of the fine relates to the final level where enforcement is enacted.

The intended recipient is both the visitor, who may have previously been unaware of New Zealand's strict biosecurity rules, and the local resident, who is encouraged to inform future visitors about the need to avoid bringing prohibited items to New Zealand. There appears to be an assumption that speakers of Asian languages may bring food and medicinal items that they may believe are unavailable or expensive in New Zealand (Sherring, 2019), while English-speaking visitors are more likely to have a piece of fruit or a sandwich that they had taken with them from the plane. The principles of audience design (Bell, 1984; Juffermans, 2012) are clearly in operation here, with both the language and the content being tailored to the imagined reader.

Places to See

When incoming passengers approach passport control, they were (at the time of data collection) divided into holders of New Zealand, Australian, UK, US, and Canadian passports, who could be processed electronically through the SmartGate system, and others (including New Zealand permanent residents) who needed to stand in line to be processed by a passport officer. Those who are directed to the queues are offered the distraction of informational signs such as the sign in the top photo in Figure 5.4. These signs have information about tourism destinations in the South Island. The sender is given as the airport, but a logo indicating the airport's carbon-neutral certification competes for attention in the sign. Visitors are referred to south.co.nz for further information. South defines itself as a "focused group of all the South Island's 13 regional tourism organisations working collaboratively with Christchurch International Airport to grow international arrivals and length of stay in the South Island of New Zealand" (south.co.nz). The website appears to be aimed at both Chinese visitors (e.g. listing places where the Chinese app Alipay can be used), and also tourism operators, explaining how they may attract Chinese visitors in particular.

The recipient of the message of the sign is assumed to be a visitor to the South Island, and they are given suggestions for places to see and taught some details in connection with the destination. One such example is the sign for Aoraki/Mount Cook shown in the top photo in Figure 5.4. Note that Aoraki/Mount Cook is the official name for this location in recognition of the original Māori name and a later English name given by European explorers. In this sign the visitor learns that Aoraki/Mount Cook is New Zealand's highest mountain, that Sir Edmund Hillary (a) was a

Figure 5.4 Tourist information before passport control (above); *kia ora* (informal greeting) sign between airbridge and duty free (below), Christchurch International Airport, September 2016.

New Zealander and (b) was the first person to climb Mount Everest and (c) climbed "Mount Cook" in his early days, and that the Aoraki/Mount Cook National Park has the longest glacier in New Zealand. Despite the use of the mountain's Māori name, Aoraki, there is no information about Māori history, cultural beliefs, or customs concerning the mountain. The sign also contains a QR code, which takes the visitor to the landing page of the south.co.nz website, which, at the time of writing, features a large photo of a smiling Asian couple.

The intention of the sign is, presumably, to show visitors possible destinations in the South Island. The south.co.nz website that it refers visitors to shows further destinations and itineraries with the stated intention "to grow the South Island economy and improve the experience that Chinese visitors enjoy when they come to New Zealand."

Māori Linguistic Landscape

Te reo Māori (the Māori language) is the indigenous language of New Zealand and is one of its official languages. Since the 1980s Māori has been the focus of renowned revitalization efforts with particular focus on the education system and public broadcasting (Author 2, 2018). Due to its status and relatively high levels of government support, Māori sits at the top of a perceived hierarchy of minority languages in New Zealand (de Bres, 2015). As a result, Māori language and visual elements are increasingly used in signage and logos developed by government and local body authorities in order to "signify 'Māoriness'" and "commitment to Māori" (Sissons, 1993: 113). However, such expression of commitment does not mean that the use of Māori comes from a normalized perspective (Harlow, 2005). Instead, the use of Māori within Christchurch Airport is marked and can be perceived as tokenistic and exoticizing.

There are several examples of Māori words on display in the international arrivals section of the airport. The first is a large mural as passengers transition from the exit corridors after deplaning and move toward entering the duty-free area (bottom photo, Figure 5.4). Although there is no explicit information on the sign as to who the sender is, it is in fact the airport itself.

The sign shown in the bottom photo in Figure 5.4 depicts a Māori elder welcoming a girl with a traditional *hongi* (noses pressed in welcome) in front of a photo of a high country scene. There is a band of woven flax along the bottom of the sign and a koru-styled Māori design in the sky of the image. Words of welcome are also included: Kia ora Welcome to Te Waipounamu (*kia ora* = welcome, greetings; Te Waipounamu = the South Island). The high-country scene matches other large textless murals of natural scenery, which could be seen in other parts of the airport at the time of the visit, including the baggage claim area. These vistas of the South Island landscape align with the airport's branding as the "gateway to the South Island."

We can consider a number of possible intentions in the use of Māori words and imagery on this sign. The words *kia ora* are in larger font, which would typically imply a higher level of importance. But, as noted by Kallen (2008: 277), font choices can also provide messaging. The cursive font used here is reminiscent of handwriting, with this particular choice invoking words written with an ink pen. Indeed, the writing of the "r" in the word *ora* uses a writing style that is no longer taught in schools in New Zealand and would be considered archaic. In other words, it is not clear that younger speakers of English would be able to decipher the word *ora*. So, while the font is large, the choice of font distances the viewer, conveying the contrasting messages of something that is both important (larger font) but also not meant to be fully understood (old-fashioned script). This message is further reinforced by the fact that none of the Māori words are translated, thus making it unclear how international visitors would read and interpret the message. If they can read English they will know that they are being welcomed somewhere, but not whether the welcome is to Christchurch, the South Island, or New Zealand? The intention of the sign, as shown by the South Island scenery, is to evoke the South Island but it is unclear whether this import is recognized by visitors.

Moving to the imagery in the photo montage, this also contains intended messages. The Māori man is wearing a traditional feathered cloak, so along with the woven flax border the message is one of exoticism. The interaction with the young girl involves a greeting ritual of pressing noses, which may be unfamiliar to many tourist visitors.

The sign can be perceived as providing some educational information to visitors in which it alerts visitors that there is another language in the landscape here and you may have some interaction with speakers of this language. However, most visitors to the South Island are unlikely to experience the encounter depicted. The formal attire of the Māori elder is something that would only be seen during a ritual welcome at a *marae* (traditional area in front of, and including, a meeting house). The *marae* setting is not depicted; instead the two people are placed in a montage in front of the high country scene.

Furthermore, this interaction is not an everyday one and not at all reflective of what a visitor might experience at one of the many tourism operations owned by the main Māori tribe in the South Island (Ngāi Tahu) or some of its subtribes. Ngāi Tahu is one of the largest tourism operators in New Zealand, owning a controlling interest in nine South Island businesses, which particularly focus on giving tourists experiences in the natural environment (Ngāi Tahu Tourism, 2018). For example, Ngāti Kurī, a subtribe, own the popular Whale Watch tours in the seaside township of Kaikōura, and

Waewae Pounamu jade enterprise is owned by Ngāti Waewae in the West Coast town of Hokitika (see Carr, 2007 for an overview of Māori-operated tourism businesses).

In addition, the messages that are intended and received from this sign are often obscured by booths and bins of discount liquor and other items, which are placed in front of the mural to entice those moving into the duty-free area that visitors next progress through in order to reach immigration.

There is a second use of Māori language as the international arrivals transition from the customs check to landside as they exit to the meet-and-greet area. Here there are three large signs, two of which are shown in Figure 5.5, both featuring a scenic destination with a Māori word alongside an English phrase (see website for Figure 5.5).

In the sign on the left in Figure 5.5 the Māori word *taonga* (treasure) is prominently displayed on photos of South Island scenery. Again, the choice of font conveys an exoticism. The English words below highlight the word *precious*, thus linking back to the meaning of the Māori word. As with most other photos of scenery in the airport actual locations are given in English in small print at the bottom. The sign on the right in Figure 5.5 is the final sign as those arriving exit to landside. The photo depicts an iconic Christchurch scene of daffodils and blossom in reference to the fact that Christchurch is often described as the most English city in New Zealand. Again, the words of the Māori welcome phrase *haere mai*, are echoed by the English below.

The placement of these photos is on the side walls directly after the final luggage X-ray machine, about 20 meters behind the final exit door (which can be partially seen in the photo on the right-hand side of Figure 5.5). At this point in the arrival process, international visitors, many of whom have arrived on long haul flights, will be focused on exiting from airside to landside and many transiting through this area will not notice these images. The educational intent of these signs is similar to the one as visitors deplane (Figure 5.4).

Both sets of signs are located at threshold points: as those arriving leave the plane and as they exit to landside. The Māori language is often used symbolically at the beginning and end of government and local body meetings (McKee & Manning, 2015) and here the placement of the signs is reminiscent of this symbolic use at the entrance and exit.

All of these signs include scenic images to cohere with the airport's branding. In fact, this seems to be the main intention of the signs. The use of Māori words appears to be symbolic; cohering to expected norms about the use of Māori in the New Zealand setting, the Māori words are not directly translated. The use of cursive, decorative fonts, and flourishes for Māori words suggests that they may not be expected to be read or even to be legible to the visitors. This may be an example of what Canagarajah (2012: 7) calls languages being "appropriated by people for their purposes."

In the interview with the airport services manager, it was revealed that the Māori words were selected and used by the marketing team without consultation or advice from the local tribe. Internationally the use of indigenous languages and cultural motifs are regularly used without approval to add an exotic flavor to the tourism experience (Gertner, 2019). This can be contrasted with the way Auckland Airport refers to how it has collaborated with local Māori in developing their thirty-year plan (Auckland Airport, 2019). Auckland Airport cites that it values "the cultural advice and services local Māori provide, including *pōwhiri* (Māori welcome ceremonies) for the new airlines we welcome to Auckland each year." Auckland Airport also supports Māori Language Week by making announcements in Māori and hosting performances by Māori cultural groups in its terminals. This is an example of the increasing engagement with appropriate Māori groups to add depth to the usage of Māori iconography and language in recognition that "the power of the tribal narrative significantly enhances the tourism experience" (Roskruge, Morrison, & Maxwell. 2017).

Discussion

We have shown that signs in airports can have a range of educative functions. From the airport's point of view, there are two central purposes: to assist the efficient movement of passengers and to market attractions at the destination. Much linguistic landscape research is done in public spaces. An airport, however, is not a street, but rather a relatively controlled area. Since it is a semi-public rather than a public space, all the signs we saw were officially generated and sanctioned by the airport and/or government agencies. As an educational arena, there are many differences to classroom-based education. In the airport, signs are more contextualized and their presence is presumably carefully thought out. The rhetorical triangle or pentad is curated to provide appropriate information to the right recipients at the right time. However, some of the implicit educational messaging, such as the strategic employment of Māori words and images, may be lost due to competition for the attention of visitors from commercial advertising in the duty-free area (Figure 5.4) and the proximity of the exit (Figure 5.5).

The signs we have focused on in this chapter have been mostly permanent and stationary, although some were temporary, such as the Chinese Language Week signs outside the airport, and also mobile (Sebba, 2010) in the case of the Chinese buttons worn by ground staff. Visitors arriving at the airport (the primary group of implicit readers of the signs in the airport) have a range of assumed educational needs. Firstly, they are given extensive guidance in key languages and pictograms to help them to successfully navigate the airport. Then they are taught how to avoid falling foul of the strict New Zealand biosecurity rules. Furthermore, they gain knowledge about what to do in the South Island through explicit tourist information and images of empty natural scenery. Signs placed where queues form offer fun facts about New Zealand and New Zealanders who may be known to visitors. Other pictures show the visitors what they might expect to see in New Zealand with images of beautiful nature and a formal encounter with Māori, but there is an absence of images of mainstream New Zealand society.

Education beyond the classroom is not only relevant for young people. Signage with an educational intention is found in many environments and this has not been the focus of much research before the current volume. The educative content of airport signage has not to our knowledge been investigated previously. Signs, like written texts in many genres, offer not only the written word but also the social semiotic context and content of the sign. Shohamy and Waksman (2009) point out that semiotic processes can only be understood by multimodal approaches and insist on attention "not only to the meanings conveyed by the language, but also to the meaning provided by the visual aspects of language like typography, placement in the semiotic layouts, color, spatial and kinetic arrangements" (Shohamy & Waksman, 2009: 316). The analysis of airport signs bears witness to this. In Figure 5.4, the stylized retro font used in the words *kia ora* amplifies the image of a Māori elder greeting a European-looking young woman in its role as a decorative evocative element superimposed in a scene of natural beauty, which is otherwise devoid of any trace of human occupation. The same theme can be seen in Figure 5.5 where a huge, ornate font marks a Māori word or phrase as decorative rather than denotative.

Similarly the use of a QR code in Figure 5.4 to link the reader to further information from other sources is a selective appeal to those who command the requisite literacies (digital savvy visitors who have a mobile device at hand with the capability of scanning a QR code along with connectivity to allow the visitor to access the linked webpage). This is covertly selective just as the use of only two languages in the left-hand image in Figure 5.2 is a way of attracting the attention of those who are being addressed while remaining invisibilized in the background for others.

We would like to extend Spolsky's (2009) enumeration of types of signs to highlight the educational function of "informative" signs. We have shown that information that is intended to facilitate learning of an imagined reader or group of readers can be considered to have an educative purpose, regardless of whether the intended learning outcomes are knowledge of how to get around independently (Figure 5.1), of the informal rules such as cultural differences and acceptable behavior or of the formal rules of the country (Figure 5.2), or of tourist attractions that could be included in a tour (Figure 5.4). The intended learning outcome of the signs referring to Chinese Language Week in Figure 5.2 is that Chinese is a valued language and Chinese speakers are especially welcome (and may even be greeted in Chinese), while Figures 5.4 and 5.5 convey multiple messages through their layered semiotic construction, but visitors may pick up on that there is a Māori language and a culture present in New Zealand, though there is a lack of links to further information. Together with the elaborate graphic design it is tempting to conclude that the presence of Māori in the airport is as a decorative, exotic element, with no real content.

In conclusion, this study reveals a range of educative functions and intended messages (as well as some unintended ones) conveyed by signage in the semi-public space of airports. Because the airport in this study is owned by a local government/government body these educative functions extend to reinforcing government priorities through the use of languages, which have identity functions and economic import.

References

Aiestaran, J., Cenoz, J., & Gorter, D. (2010). Multilingual cityscapes: Perceptions and preferences of the inhabitants of Donostia-San Sebastián. In E. Shohamy, E. Ben-Rafael, & M. Barni (Eds.), *Linguistic Landscape in the City* (pp. 219–34). Bristol: Multilingual Matters.

Auckland Airport. (2008). *Our Brand New Welcome Experience*. Auckland: Auckland Airport. Retrieved from https://www.aucklandairport.co.nz/~/media/426D09A08C684 F12B16866D049227C92.ashx?sc_database=web

Auckland Airport. (2019). *Engaging with Local Māori*. https://corporate.aucklandairport.co.nz/corporate-responsibility/engaging-with-local-maori.

Bell, A. (1984). Language style as audience design. *Language in Society*, 13(2), 145–204.

Blow, C. J. (2013). *Airport Terminals: Butterworth Architecture Library of Planning and Design*. Oxford: Butterworth-Heinemann.

Bradley, G. (2017). Tourism roars past dairy as NZ's biggest export earner. *New Zealand Herald*, April 30. Retrieved from https://www.nzherald.co.nz/business/news/article.cfm?c_id=3&objectid=11847120

Burke, K. (1969). *A Rhetoric of Motives*. Berkeley: University of California Press.

Carr, A. (2007). Māori nature tourism businesses: Connecting with the land. In R. Butler & T. Hince (Eds.), *Tourism and Indigenous Peoples* (pp. 113–27). Amsterdam: Butterworth-Heinemann.

Canagarajah, S. (2012). *Translingual Practice: Global Englishes and Cosmopolitan Relations*. New York: Routledge.

Castro, R., & Lohmann, G. (2014). Airport branding: Content analysis of vision statements. *Research in Transportation Business and Management*, 10, 4–14.

Cenoz, J., & Gorter, D. (2006). Linguistic landscape and minority languages. *International Journal of Multilingualism*, 3, 67–80.

Christchurch Airport (2016). *Our Place in the World: Annual Report*. Christchurch: Christchurch Airport. Retrieved from https://www.christchurchairport.co.nz/media/830702/cial_annual_report_main_report_spreads.pdf

Coupland, N., & Garrett, P. (2010). Linguistic landscapes, discursive frames and metacultural performance: The case of Welsh Patagonia. *International Journal of the Sociology of Language*, 2010(205), 7–36.

de Bres, J. (2015). The hierarchy of minority languages in New Zealand. *Journal of Multilingual and Multicultural Development*, 36(7), 677–93.

Fewings, R. (2001). Wayfinding and airport terminal design. *Journal of Navigation*, 54(2), 177–84. doi: 10.1017/S0373463301001369

Fodness, D., & Murray, B. (2007). Passengers' expectations of airport service quality. *Journal of Services Marketing*, 21(7), 492–506.

Gertner, R. K. (2019). The impact of cultural appropriation on destination image, tourism, and hospitality. *Thunderbird International Business Review*, 61(6), 873–77.

Gibbs, J. (2014). Passenger perceptions of depersonalisation of the airport experience. master's thesis, University of Otago.

Gorter, D. 2018. Linguistic landscapes and trends in the study of schoolscapes. *Linguistics and Education*, 44, 80–5.

Guilford, G. (2013). Chinese government publishes guide on how to avoid being a terrible tourist. *The Atlantic* (October 7). https://www.theatlantic.com/china/

archive/2013/10/chinese-government-publishes-guide-on-how-to-avoid-being-a-terrible-tourist/280332/

Gupta, I. (2008). Public signage system to combat problems of illiteracy and multilingualism. *Journal of International Social Research*, 1(4), 268–78.

Harlow, R. (2005). Covert attitudes to Māori. *International Journal of the Sociology of Language*, 172, 133–47.

Hayward, J. (2012). Biculturalism—Biculturalism in the state sector, *Te Ara—the Encyclopedia of New Zealand*, http://www.TeAra.govt.nz/en/biculturalism/page-2

Hoaxbuster. (May 1, 2013). *Panneau anti-chinois au Louvre*. https://www.hoaxbuster.com/societe/2013/10/04/panneau-anti-chinois-au-louvre

Jameson, J. (2019). Jewel Changi Airport, Singapore: First look at game-changing new development. *Stuff* (April 12). Retrieved from https://www.stuff.co.nz/travel/destinations/asia/111985651/jewel-changi-airport-singapore-first-look-at-gamechanging-new-development-jewel (accessed August 25, 2019).

Juffermans, K. (2012). Multimodality and audiences: Local languages in the Gambian linguistic landscape. *Sociolinguistic Studies*, 6(2), 259–84.

Kallen, J. (2008). Tourism and representation in the Irish linguistic landscape. In E. Shohamy & D. Gorter (Eds.), *Linguistic Landscape: Expanding the Scenery* (pp. 270–83). New York: Routledge.

King, J. (2018). Māori: Revitalization of an endangered language. In K.L. Rehg & L. Campbell (Eds.), *The Oxford handbook of endangered languages* (pp. 592–612). Oxford: Oxford University Press.

Kinneavy, J. L. (1980). *A Theory of Discourse: The Aims of Discourse*. New York: W. W. Norton.

Landry, R., & Bourhis, R. Y. (1997). Linguistic landscape and ethnolinguistic vitality: An empirical study. *Journal of Language and Social Psychology*, 16, 23–49.

Le Figaro. (August 22, 2013). *La Chine s'inquiète de l'incivilité de ses touristes*. http://www.lefigaro.fr/international/2013/08/22/01003-20130822ARTFIG00340-la-chine-s-inquiete-de-l-incivilite-de-ses-touristes.php

Macalister, J. (2006). The Maori presence in the New Zealand English lexicon, 18502000: Evidence from a corpus-based study. *English World-Wide*, 27(1), 1–24. doi: 10.1075/eww.27.1.02mac

McKee, R. L., & Manning, V. (2015). Evaluating effects of language recognition on language rights and the vitality of New Zealand Sign Language. *Sign Language Studies*, 15(4), 473–97.

Miller, C. (2016). How racist are we New Zealand? *New Zealand Herald* (January 5). https://www.nzherald.co.nz/nz/news/article.cfm?c_id=1&objectid=11776745

New Zealand Government. (2019). Māori culture and heritage. https://www.govt.nz/browse/history-culture-and-heritage/maori-language-culture-and-heritage/maori-culture-and-heritage/

Ngāi Tahu Tourism (2018). https://www.ngaitahutourism.co.nz/

Pakarinen, S., & Björklund, S. (2018). Multiple language signage in linguistic landscapes and students' language practices: A case study from a language immersion setting. *Linguistics and Education*, 44, 4–11.

Paranihi, R. (2019), New Māori look for Auckland Int. Airport, *Te Ao Māori News* (May 23). Retrieved from https://teaomaori.news/new-maori-look-auckland-int-airport

Roskruge, M., Morrison, S., & Maxwell, T. K. (2017). *Measuring the Value of the Contribution of Māori Language and Culture to the New Zealand Economy*. Retrieved from https://www.tetaurawhiri.govt.nz/assets/Uploads/46b6fdcf03/Measure-the-value-of-te-reo-Maori2.pdf

Royal Society of New Zealand. (2013). *Languages in Aotearoa New Zealand*. Retrieved from https://www.royalsociety.org.nz/assets/Uploads/Languages-in-Aotearoa-New-Zealand.pdf

Scollon, R., & Wong Scollon, S. (2003). *Discourses in Place: Language in the Material World*. London: Routledge.

Sebba, M. (2010). Discourses in transit. In C. Thurlow, & A. Jaworski (Eds.), *Semiotic Landscapes: Language, Image, Space* (pp. 59–76). London: Continuum.

Sherring, P. (2019). Declare or dispose: Protecting New Zealand's border with behaviour change. *Journal of Social Marketing*. doi: 10.1108/JSOCM-09-2018-0103

Shohamy, E., & Waksman, S. (2009). Linguistic landscapes as an ecological arena: Modalities, meanings, negotiations, education. In E. Shohamy & D. Gorter (Eds.), *Linguistic Landscape: Expanding the Scenery* (pp. 313–31). New York: Routledge.

Sissons, J. (1993). The systematisation of tradition: Maori culture as a strategic resource, *Oceania*, 64(2), 97–116.

Spolsky, B. (2009). Prolegomena to a sociolinguistic theory of public signage. In E. Shohamy & D. Gorter (Eds.), *Linguistic Landscape: Expanding the Scenery* (pp. 25–39). New York: Routledge.

Spolsky, B., & Cooper, R. L. (1991). *The Languages of Jerusalem*. Oxford: Clarendon Press.

Stats N. Z. (2018). International visitor arrivals to New Zealand: December 2017. Retrieved from www.stats.govt.nz/information-releases/international-visitor-arrivals-to-new-zealand-december-2017

Tan, M. S., & Said, S. B. (2015). Linguistic landscape and exclusion: An examination of language representation in disaster signage in Japan. In R. Rubdy & S. B. Said (Eds.), *Conflict, Exclusion and Dissent in the Linguistic Landscape* (pp. 145–69). London: Palgrave Macmillan.

Tsui, K., & Henderson, I. (2018). The changing dynamics and roles of New Zealand's airports: An overview. *Airline Economics in Asia (Advances in Airline Economics)*, 7, 245–66.

6

English Learning Experience in a Textile Company in Turkey

Yasemin Kırkgöz

Introduction

In addition to being spoken, languages are also displayed in public space for functional or symbolic purposes, offering stimulating texts on multiple levels such as single words, colorful images, and a variety of text types displayed in multiple languages and varieties. The field of linguistic landscape (LL) thus refers to studies related to the representation and interpretation of languages displayed in public places. LL studies aim to explore patterns and meanings underlying languages in public spaces and to interpret the meanings, ideologies, and decision-making of people, leading to the creation of such landscape in its varied forms. Recently, however, the definition of the notion of LL has been broadened. It has been argued that LL research should go beyond the varied text types displayed in public spaces of written languages on signs and also include images, sounds, drawings, and movement (Gorter, 2006). Accordingly, for researchers engaged in LL, language in public spaces is said to be not arbitrary; rather, they attempt to explore these systematic patterns in the relationship between LL and people, ideology, policy, in order to describe and analyze various forms of representation.

The present study was initiated to support the English language development of Turkish personnel working in a textile company. The research aimed to explore how images and their corresponding texts provide language learning experience beyond the boundaries of a classroom in the space of a textile company. The theoretical frame of the study is peripheral language learning (PLL) theory, which offers an indirect method of educating adults efficiently. Qualitative approach was adopted as the methodology of the study. The research context, the creation of PLL experience in a Turkish textile company as well as the procedure for collecting qualitative data from individual and focus group interviews are presented in the methodology section. The same section also presents analysis of the qualitative data from related research tools. The impact of PLL on the textile personnel's English language development is discussed in accordance with each research question in the findings section of the chapter. The study concludes with some suggestions for future directions that research in this specific area can take.

Peripheral Language Learning

The concept of peripheral learning was originally coined by the Bulgarian psychologist, Georgi Lozanov, in the 1970s as a part of the language teaching method, *Suggestopedia* (Larsen-Freeman & Anderson, 2011). Lozanov attributed the reason for learning inefficiency to psychological barriers such as the fear of being unable to perform, failure, and having limitations in our ability to learn. Lozanov (1978) believed that students underutilized their mental capacity, and if given ideal conditions and a more pleasant learning environment learners would use their full mental capacity, considerably more material could be processed and retention of material would reach to its maximum potential. In other words, Lozanov asserted that in order to make better use of our mental power, the limitations we perceive needed to be "desuggested." Suggestopedia also came to be known as *Desuggestopedia*; the application of the study of suggestion to pedagogy refers to eliminating the feeling that one cannot be successful and/or the negative association one may have toward studying.

Suggestopedia considers the physical environment and the classroom atmosphere significant. Accordingly, teachers should "suggest" whatever students like and "desuggest" whatever they dislike. This application helps to overcome the barriers to learning (Harmer, 2001). One of the fundamental principles of Suggestopedia is PLL, which depends on the possibility that we see more in our surroundings than we intentionally see. Larsen-Freeman (2011) supports the view that learners learn not only from direct instructions but also from the surrounding environment and stresses that posters and pictures illustrating language elements help students to take advantage of peripheral learning.

Fatemipour (2013) views PLL as "learning from the environment" and states that "[it] is encouraged through the presence in the learning environment of posters and decorations" (p. 1395). Supporting and enriching the learning environment with images of posters containing target words, phrases and structures, pictures or realia demonstrating meaning can be considered as a means of creating a target language (L2) environment and thus increasing the learner's exposure to the displayed information.

PLL can also be considered as a type of incidental and implicit learning as opposed to explicit and intentional learning owing to continuous exposure to information (Bahmani, Pazhakh, & Raee Sharif, 2012; Ellis, 2008). Marsick and Watkins (1990) define incidental learning as "a by-product of some other activity, such as task accomplishment, interpersonal interaction, sensing the organizational culture, trial-and-error experimentation, or even formal learning" (p. 12). It occurs when learners are unaware of its occurrence and is often used interchangeably with the term, *peripheral learning*. As reported by Reider (2003), it is composed of implicit learning processes that happen without the learner's awareness and/or explicit learning processes that take place without learning intention but nevertheless involve an awareness and hypothesis formation. Hulstijn (2005) maintains that in the former situation, learners are informed prior to their engagement in a learning task that they will be tested afterward on their retention of a particular type of information. In the latter case, however, learners are not forewarned of an upcoming retention test for a particular type of information.

PLL is considered to offer great potential for learning English as a foreign language (EFL) efficiently within the classroom context. As pointed out by Larsen-Freeman

(2011), "we perceive much more in our environment than that to which we consciously attend" (p. 84). The author further articulates that EFL learners can effortlessly absorb such information as vocabulary and grammar items displayed on the classroom walls. Likewise, Wong (2001) believes that EFL learners' exposure to vocabulary might trigger incidental vocabulary acquisition and other linguistic elements such as verbs.

A number of studies have been conducted in different environments examining the effect of peripheral learning on vocabulary acquisition (Badri, Badri, & Badri, 2015; Bahmani, Pazhakh, & Raee Sharif, 2012; Reider, 2003), reading comprehension (Rashidi & Ganbari Adivi, 2010), grammar (Doost & Tahmasbi, 2017), and word spellings (Rokni, Porasghar, & Taziki, 2014). These studies have consistently reported that peripheral learning is effective in improving learners' vocabulary retention and recall and spelling ability. All of these studies seem to suggest that creating peripheral learning conditions as a supplement to more explicit learning methods has a positive effect on the acquisition of vocabulary and some linguistic features.

Despite its potential benefits, the phenomenon of PLL and its possible uses outside the classroom context such as in a workplace have not been adequately investigated. Hence, in recognition of the potential benefits of PLL, the present study was initiated, as will be described in the following section. The study is unique in many respects from the studies reported here. First, the previous studies were conducted in the classroom environment with the researchers created PLL experiences by displaying posters on the classroom environment whereas the present study explores the potential benefits of PLL outside the classroom context in a work place. In addition, these studies mostly draw on well-known existing research methods and techniques including questionnaires to produce quantitative data that carry numerical values. The present study is qualitative in nature that aims to understand and interpret the meaning adult textile workers ascribe to this novel experience from their own perspective of reality (Berg, 2001; Creswell, 2013). As such, the present study uses such qualitative research tools as individual and focus group interviews.

In line with the above discussion, the present research seeks answers to the following questions:

- What are the participants' views and opinions toward images being present in the company?
- To what extent do the participants tend to notice and examine such images presented in the company?
- How can images and their corresponding texts provide language learning experience beyond the boundaries of a classroom in the space of a textile company?

Research Context

Turkey is one of the world's most prominent textile and clothing producers. The textile and clothing industry is a major contributor to the Turkish economy and is by far the largest employer within the manufacturing sector. The context for this study is an international textile company in Turkey employing over 250 people, including managers, line supervisors, shop-floor employees, sales representatives, and foreign specialists (Kırkgöz, 2013). In this company not only Turkish personnel participate in the process of production but foreign personnel, mainly by British and American, participate as well. Thus, effective communication in English between the Turkish and foreign personnel is critical to perform the required tasks and for the well-being of the company. The company had two sections; the administration section consisted of offices for managers, sales representatives, and Turkish and foreign textile specialists; and the factory section where garments were manufactured.

The research was conducted to examine the impact of English words and images related to a particular domain, textile engineering, which were used to create implicit and peripheral language learning opportunities in the context of a workplace, that is, a textile company. What motivated the initiation of this research was that I was invited by the director of this textile company to support English language development of Turkish textile personnel. I designed a Professional English course, scheduled as two hours weekly to meet the language needs of participants and to give them the skills and confidence to use English effectively in the workplace and beyond with foreign textile engineers. The weekly two lessons, each forty-five minutes, were taught in the factory. Although the staff was motivated to improve their English language and communication skills they had one major problem. As they had insufficient time to do out of class revision of the materials taught, they failed recalling and remembering what was previously taught. Therefore, I decided to create language learning opportunities beyond the classroom boundaries in order to support the English language development of Turkish textile personnel. The course lasted ten weeks. Participants of the course were thirty-six textile personnel (16 male and 20 female) with an average age of twenty-eight and elementary level of language proficiency in English corresponding to A2.

Procedure

Within the philosophy of learning beyond the classroom boundaries, textile-related signs were posted as educational materials in various spaces of the textile company, both in the administration section and the factory section, by the researcher in a structured and purposeful manner. In the administration section of the company, I posted the signs to the office doors of the assistant managers, sales representatives, and supervisors, and also to the main corridors. These were the places where staff walked by the most. In the factory component where shop-floor employees worked, I hung up the images mostly on the walls. The company had a large entrance, which was a suitable place to put up posters. Therefore, the final place was the walls of the entrance where the posters were neatly displayed. All of these places were suitable for the personnel to notice the signs around the factory and give staff an opportunity to notice.

The selection process of the images and related textual materials (terms, etc.) largely depended on the in-class topics covered in the Professional English course. Images were in the form of a poster prepared on a separate piece of paper, containing some sort of textual message, and being displayed out in the open space with the aim of fostering "sporadic, individual, incidental learning" (Hubenthal, O'Brian, & Taber, 2011: 196). Images served a number of purposes including (a) illustrating a concept or a thing, (b) demonstrating a process, (c) differentiating between similar things, and (d) drawing interest (Demirağ, 2018). Each image accompanied textual information to help the passersby make an association between the images and their corresponding textual message.

The size of the images printed in A2 size or smaller depended mainly on the size and quantity of linguistic and visual material in order to catch the attention of the passersby (Rubdy, 2015). The "image quality" is another issue that I considered, making sure that each image is free from defects such as blur, low readability, and so on (Dock, 2019). Each poster was colorful and linguistic elements were readable to enable the personnel to figure out the published images. Initially, the most basic type of sign was displayed; featuring textile terms comprised of one or a few words and paired with an image. These are illustrated in the three posters in Figure 6.1, placed on a door and the walls of a corridor.

The complexity of the materials gradually increased to include a larger set of textile terms and expressions with their corresponding textual material in an attempt to educate the passersby to implicitly and/or incidentally become familiar and adept with these signs and expressions as a result of continuous *exposure* to the increasing quantity of information. An example of this is given in the following images:

As is evident from the illustrations below, the textile terms are repeated intentionally to create the recycling effect in the learning process. Recycling is reintroducing and practicing language that learners have seen previously in a different context (Brown, 2000). As seen in Figure 6.2, the newer version contains more information and more texts than the previous one. The newer sign contains the same lettering of the texts with some textual and pictorial additions to the older sign. The positioning of the pictures and posters was changed at two- or three-week intervals to make learning more interesting and effective. In fact, the posters were moved around every three weeks, and every week new ones were posted. To create a long-lasting effect on learning the signs remained in their places for three weeks, and I added new ones every

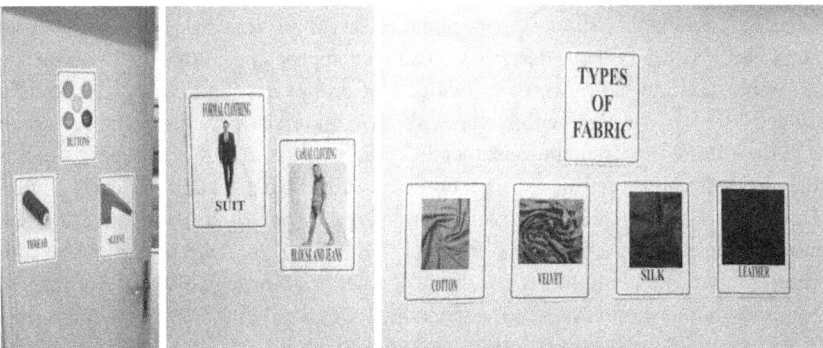

Figure 6.1 Placement of the posters of textile terms

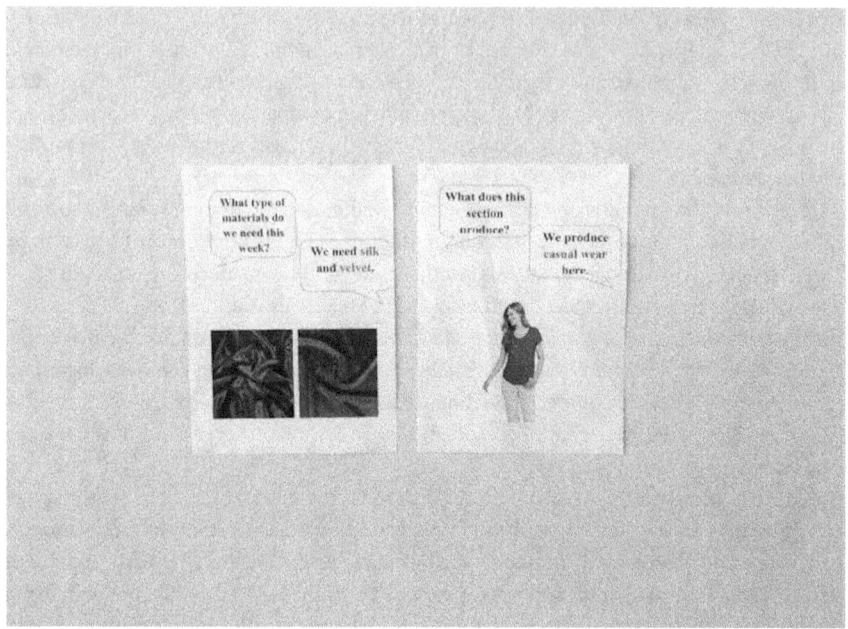

Figure 6.2 Placement of a poster of a dialogue in the corridor

week. Twenty-six posters were prepared by the researcher and displayed in various places in the company in order to provide personnel with a visual and verbal source of peripheral information. The posters were colorful and contained illustrative images to create a source of motivation and to catch the personnel's attention.

Research Method

In this study qualitative methods were used, and the research drew upon several research instruments including participant observation, individual and focus group interviews. Creswell (2009) describes qualitative approach as "a means for exploring and understanding the meaning individuals or groups ascribe to a social or human problem" (p. 4). Working within the qualitative approach paradigm, the researcher took the role of a participant observer to explore the activities of the people under study in their natural setting through observation and participation in those activities (DeWalt & DeWalt, 2002) over an extended period of time to facilitate a better understanding of those behaviors. Bernard (1994) notes that participant observation requires the researcher to maintain a sense of objectivity through distance. He suggests that more than just observation be used in the process of being a participant observer, also recommending the use of interviews and field notes.

Accordingly, in this study, participant observation has been complemented with individual and focus group interviews. Anderson (1990) defines a focus group as comprising "individuals with certain characteristics who focusses discussions on a given issue or topic" (p. 241). According to Denscombe (2007) "focus group consists of a small group of people, usually between six and nine in number, who are brought together by a trained moderator (the researcher) to explore attitudes and perceptions, feelings and ideas about a topic" (p. 115).

An initial focus group discussion, held mainly in English, especially for the picture portion, with different groups of personnel, enabled the researcher to determine textile personnel's existing knowledge with textile-related words and expressions. In addition, pictures of textile-related terms were shown to participants and they were asked what those terms meant to them. Out of thirty-six participants, only eight were able to recognize the true meaning of the terms demonstrated in English. In addition, participants were given some more complex pictures such as a dialogue, and they were asked what the people could be talking about in L2. In each group, only one or two participants were able to respond to such questions accurately. The same focus group discussions were held at the end of the ten-week period. These focus groups at the end had the same composition of textile personnel as the ones at the beginning. Unlike the initial focus group interviews, most participants were able to respond with great accuracy to the questions posed by the researcher.

At the end of the study, the researcher interviewed each participant, asking for their individual reflections on this learning process; the discussions were audio-recorded. The interview questions were asked in Turkish (L1) to make the participants feel at ease. In the interview, the participants were asked to express (a) what they personally felt and thought about the images being displayed in various places in the company, (b) how frequently they were able to notice and examine posters presented in various places in the company, and (c) what their overall language learning experiences were in relation to the use of images.

The qualitative data from multiple sources were analyzed using content analysis, and audio-recorded interview responses by the participants were transcribed verbatim. They were then translated into English by the author. Each participant was coded as P1, P2, P3, etc., using procedures suggested by Creswell (2013) as the framework for analysis. The responses given by each participant were then examined in order to develop categories following a three-step process: read the transcribed interview data, identify themes, and place the matching responses to the appropriate themes. The overall response patterns were evaluated for each research question, enabling the analysis of the qualitative data to be performed in a recursive and iterative manner. To ensure reliably, another coder was invited to cross-code the data independently and 96 percent of inter-coder agreement was attained.

A similar procedure was followed to analyze the data from focus group interviews. Finally, data from these sources were compared and the researcher's field notes from observations were used to validate and support the emerging themes found in the focus group discussions and the interview data. Interview extracts from the participants are used for illustrative purposes in the findings section of the study.

Findings

It has been found that the presence of a multitude of informational and illustrative images and posters displayed in various outdoor places in the company affected the textile personnel's acquisition and retention of textile-related terms and related materials. In this section, responses to each research question are presented and discussed.

The Participants' Views and Opinions toward Posters Being Present in the Company

In the interview, participants were asked to express what they personally felt and thought about the images being displayed in various places in the company. The responses were overwhelmingly positive. Most participants stated that the presence of posters has affected their learning vocabulary, textile-related terms, and expressions, as illustrated in the following interview extracts:

> *I think the pictures on the walls are really interesting and helpful. I don't need translations. I can understand the words' meanings from the pictures.*
>
> *(P8)*

As noted earlier, learning through PLL is implicit since it is implied and takes place indirectly, and it is incidental. The interview extract below indicates a clear evidence of this principle happening in the participant. One of the aims of Suggestiopedia is to eliminate the fear of learning. The last statement in the extract shows the removal of classroom tension.

> *I learned the words unconsciously. When I hear someone say the word, the picture comes to my mind. It's better to learn like this than a classroom because there is no pressure.*
>
> *(P18)*

Many participants acknowledged that images and pictures displayed around the company created a lively and colorful environment. The posters were found to be eye-catching for the passersby, and participants were found to engage with the linguistic landscape and liked the continuous change in the linguistic landscape, as shown in the following extracts:

> *The presence of colorful posters made the environment special. This made us feel good and happy. We felt relaxed and peaceful in our workplace. Looking at the posters we felt interested and inquisitive to learn new information.*
>
> *(P3)*

> *The pictures on the walls were really noticeable. I notice the pictures the day they were put up. It is impossible to overlook them. The colorful pictures made me curious about what the posters were about.*
>
> *(P9)*

Many of the participants found this PLL learning experience new and innovative, as clearly stated by the following participant:

> *It was a different experience to have these pictures on our walls because they were decorative and useful at the same time. I liked that the pictures were in different colors.*
>
> (P12)

> *I feel happy and peaceful because the design of the posters and pictures are very pleasing. Having illustrative posters as opposed to blank walls has made the workplace feel special.*
>
> (P32)

The Extent to Which Participants Tend to Notice and Examine Such Posters Presented in the Company

In the interviews, participants were also asked how frequently they were able to notice and examine such posters presented in various places in the company. As illustrated in the following extracts, while walking around the building, posters frequently caught their attention:

> *I see the pictures everyday while I walk through the building. I look at the pictures for a couple of minutes. They help me a lot to learn new vocabulary.*
>
> (P19)

> *I saw my co-workers examining the pictures the first day. I was curious about what they were looking at.*
>
> (P11)

> *I look at the posters a couple of times every day. Since they are part of our immediate surroundings, it's easy for us to see them. As they are informative when we look at them, we see new things each time.*
>
> (P15)

Almost all participants acknowledged that while passing by the corridors or walking around the building those colorful posters attracted their attention unintentionally. They also agreed that in due course they developed a habit of looking up at the posters and wondering about what new images were going to be displayed.

The expressions of most participants confirmed the argument that PLL is an unconscious act. However, there were also cases showing that noticing the signs and learning from them are not always fully conscious, as can be seen in the comment of the participant (P10), nor fully unconscious, as stated by P22 below, but that the employees' attention might be more captured at certain times rather than others.

> *Initially, I didn't care much about them. But after a while, walking along the corridor or walking into an office ... or even walking around the entrance to the company posters with their textual materials began to draw my attention.*
>
> (P10)

I always look at the posters very attentively. When I forget some words or I feel uncertain about their spellings, I mean ... how a word is written in English ... Looking at the posters makes me feel happy and peaceful. I feel happy to see some words that I learned before ... this time in different sentences. So I feel confident.

(P22)

By analyzing the results, it has been observed that the peripheral exposure of textile-related terms and expressions had a very significant impact on the participants' vocabulary acquisition, retention, and recall. Unlike the language classroom, which provides formal spaces, PLL seemed to offer indirect methods of educating adults efficiently and the structured landscape provided opportunities for learning for the whole staff in the company. The present study provided an opportunity where the passersby textile company staffs were able to learn in some way, peripherally.

How Images and Their Corresponding Texts Provide Language Learning Experience beyond the Boundaries of a Classroom in the Space of a Textile Company

In the present study, peripheral learning is encouraged through the presence of posters and decorations featuring the target language and different grammatical information in the learning environment. It has been revealed that while passing by many participants were able to notice new terms with their meaning and thus acquire knowledge related to the textile field without concentrating much on the images and related text. It was found that the peripheral exposure to signs and posters had a very significant impact on the personnel's vocabulary acquisition, retention, and recall. As revealed from the interview findings, and the researcher's own observation of the personnel speaking to native English speakers working in the company, many participants were able to speak with confidence using the terms and expressions displayed for peripheral learning purposes. The following interview extracts illustrate this finding:

Images and posters with some textual materials displayed in various outside places helped me recall terms and dialogues, and I used them when I needed them in the proper places.

(P31)

Images and posters have affected my speaking very positively. I've learned many words from the posters, and whenever I saw these words when I was reading some articles related to my job, or writing an email to my British co-worker, the picture in the poster would come up in my mind and I'd just recall the right word. I also learned some grammar structures by looking at the dialogues in the posters. They just stuck in my mind.

(P16)

As we keep seeing the same things, learning becomes easier and more permanent. We can look at the posters any time during and outside the working hours and make use of them whenever we need.

(P22)

I looked at the posters, and because I saw the posters every day, most vocabulary and dialogues have become familiar to me. The posters helped me to remember certain words and grammar structures.

(P18)

Posters helped me a lot. I learned many words related to textile engineering. I learned garment, yarn, buttons and many others. Even just looking at the pictures is a great help in understanding what the word would mean in English.

(P16)

Thanks to these posters, I was able to remember vocabulary and many dialogues related to my job. I now think putting up such posters is something indispensable.

(P10)

Especially the posters with pictures right in front have stuck in my mind. There has been information that I remembered later. Also, I believe that being constantly exposed to information makes it easier to remember later. That's why there was a positive effect.

(P10)

The participants stated that they preferred to learn vocabulary through images with texts and posters displayed on the wall, rather than learning in the classroom environment. The following extracts illustrate the participants' opinion related to this:

I looked at the posters with pictures every day. Especially seeing words that I had trouble remembering.... Terms illustrated with pictures allowed many words to stick in my mind.

(P28)

There were some difficult words, but I think these pictures were really helpful. I liked that they changed the words and pictures so we can learn more. I have improved my vocabulary and speaking skills by learning many things.

(P15)

The posters have improved my talk with my foreign colleagues working in the company. As a result, I can talk with more confidence.

(P4)

In addition, it has been found that the textile personnel found the signs highly meaningful, as illustrated below:

When we look around, even if randomly, we see subject information or words related to my job. Since they are relevant to textile, I am able to remember them. Honestly, I think that they have helped me with my English.

(P31)

To summarize, by purposively displaying images and posters, peripheral learning opportunities were created to seek answers to the three main questions: (1) What are the participants' views and opinions toward images being present in the company? (2) To what extent do the participants tend to notice and examine such images presented in the company? (3) How can images and their corresponding texts provide language learning experience beyond the boundaries of a classroom in the space of a textile company?

This study suggests that when participants are provided with continuous exposure to images from the environment that they are present in, a kind of peripheral learning does occur with a positive effect on the learners' later recall of knowledge (Ramsoy & Overgaard, 2004) and is reflected in various behaviors, i.e., speaking. The findings confirm several studies (Badri, Badri, & Badri, 2015; Bahmani, Pazhakh, & Raee Sharif, 2012) stating that posters with text that are displayed for a longer period of time drive learner attention, as well as facilitating acquisition and retention of vocabulary and grammar. Thus, if a combination of both peripheral perception and intentional learning can take place simultaneously, the learning of, especially, terms and dialogues can be optimized.

These results are also consistent with previous studies investigating the effects of the poster and visual aid on student motivation (see Dolati & Richards, 2012). As evidenced by the present study, the majority of participants preferred a peripheral learning environment because it helped them enhance their knowledge of textile-related vocabulary, grammar, and dialogues. Moreover, almost all participants approved that images and posters with text on the linguistic landscape helped them to remember and utilize later when needed.

The findings of the study indicate that adults of varying ages, in this case, textile workers, can become a student provided the right context is created. From this perspective, the whole system of landscape supports the idea that learning is a lifelong, dynamic and emergent process worked beyond the classroom boundaries into a company environment.

Limitations and Future Directions

The current study was conducted with textile personnel and the posters used consisted mainly of language content accompanied by some relevant images related to a particular domain, textile engineering lasting ten weeks. A similar study may be carried out to observe longer-term benefits of this type of learning. Moreover, studies investigating peripheral learning have focused on visual input in the periphery, whereas the effect of audial input that may be present in the environment such as background sounds may also provide better insight into peripheral learning beyond classroom educational settings.

The important pedagogical implication of this study is to characterize peripheral learning as an effective way of learning the target language particularly vocabulary, spelling, and dialogues, through exposure to educational images and posters outside the classroom environment. By making use of the periphery of the environment as an educational tool, adults keep the acquired knowledge in mind, use their focused and/or peripheral attention, improve their self-learning ability, and enhance motivation and confidence. This study has showed that adult learners with different working schedules can use the periphery of the workplace education setting to acquire knowledge.

The results of this research can lead future researchers to investigate other related areas. In this regard, the following potential subjects are suggested for further research:

- First, this study focused on the effect of peripheral learning on adult learners' vocabulary acquisition in a physical environment. So comparative studies might be undertaken to investigate the above-mentioned effect in different workplace settings.
- Second, this research was conducted with adults at elementary level of language proficiency. Other levels of language proficiency can also be the subject of future studies.
- Finally, the amount of time allocated for this study was ten weeks. Future studies can allocate more time to this kind of investigation to observe the long-term effect of peripheral learning on the participants.

Conclusion

This study examined the potential benefits of English words and images, an aspect of linguistic landscaping, related to textile engineering that have been used to create PLL opportunities in the context of a workplace, a textile company. Taking advantage of peripheral learning via the use of colorful and illustrative posters, the employees were exposed to the target language in the workplace beyond a formal classroom context. The results of multiple data collection tools have shown that display of the posters in the learning environment has been beneficial to textile personnel in incidental learning, recall, and the use of textile-related vocabulary and related language. Participants tended to make use of the posters by observing and viewing them frequently and that the presence of such images was found to be well received by the passersby. Such benefits deriving from the continuous exposure stem not only from the role that the environment plays in giving the personnel information incidentally but also it shows that creating language learning beyond the classroom boundaries would appropriate more for the personnel having different working schedules. Thus, the findings confirm the argument put forward by Kolb and Kolb (2005) who stated that "learning results from synergetic transactions between the person and the environment" (p. 194).

References

Anderson, G. (1990). *Fundamentals of Educational Research*. London: The Falmer Press.
Badri, A., Badri, A., & Badri, G. (2015). The effects of peripheral teaching on Iranian EFL vocabulary improvement. *International Journal of Educational Investigations*, 2(1), 10–18.

Bahmani, M., Pazhakh, A., & Rae Sharif, M. (2012). The effect of peripheral learning on vocabulary acquisition, retention and recall among Iranian EFL learners. *Higher Education of Social Science*, 3(1), 44–52.

Berg, B. L. (2001). *Qualitative Research Methods for the Social Sciences*, 4th ed. London: Allyn and Bacon.

Bernard, H. R. (1994). *Research Methods in Anthropology: Qualitative and Quantitative Approaches*. Thousand Oaks, CA: Sage.

Brown, H. D. (2000). *Principles of Language Learning and Teaching*, 4th ed. White Plains, NY: Longman.

Creswell, J. W. (2009). *Research Design: Qualitative, Quantitative, and Mixed Methods Approaches* (3rd ed). Thousand Oaks, CA: Sage.

Creswell, J. W. (2013). *Qualitative Inquiry and Research Design: Choosing among Five Approaches*. Thousand Oaks, CA: Sage Publications.

Demirağ, N. B. (2018). *Peripheral learning and Its effectiveness in intensive English classes*. Unpublished Master thesis. Hacettepe University, Ankara.

Denscombe, M. (2007). *The Good Research Guide for Small-Scale Social Research Projects*, 3rd ed. New York: McGraw-Hill.

DeWalt, K. M., & DeWalt, B. R. (2002). *Participant Observation: A Guide for Fieldworkers*. Walnut Creek, CA: AltaMira Press.

Dock, G. (2019). Methods and techniques for linguistic landscape research: About definitions, core issues and technological innovations in expanding the linguistic landscape. In M. Pütz & N. Mundt (Eds.), *Multilingualism, Language Policy and the Use of Space as a Semiotic Resource* (pp. 38–57). Bristol: Multilingual Matter.

Dolati, R. I., & Richards, C. (2012). The perception of English language teachers in the use of visual learning aids. *Journal of Applied Sciences Research*, 8(5), 2581–95.

Doost, I. N., & Tahmasbi, S. (2017). The effect of peripheral learning on elementary EFL learners' grammar improvement: The case of prepositions of time and place. *Global Journal of Foreign Language Teaching*, 7(2), 91–100.

Ellis, N. C. (2008). Usage-based and form-focused SLA: The implicit and explicit learning of constructions. In A. Tyler, Y. Kim, & M. Takada (Eds.), *Language in the Context of Use: Cognitive and Discourse Approaches to Language and Language Learning* (pp. 93–120). Amsterdam: Mouton de Gruyter.

Fatemipour, H. (2013). Peripheral learning of English language: A comparison between ESL and EFL contexts provided for university students. *Procedia-Social and Behavioral Sciences*, 93, 1394–7.

Gorter, D. (2006). Introduction: The study of the linguistic landscape as a new approach to multilingualism. *International Journal of Multilingualism*, 3(1), 1–6.

Harmer, J. (2001). *The Practice of English Language Teaching*, 3rd ed. Essex, England: Longman.

Hubenthal, M., O'Brien, T., & Taber, J. (2011). Posters that foster cognition in the classroom: Multimedia theory applied to educational posters. *Educational Media International*, 48(3), 193–207.

Hulstijn, J. H. (2003). Incidental and intentional learning. In C. Doughty & M. Long (Eds.), *Handbook of Second Language Acquisition* (pp. 349–81). Oxford: Blackwell.

Kırkgöz, Y. (2005). The use and uptake of information and communication technology: A Turkish case of an initial teacher education department. In J. E. Aitken (Ed.), *Cases on Communication Technology for Second Language Acquisition and Cultural Learning* (pp. 140–71). (An imprint of IGI Global). New York: IGI Global Publications.

Kolb, A. Y., & Kolb, D. A. (2005). Learning styles and learning spaces: Enhancing experiential learning in higher education. *Academy of Management Learning & Education*, 4(2), 193–212.

Larsen-Freeman, D., & Anderson, M. (2011). *Techniques & Principles in Language Teaching*. Oxford: Oxford University Press.

Lozanov, G. (1978). *Suggestology and Suggetopedy: Theory and Practice*. New York: United Nations Educational, Scientific, and Cultural Organization.

Marsick, V. J., & Watkins, K. (1990). *Informal and Incidental Learning in the Workplace*. London and New York: Routledge.

Ramsoy, T. E., & Overgaard, M. (2004). Introspection and subliminal perception. *Phenomenology and the Cognitive Sciences*, 3, 1–23.

Rashidi, N., & GanbariAdivi, A. (2010). Incidental vocabulary learning through comprehension focused reading of short stories. *Journal of English Language Teaching and Learning*, 53(217), 111–29.

Reider, A. (2003). Implicit and explicit learning in incidental vocabulary acquisition. *VIEWS*, 12, 24–39.

Rokni, S. J., Porasghar, H., & Taziki, Z. (2014). The effect of peripheral learning on EFL learners' spelling. *International Journal of English Language, Literature and Humanities*, 1(V), 201–15.

Rubdy, R. (2015). A multimodal analysis of the graffiti commemorating the 26/11 Mumbai terror attacks: Constructing self-understandings of a senseless violence. In R. Rubdy & S. B. Said (Eds.), *Conflict, Exclusion and Dissent in the Linguistic Landscape* (pp. 280–303). Basingstoke: Palgrave Macmillan.

Wong, C. K. (2001). *What We Know after a Decade of Hong Kong Extensive Reading Scheme*. Washington, DC: University of Connecticut (ERIC Document Reproduction Service No. ED 458 806).

7

The Public Discourse and Presentation of Migrant Groups within a Museum Space

Barbara Loester

Introduction

Public discourses about immigration and its perceived advantages and disadvantages are nothing new but have dominated headlines over a number of years in most European countries—whether it is the refugee crisis, partly triggered by the war in Syria, or the Brexit discussions in the UK, and whether immigrants are "beneficial" for the UK or a drain on resources. As a result, arguments about different types of immigrants, such as the "good" immigrant versus the "bad" immigrant, have resurfaced, polarizing heated and controversial debates even further. Traits that migrant communities display, such as physical appearance, religious affiliation, ethnic background, the languages, and cultural traditions, are also evaluated and often judged on the basis of how similar or different they are to the host community, even if the former are not homogenous entities. Additionally, these perceptions of "usefulness" that come into play in the UK are often closely tied to ideas of class. When the economic circumstances are good and the incomers fill gaps in the labor market, they are tolerated or even welcome, whereas in times of an economic downturn, immigrants are more likely to be blamed for the changes, particularly by those in the lower socioeconomic strata of society (Guibernau, 2007: 58).

While learning is often associated with the formal education of children and young adults, lifelong learning can occur at all stages of life. When it comes to the topic of immigration and the presence of a diverse set of communities in the UK, key stage 4 in the national curriculum for England and Wales for the citizenship programs clearly lists as one of its objectives that "[p]upils should be taught about: diverse national, regional, religious and ethnic identities in the United Kingdom and the need for mutual respect and understanding" (Department of Education, 2013).[1] Museums provide learning opportunities for both adults and children and this can take place within structured frameworks such as educational programs and outreach events for schools or in the form of much less formalized opportunities that encourage and support lifelong learning. Therefore, they are spaces to experience other cultures, acquiring new knowledge, and potentially change attitudes.

Set against this backdrop, this chapter explores the presentation of mainly non-British groups within a museum dedicated to Southampton—a major port city in the south of England. The permanent "Gateway to the world" exhibition is analyzed in conjunction with a complementary and temporary exhibit focused on twentieth-century immigration. The "Gateway" displays are further subdivided into the themes of settlers, exiles, traders and soldiers, and the presence of these groups, alongside the more traditional labeling of ethnic belonging, in the city. Large segments are focused on what could be seen as ordinary people or groups that are excluded from the "official" narrative of the location, such as Jewish transmigrants from Russia or Basque child evacuees during the Spanish Civil War and their legacies. The temporary "Storyboxes" exhibit provides an interesting counterpoint and together these two approaches attempt to present an authentic and personalized approach to the role migration plays for Southampton, highlighting its benefits for the population overall.

Southampton—Profile of the City

Southampton is a major port city on the English south coast and, based on the last census figures from 2011,[2] recorded a population of 236,882 overall, with 17.6 percent of its population having been born outside the UK—0.6 percent were born in Ireland, 6.7 percent in Europe, and 10.3 percent elsewhere (Southampton City Council, n.d.b: 9). With the national average for this category standing at 13.8 percent (Krausova & Vargas-Silva, 2014: 2), this makes Southampton slightly less "British" than other locations; however, it still sits comfortably in the middle of the ranking of core cities in the UK with regard to ethnic composition (see Table 7.1 below). Only Newcastle, Liverpool, Sheffield, Leeds, and Portsmouth record higher percentages for the White British group (Southampton City Council, n.d.b: 2). Like other port cities, Southampton has attracted migrant communities, some of whom are transient and others eventually settle permanently. As highlighted by Cadier and Mar-Molinero (2012, 2014) and as will be shown in the discussion of the "Storyboxes" exhibit, twentieth-century migration was characterized by the arrival of groups from the (former) British Empire, including the Indian subcontinent and the Caribbean, and from a number of European countries, such as Poland. With the eastern enlargement of the European Union, starting in 2004, a rise in the number of migrants from former Eastern Bloc states moving there can also be noticed in the census data, especially as the UK did not insist on any restrictions to Freedom of Movement.[3] While much smaller in number, Southampton is also home to refugees, from countries such as Afghanistan, Iraq, and Somalia.

While Southampton had strategic importance during the Second World War and thus fell prey to extensive bombing raids by the German forces, it was of less significance in comparison to Portsmouth, which played a major role in the Dunkirk evacuations. This is a fact that was brought back during the recent commemoration events, such as the 2019 celebrations that centered around the port's crucial role in staging the Allied landings in Normandy in 1944 (Deutsche Welle, 2019). Based on these war developments, Southampton's city center had to be extensively rebuilt in the postwar era and therefore displays comparatively little remaining medieval building

Table 7.1 2011 census figures according to ethnicity in percent (Southampton City Council, n.d.b: 8)[4]

Ethnic groups in Southampton	White British	Irish, Gypsy or Irish traveler	Other white	Mixed, multiple ethnic groups	Asian, British Asian	Black, African, Caribbean, Black British	Other	Total Non-white British population
	77.7%	0.8%	7.4%	2.4%	8.4%	2.1%	2.1%	22.3%

structure when compared to other cities in Hampshire, such as Winchester, despite having a similarly long history of settlement.

The city itself is now a regional commercial center; its docks, particularly those for the cruise ships, have been well known for roughly a century, having gained notoriety as the Titanic's maiden voyage started from Southampton. Due to the position of the waterways and existing settlement patterns, the docks have essentially remained within the city environs and have shaped the image and appearance of Southampton as an industrial urban area. It should be noted that a significant number of the workforce are employed in the service and the education sector as Southampton has two universities and multiple hospitals, including a teaching hospital. Such factors are reflected in the student population standing at over 10 percent of the overall population, employment, and occupation patterns across the area and the comparatively low unemployment rate of 4.2 percent (Southampton City Council, n.d.b: 29; 33–9).

Brexit, Immigration, and Superdiversity in Southampton

As the city profile and census data show, Southampton might not be seen as affluent as some areas of Hampshire or the New Forest, counties, and regions that border on the city. Similarly, it cannot be seen as a social hotspot in the same way as some of the northern cities in England, with regard to race relations or a lack of employment opportunities. Looking at the census data it is clear that the city of Southampton can be described as a multiethnic, diverse city that has been shaped by migration. Three wards stand out: Bevois, Bargate, and Freemantle. All three are located within the city center, west of the River Itchen, with Freemantle just west of central Southampton.[5] They noticeably have the highest percentages of non-white residents and of those born outside of the UK; most other wards are diverse but to a lesser extent.[6]

In the run-up to and since the referendum in June 2016, which returned the result that the UK should leave the European Union, Brexit has brought immigration discussions to the forefront again.[7] The Leave vote is generally seen to be closely tied to fears of spiraling immigration, a rising number of refugees, and resulting economic and social pressures from these and other political developments, such as the reactions to financial crisis in the late 2000s. The Southampton count for the referendum showed a result slightly more in favor of leaving the European Union (53.8 percent Leave; 46.2 percent Remain) than the UK overall (51.8 percent Leave; 48.2 percent Remain) (Southampton City Council, 2016a, 2016b). When looking at the results for the 2019

Table 7.2 Wards with the highest percentages of non-white and non-UK-born residents (Southampton City Council, n.d.b: 8–9)

Wards in Southampton	Non-white residents (in percent)	Residents born outside the UK (in percent)
Bevois	55.4	39.2
Bargate	35.5	27.9
Freemantle	32.7	26.7

EU parliament election for the southeast region into which the Southampton area falls, the Brexit party heavily dominated. The party gained four (out of ten) MEPs for the region, an outcome comparatively representative of the English results overall.[8] While Southampton is undeniably ethnically diverse, politically it is not particularly extreme with regard to anti-immigrant sentiment.

Diverse and superdiverse communities are shaped by various forms of migration and Southampton is no exception: "Nonetheless, in common with all modern cities, Southampton contains many different, diverse and hybrid communities defined more by people than spaces" (Cadier & Mar-Molinero, 2014: 506). As Vertovec (2007: 1) established, superdiversity comes as a result of "transformative 'diversification of diversity'" with regard to the countries of origin and the ethnicities of communities themselves but also in light of "a variety of significant variables that affect where, how and with whom people live." This was portrayed in the 2015 program *Immigration Street*, set in Derby Road in Bevois. The program was designed as a spin-off of the controversial series *Benefits Street*, widely labeled as "poverty porn" and criticized as exploitative and painting a biased, negative picture of people in receipt of benefits. *Immigration Street* was supposed to portray how immigration has changed a community by focusing on one street. Only one episode was broadcast and the show was canceled as the residents were largely unhappy with how they had been portrayed and a rising fear of racist attacks, among other factors. What the program highlighted was that prejudice in and of itself is perceived as unacceptable by those featured in the program and the residents of Southampton generally. However, if there appears to be a reason for displaying prejudice, such as a minority group being treated favorably with regard to access to work or housing over a majority, or in the case of the UK an indigenous group, then the prejudice would be seen as "rational" and justifiable (Valentine & McDonald, 2004: 13). This also leads back to the discussion of the "good" versus the "bad" immigrant as discussed above and how such perceptions can be challenged through education.

The Post-Museum, Linguistic Landscapes, and the Question of Identity

Museums have always had an educational role, both for the individual and also for society as a whole; according to the Museums Association (1998), "[m]useums enable people to explore collections for inspiration, learning and enjoyment. They are institutions that collect, safeguard and make accessible artefacts and specimens, which they hold in trust for society." The audiences and the ways of fulfilling the educational role, however, have changed over time. From the 1980s onward the field has seen considerable changes. In the 1980s and 1990s these included revising the approach to studying museums; partially, this was influenced by the emergence of museums funded by private organizations, independently of the public sector. The subsequent two decades saw an increasing focus on attracting new and diverse audiences, such as ethnic minorities, working-class visitors, people with disabilities, and children (Candlin, 2012: 28ff). This new type of museum, the "post-museum," needed to review its function: "The post-museum must play the role of partner, learner (itself), and service provider in order to remain viable as an institution" (Hooper-Greenhill, 2000: xi). It entailed giving a voice to the communities featured and involved in it, as well as presenting different perspectives and discourses. Additionally, it should also provide constructivist approaches to learning, challenging established discourses, e.g., questioning the dominant social and cultural norms, thus making the museum also a site of resistance (Hooper-Greenhill, 2000).

This presents a marked shift in approach as previously museums revolved around the establishment of a canon. Such a canon creates a hierarchy through ranking narratives, figures, and ideas, determining whose voices can be heard, often to the exclusion of others:

> This is a strategy of boundary maintenance through which some are enabled to speak and are empowered but others are silenced and marginalised. [...] New statements may speak old messages, but also have the potential to construct different ones. Through displays, museums can make new meanings which are produced through new equivalences. Museums thus have the power to remap cultural territories, and to reshape the geographies of knowledge. These are political issues, concerned with the opening up or closing down of democratic public life.
>
> (Hooper-Greenhill, 2000: 21)

Museums can and do have a role to play in changing social attitudes, such as those about immigration. While it appears to be the case that most museums focused on natural history or science can implicitly or openly promote values, such as care for the environment, without having to justify such support, equivalent advocacy for societal issues, with a view to changing visitors' attitudes, appears to be viewed with more apprehension if it is made explicit at all (Sandell, 2007: 177). It is not surprising that support for a potential social or cultural agenda on display is regarded with caution by museum staff as this can easily be interpreted as pushing a particular, often politically oriented program and its associated ideologies. Particular narratives and perspectives are likely to be conveyed through the artifacts on display, the accompanying texts and even the architecture of the building, and how visitors are guided through it. There are also two different agendas at play: the top-down agenda of the museum makers and the bottom-up agenda of the visitors, and these can conflict with each other. The former can promote a particular narrative and ideology, e.g., the inclusion of specific community groups, and the construction of the space and language used are therefore not necessarily neutral (Clifford, 1997: 107ff.; Ravelli 1996; Shohamy & Waksman, 2012), while the latter involves drawing conclusions different from the ones intended or designed by the museum makers.

It is at this point where the connections between museums, their educational mandate, and the study of linguistic landscapes very clearly intersect, an aspect that rarely has been pointed out explicitly in either museum or linguistic landscape studies. Hooper-Greenhill's (2000) exploration of visual culture in the museum hints at this; she highlights the space and the place of museums as "cultural borderlands" (2000: 140) that present opportunities to challenge the cultural and social status quo:

> [A] range of practices are possible, a language of possibilities is a potential, and [...] diverse groups and sub-groups, cultures and sub-cultures may push against and permeate the allegedly unproblematic and homogenous borders of dominant cultural practices. By viewing museums as a form of cultural politics, museum workers can bring together the concepts of narrative, difference, identity and interpretative strategies for negotiating these practices. In the post-museum, multiple subjectivities and identities can exist as part of a cultural practice that provides the potential to expand the politics of democratic community and solidarity.

The aspect of museum workers' apprehension with regard to challenging and changing visitors' social attitudes, as highlighted by Sandell (2007), is not fully echoed here. To some extent, as Sandell argues, it is the visitor's decision how deeply they engage in the learning process (2007: 71ff) and larger, more mainstream museums might be more successful in achieving this as they are perceived to present a more authoritative voice (2007: 105) that can challenge established views. In a similar vein, Cooke and McLean (2002: 117) discuss the visitor experience in the Museum of Scotland, stating that Scottish visitors, on the whole, reported coming away with a positive image of the nation. Non-Scottish visitors from elsewhere in the UK felt their British identity, specifically their English one, threatened, "either through closer involvement in the European Union, or the rise in Scottish and Welsh identities, [and] necessitated a rethinking of what it mean to be 'English'" (2002: 117).

Museum makers might feel conflicted about their work displaying a social or political agenda but, as Clifford highlights in his work about borders and contact zones, they often already engage in such discussions: "museums understand themselves to be interacting with specific communities across such borders, rather than simply educating or edifying a public, they begin to operate—consciously and at times self-critically—in contact histories" (Clifford, 1997: 204). In a number of linguistic fields and approaches, e.g., sociolinguistics, critical discourse studies, or LL, researchers frequently challenge boundaries and question the status quo and associated social and cultural practices. While the study of linguistic landscapes is often focused on multilingualism, public signage and texts in the widest sense, monuments, museums, and architectural features also contribute to the landscape (Shohamy & Waksman, 2012: 109) but have, comparatively speaking, received little attention so far, despite their prominent role in the cultural, educational, and also ideological landscape of towns and cities, or even nations.⁹ In this vein, museums and their exhibitions constitute such spaces, even if they are—like in the case of the SeaCity Museum—not fully public, as they charge an entry fee, thus potentially excluding access for some. The objects, displayed texts, and the spatial arrangements all form elements of the linguistic landscape and should be seen and analyzed in conjunction, an approach which to some extent is already laid out in museum pedagogy:

> Museum pedagogy is structured firstly through the narratives constructed by museum displays and secondly through the methods used to communicate these narratives. Museum pedagogy produces a visual environment for learning where visitors deploy their own interpretative strategies and repertoires.
> (Hooper-Greenhill, 2000: 3)

Newman and McLean (2002: 58) present the museum visit as a social activity which involves exploring the stories presented in the museum space, which will have been shaped by the people who created the exhibits; while research in the field of museums studies does not make it explicit, the links to Scollon and Scollon's (2003: 108ff) work on spatial semiotics and indexicality are clear. The way the audience navigates the space and interacts with the displays will vary as they reinterpret them or see very different meanings to ones intended; this can also be affected by the visitors' experience, cultural situation, and background knowledge. In doing so, the narratives are reshaped and can be accepted or rejected in their entirety or only certain aspects of them. It is not only how exhibits are presented but also where they are placed and how they are arranged within a designated space on a site or in a building. Garvin and Onodera (2020: 156) highlight in their study about a Japanese American memorial site that "the LL is a powerful tool of remembrance that shapes, mediates and to a certain extent controls public history."

Taking into account the educational aspects of the museum and the social commentary they can provide everyday objects and a focus on ordinary people rather than important historical figures, delivering more accessible points for visitors. Pahl and Rowsell (2010) suggest the use of everyday objects for storytelling, such as photos or family narratives when employing museum visits for literacy programs (Vaughan, 2012: 684–5), and Aronin and Ó Laoire's (2013) work, focusing on university students, follows a similar approach but does so from the LL and material culture perspective, again highlighting the close connection that can be established between these fields. Pahl's (2012) discussion of an exhibition focusing on everyday objects and narratives of Pakistani-heritage families in the UK provides an entry point for examining one of the two exhibitions in this chapter, the "Storyboxes" (see below) as a linguistic landscape.

> The representation of home objects, she [Hurdley] argued, is mediated by the way in which they are displayed and the narratives told about them. Objects relate both to the display practices that circulate around them, and the space they are placed in, but also to the timescales attached to the object. Space and time, taken together, are relevant lenses that help us understand the meanings and uses of objects in the home.
> (Pahl, 2012: 305)

This brings the idea of the chronotope into the discussion to allow for a way to approach a complex system of dealing with (super)diverse identities, time and space, especially with regard to effects of migration and how these factors affect narratives (Blommaert & De Fina, 2015; Brandão, 2006). Migration therefore entails objects changing meaning due to changes in space and time for those involved. Something banal, like a bag of rice, can become significant, influenced by other value systems in the host culture, as the storybox of the Cookery Exchange illustrates. Pahl (2012: 306) also draws on Clifford's (1997) term of the "contact zone" to signify the varying experiences of the immigrants and provide an identity narrative. Having borrowed the term from Pratt (1992), Clifford originally discussed the "contact zone" of the museum in relation to dealing with colonial encounters,[10] highlighting the aspect interaction between the parties involved but this can also be applied to immigration setting and also in relation to questions of access and inclusivity: "When museums are seen as contact zones, their organizing structure as a collection becomes an ongoing historical, political, moral relationship—a power-charged set of exchanges, of push and pull" (Clifford, 1997: 192).

By placing objects in an exhibition and situating them in a different context, the meaning changes and in turn affects the relationship between space, place, and identity. Pahl avoids the use of "contact zone" for the museum as a whole in this context and introduces the "boundary objects"; these, similar to Clifford's (1997) discussion, hint at signs of dislocation or disruption (Pahl, 2012: 312ff), giving visitors the opportunity to look at them in a new light and to challenge or reevaluate their own views. In this respect the museum's linguistic and semiotic landscape provides them with an alternative educational approach. Such a repositioning and recontextualization have an impact on attitudes and identity formation and provide the opportunity for giving a voice to previously marginalized communities that had been excluded from the narrative of the location. In the UK, immigrant communities from the former British Empire can be taken as a prime example to move from the traditional presentation of them in the museum to the possibility of seeing new identities (Candlin, 2012: 34; Pahl, 2012: 322ff).

The SeaCity Museum

In 2012, a new museum was opened in Southampton—the SeaCity Museum, "tell[ing] the story of the people of the city, their fascinating lives, and historic connections with Titanic and the sea" (SeaCity Museum, 2019a). Unlike many other museums in the country, this one charges an entry fee and its existence is not entirely uncontroversial. The city considered selling parts of its art collection to fund the new museum and while the artworks considered for sale were not on public display due to size of the collection itself, this move triggered a public outcry, and alternative sources of funding, such as lottery funding, had to be identified for realizing the project (Loester, 2016). Criticism has never fully abated since the initial funding proposal, in particular because the venue is not generating as much income as was hoped.

The museum itself now houses two established, permanent exhibitions and a third evolving exhibition. It also has space for a smaller temporary exhibit. The Titanic exhibition is the main focus of the museum and encompasses several rooms, functioning as the main point of attraction for the museum overall. The smaller, so-called Gateway to the world exhibition is treated and advertised on an equal footing to the Titanic exhibition but attracts fewer visitors, an aspect also reflected in comments on and the reviews of the museum. The Gateway exhibition is focused on telling the story of the city and its relevance as a port through the arrivals and departures of various population groups and, where possible, through the stories of individuals within these groups. This is also indicated by the subheading: "200,000 years of seafaring," which highlights the time period of settlement in the area. The latest, evolving exhibition is "Southampton stories" and explores particular eras, such as both world wars, and aspects of daily life, such as sport, with a focus on Southampton Football Club, and work.[11] The latter is mainly centered on various aspects related to the docks (SeaCity Museum, 2019a). As Ben-Rafael et al. (2006: 8) highlight, a particular place can be read as emblematic of the space; therefore, this museum can be regarded as a representation of the city itself as the name would also hint at. The SeaCity Museum, particularly with its focus on the Titanic, acts as a major branding project to (re)claim the city's heritage as there is comparatively little in the way of old buildings to illustrate the long-standing history of the place (Loester, 2016).

Throughout the exhibitions all displays are in English only; the museum booklet is available in various languages (French, Spanish, German, Russian), mostly influenced by those relevant for local tourism, including those visitors brought by cruise ships. The booklet is supplemented by a free city and sightseeing map, the "Southampton Heritage Experience" that features recommendations in Spanish, German, Portuguese, French, Russian, and Italian.

The Gateway Exhibition

The Gateway exhibition is given equal coverage with the Titanic exhibition on the museum's website, and in the building both are treated the same with regard to access from the main entrance. Sandell (2005, 2007) argues that temporary displays, often situated away from the main routes through museum displays, are less advantageous for minority and marginalized groups. Rather than consign such displays to less accessible or visible spaces, thus marginalizing them, these benefit from being included as part of the permanent, "mainstream" exhibitions as they "might serve to more powerfully confer equality and convey a sense of inclusion and legitimisation" (Sandell, 2007: 129).

This part of the SeaCity museum is, unlike the Titanic one, characterized by making more generous use of the space available, giving visitors the opportunity to move freely around the gallery, without a prescribed or obvious path. On entering the space, there is a world map with an eye-catching feature, highlighting where sea routes to and from Southampton lead, thus reinforcing the exhibition's subheading of "200,000 years of seafaring" to highlight the movement of people in and out of the area based on its geographical position. Following that, the visitors are introduced to a set of questions to guide them, including "Why did they [the migrants] leave their country?" and "What did they hope for?" (see Figure 7.4 on the companion website). These questions encourage seeing immigrants as well as emigrants, whether they become part of the permanent or a transitory community in Southampton, as individuals with motives and skills rather than as a homogenous, faceless group. This approach is reinforced by focusing on specific, identifiable people and presenting their stories.

While early migratory groups, such as the Romans and the Anglo-Saxons, are presented mainly through the display of artifacts and short texts, from the Middle Ages onward the focus shifts to specific individuals, partly because records have survived. One of four such examples is the display dedicated to Huguenot immigration in the 1600s, and the individual giving a face to the group is Judith de la Motte. In line with the other groups and the representative individuals, the museum has produced a profile card (see Figure 7.1 below), detailing place of origin, occupation, languages spoken, and which skills they bring. In the case of Roger Machado, a French diplomat who was resident in Southampton in the late fifteenth century, the language skills (French, Breton, Portuguese, English) and the products he also traded (Venetian glass, Italian pottery, fine fabrics) are listed. By highlighting these attributes in the profiles, a positive image of immigrants is created as the focus is on what they can bring and contribute to the local community, such as improving the cloth-making skills in the case of Judith de la Motte. Equally, listing the languages spoken alongside the skills and professions confirms that these newcomers are generally not unskilled and therefore "useful" for the host community and therefore less likely to be negatively stereotyped as often happens with migrants or refugees.

In a similar setting, Szekeres (2002: 142) discusses the presentation of immigration in the Migration Museum in Adelaide, questioning the decision process in relation to whose histories are to be represented and how those stories could be told as this influences the (re)presentation of reality and creates potential for stereotyping. There, as in the Gateway exhibition, the danger is that "good" immigrants, such as traders or diplomats, are pitted against the "bad" immigrants, such as the transmigrants who are the representation of a transitory group. As the display texts in the Gateway exhibition highlight, the transmigrants also come from diverse linguistic backgrounds and have occupations, such as farm worker or shopkeeper. However, the group is very diverse, and records are scant, thus making it much harder to personalize anyone. In turn, it is harder to see them as being positive for the host community. This is reinforced by the display stating that they were held in transit camps at a considerable distance outside the city, making the statement on the introductory display about exiles sound hollow: "Arriving or leaving, they never forget the welcome we give them."[12] Looking at the color of the transmigrants' display texts it is notable that, except for the description, they are all provided on a dark gray background with white writing, in contrast with the more vibrantly colored texts of the other cases.

As one of the few interactive elements of the exhibition, the installation (see Figure 7.2 below) at the end also invites the visitors to plot their places of origin and thus contribute their "stories" to that of Southampton. The screen dominates the wall adjacent to the entrance to the gallery and the keyboard is placed in the center of the

Public Discourse within a Museum Space   143

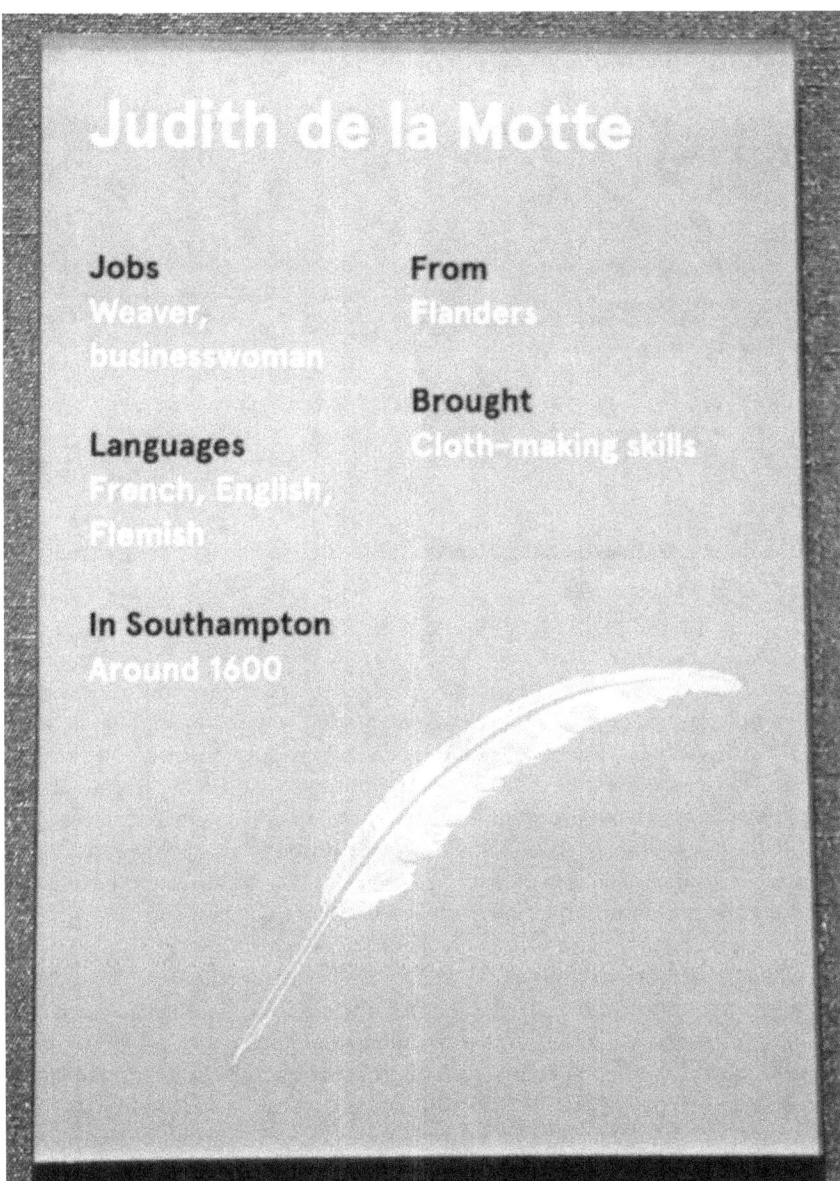

Figure 7.1 Description of Judith de la Motte

space; this arrangement makes the installation the visually most dominant element and also highlights its planned and perceived importance (Scollon & Scollon, 2003: 169ff).

This is an interesting feature and would help to turn the museum into a genuine "post-museum" by allowing the visitors to interact with it. While observing the space, it was clear that the space around the keyboard was the most popular location,

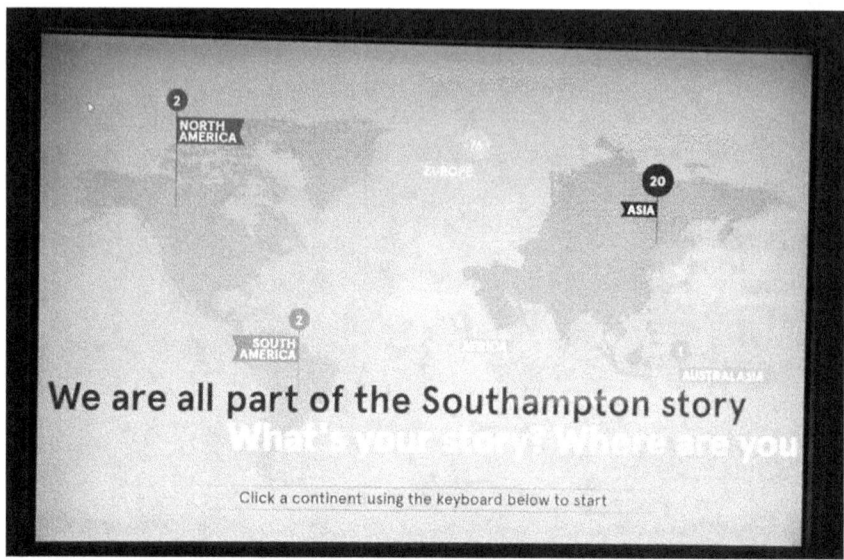

Figure 7.2 Interactive display

particularly with children. However, this still raises the question as to what extent the Gateway displays go beyond a superficial engagement with the minority groups and make the diversity of visitors, including residents as well as tourists, more tangible. Simply plotting a location on the map adds little information to the discourse of migration and travel; however, tourists are generally a transient group that leave very little in the way of visible traces, and this interactive display does take their short-lived presence into account (Kallen 2009).[13] The questions how Southampton has affected migrants and how in turn they have shaped the city are not clearly answered in this part of the museum.

While telling history in this form, "from below," where specific names and people are the focus of the narrative, it helps the visitor to engage and, potentially, learn and change perceptions. It is fairly common that immigrant communities, even those whose presence often dates back a considerable time, are not afforded space in the official narrative of a place, as O'Keeffe (2007: 10) notes: "Heritage tends to be white, yet it need not be so." While the Gateway exhibition does indeed highlight the contribution of (white) migrants, they tend to be mostly of European origin (see Figure 7.2) as the temporary "Storybox" exhibition attempts to address this gap.

The Temporary Display—the "Storyboxes"

Accessible via the Gateway gallery, the SeaCity museum provides a small space to host temporary exhibitions. In spring 2016, it was used for ten displays, presenting stories of migration relating to distinct groups, thus tying it closely to the Gateway exhibition. From a chronological perspective, the time period covered starts roughly where the Gateway exhibition ends—the Second World War. The exhibits were focused on evacuee children during the Second World War, prisoners of war, the so-called Ten Pound Poms,[14] immigrants from India and Pakistan in the 1950s, the Caribbean in 1960s, Uganda in the 1970s, China in the 1980s, and Poland in the 2000s. The only display without an explicit time frame is the one dedicated to the International Cookery Exchange. While this made sense thematically, as the Storyboxes can be seen as complementary to the permanent displays, it also highlights that the exhibits are curated differently. Based on the observations for this project, the temporary space was frequented even less than the permanent Gateway exhibition, raising questions not only about the popularity but also about how the display is perceived in terms of authority. Do temporary ones, when co-curated with community groups, command less authority than permanent ones? The lack of foot traffic would indicate so but unless they are advertised well, visitors might be more accidental or include only people who were already aware and make the effort to see them.

The displays dedicated to particular decades and ethnic groups were all designed by the same person (Mark Woods) with input from local community groups (see Figures 7.7–7.9 on the companion website). This challenges traditional museum practices, as the heritage industry generally sets its own criteria as to what cultural-historic "things" are; these are generally based on antiquity, uniqueness, history, and/or historical association (O'Keeffe, 2007: 10). The storyboxes break with this convention as they provide everyday objects chosen by the community members and feature narratives related to the immigrant experience, thus giving those involved an authentic voice and moving the exhibition into the post-museum setting.

As can be seen from the Caribbean storybox, the display is colorful, often aligned with one or several colors of the national flag; in this case, the green contours on the writing of some segments are eye-catching.[15] The display text is comparatively short, often comprised of only a handful of sentences, highlighting the motives for emigrating, the sectors in which they found work, and whether they decided to settle. The objects in the case tend to be everyday items, such as a bottle of rum. The Indian display features samples of various fabrics, making reference to a personal testimony of one community member who worked as a peddler; the Chinese display focuses on a Chinese-English dictionary as a symbol for the number of students who have come to the city.

With regard to narratives, in addition to the short summary, the cases all display sound bites of community members relating to their experiences, including statements such as the following one: "YOU PEOPLE [emphasis in the original] come here/expect your fare back/to be paid/and she was/my boss that woman" or "where I grew up there was no such thing as colour prejudice" (see Figure 7.8 on website). Here the discrepancy between personal experience of racism is contrasted with the political drive and economic necessity of immigrant labor while, at the same time, highlighting the differences in perceived and experienced social status. These authentic voices serve to illustrate larger themes, such as racism (Caribbean), refugees (Uganda), or science and technology (China), which are used to give a focus to each display as well as providing what can be seen as an authentic voice. In addition, family photos and postcards are also used as additional visually engaging elements to recount intergenerational experiences, comparable to what Pahl (2012) observed in her project.[16] Such use of family photos and narratives relating to everyday life as intangible heritage (Alivizatou, 2006: 50ff) are regarded as a characteristic of the post-museum.

The displays on evacuees, POWs, £10 Poms, and the Cookery Exchange are designed by a different artist (Al Johnson) and, with exception of the last one, without community input. Their styles are distinctly different, as can be seen when comparing Figures 7.3 and 7.5 on companion website, for example. The display texts are significantly longer, generally twice the length of the others and the cases feature more artifacts, such as items of clothing with letters stitched onto them (evacuees), advertising posters and maps (£10 Poms; see Figure 7.3), and bags of ingredients (Cookery Exchange, see Figure 7.10 on companion website).

Overall, the selection of objects was not solely in the hands of the artist or curators but carried out in cooperation with community groups whose input is acknowledged on the display cases. This makes parts of the exhibition more inclusive and ensures mutual engagement and thus can be seen to conform, at least to some extent, to Hooper-Greenhill's (2000) concept of the post-museum. The Cookery Exchange was founded to provide a meeting place for women from different cultural backgrounds "to swap culinary skills and build confidence."[17] The display for this community initiative makes this particularly clear by placing everyday objects, in this case bags of ingredients, such as rice, at the center of the display. As rice is a foodstuff commonly used across many cultures and communities, it can be seen to highlight the similarities between "us," i.e., the host community, and "them," the newcomers, thus removing the "justification" for prejudice on some level (Valentine & McDonald, 2004). The display presents physical

Figure 7.3 Storybox "Ten Pound Poms"

objects (bags) and alongside them intangible heritage in the form of cultural practices; human universals, like cooking and storytelling, are implied through the narrative provided on the texts (Alivizatou, 2006: 52). While such encounters take place in the host community, and therefore more likely to be placed within their social and cultural values, the meeting also provides what Hooper-Greenhill (2000: 13) describes as "a site of resistance where dominant shared codes may be disrupted or displaced, and where alternative shared codes can be produced." That means within the setting of this group we can see the "contact zone" (Clifford, 1997) emerge where new knowledge can also be generated, thus potentially challenging stereotypes and prejudices while, at the same time, focusing on shared human practices.

Conclusion

According to Moore, cities are characterized by ties to their past and the present and how they shape identities and the heritage:

> [C]ities are not simply blank canvases on which new stories can be written and although undergoing change, do remain intimately tied to their past. The landscape of a particular place will tell us much about the history of the people, particularly if the memory held by those living there or associated with it the longest remains strong. In a world characterized as runaway and constantly in flux, memory is critical in the formation of both personal and place identity.
>
> (Moore, 2007: 97)

Southampton's landscape and identity are shaped as much by locals as it is by incomers, and consequently, the location's and the community's identity changes and adapts over time. While Moore primarily looks at the physical heritage, such as buildings, all of these also apply to people and their stories, and the everyday objects they bring with them as intangible heritage. Being a port city, Southampton has always been a primary point of entry or exit, thus displaying a more diverse and often transient population.

Heritage is a problematic term both with regard to superdiversity and the concept itself as it throws up the question of who decides what the heritage is and whose voices should be heard. The SeaCity Museum attempts to address these questions by placing the often unheard voices and stories at the center of attention. The Titanic exhibition, while not the focus of this chapter, explores the lives and fate of the crew members on how the high death toll affected life in Southampton. The Gateway exhibition highlights the lives of various immigrant communities in the city over time. It gives focus to the questions, such as who belongs to Southampton and how long someone needs to have lived there before they become part of the community. Blommaert remarks on the societal and technological changes over the last few decades and their effects on communities: "The Other is now a category in constant flux, a moving target about whom very little can be presupposed; and as for the We, ourselves, our own lives have become vastly more complex and are now very differently organized" (Blommaert, 2013: 5–6).

By not only including but focusing on marginalized communities, such as immigrants, the exhibition presents a more inclusive approach to museum learning. At the same time, the presentation of display texts addresses the issue of empowering previously excluded or silenced voices. Using a person, like Judith de la Motte, or the group of Basque child refugees, for telling the stories diverts the attention away from what visitors might otherwise regard as people of historical importance, such as explorers, and provides more relatable narratives that can enable them to review their own histories. Both the Gateway and the Storyboxes galleries succeed in moving toward a post-museum approach that can also help to open up the museum experience to audiences that might generally not consider visiting as the encounter becomes relevant to them and their lives.

While SeaCity is not a national museum and therefore might lack the "authority" attributed to others, discussions—like Cooke and McLean's (2002)—highlight the political nature of museums and their exhibitions, their role and contribution when it comes to discussions about culture, and social inclusion or exclusion should not be underestimated. The museum undoubtedly provides opportunities to explore aspects of Southampton's multiethnic past and background using a variety of tools. It gives the local visitor and the tourist the opportunity to review their own experiences and attitudes. Having said that, to some extent it remains questionable as to who will take advantage of these.

Notes

1. Key Stage 4 in the English education system refers to Years 10 and 11; that means pupils are aged 14–16.
2. In the UK a census is taken every ten years with the most recent data collected in 2011. Due to demographic developments, a change in migration patterns, and other factors, the population for 2017, the latest, projected figure available, is estimated to have risen to 252,359 (Hampshire County Council, n.d.).
3. These developments can be observed by comparing 2001 and 2011 census data. For a summary and further data gathered from community sources, see Cadier and Mar-Molinero (2012).
4. A more detailed breakdown according to ethnic group membership can be found in the "2011 Census briefing: Ethnicity, religion and origins" (Southampton City Council, n.d.c: 1).
5. See map (Southampton City Council, n.d.b: 4).
6. Some of the numbers are to be expected as both universities are located in central Southampton and therefore the area hosts a sizeable student population.
7. Discourse about immigration, from EU/European countries, the Commonwealth and elsewhere, has featured regularly in the British media, also prior to the 2016 referendum (e.g., Amin, 2002; Fielder & Catalano, 2017; KhosraviNik, 2014; Van Dijk, 2018).
8. The results for London, Scotland, and Northern Ireland buck this trend.
9. Until the publication of Blackwood and Macalister's (2020a and 2020b) edited collection, comparatively few articles and chapters have investigated monuments, memorials, and museums as linguistic landscapes, e.g., Abousnnouga and Machin

(2010, 2013), Aronin and Ó Laoire (2013), Kelly-Holmes and Pietikäinen (2016), Shohamy and Waksman (2011) or Xiao and Lee (2019).
10 Pratt defines contact zone as "the space of colonial encounters, the space in which peoples geographically and historically separated come into contact with each other establish ongoing relations, usually involving conditions of coercion, radical inequality, and intractable conflict" (1992: 6–7).
11 This new, permanent exhibition is still developing. It also features space for a community project that will be of a temporary nature, i.e., changing on a regular basis (SeaCity Museum, 2019b).
12 See Figure 7.5 on the companion website.
13 I am deliberately excluding transgressive signs (Scollon & Scollon, 2003: 146), such as graffiti or litter, from this discussion.
14 The term refers to British emigrants to Australia and New Zealand who were part of an assisted passage scheme, hence the reference to £10 as the cost of the passage for each emigrant. The scheme started after the Second World War and continued until the early 1970s.
15 See companion website, Figure 7.9. The font color in the Poland display is kept entirely in red and white.
16 See Figure 7.7 "Pakistan" on the companion website for illustration.
17 See Figure 7.10 on the companion website.

References

Abousnnouga, G., & Machin, D. (2010). War monuments and the changing discourses of nation and soldiery. In A. Jaworski & C. Thurlow (Eds.), *Semiotic Landscapes: Language, Image, Space* (pp. 219–40). London: Continuum.

Abousnnouga, G. & Machin, D. (2013). *The Language of War Monuments*. London: Bloomsbury.

Alivizatou, M. (2006). Museums and intangible heritage: The dynamics of an "unconventional" relationship. *Papers from the Institute of Archaeology*, 17, 47–57.

Amin, A. (2002). Ethnicity and the multicultural city: Living with diversity. *Environment and Planning*, 34(6), 959–80.

Aronin, L., & Ó Laoire, M. (2013). The material culture of multilingualism: Moving beyond the linguistic landscape. *International Journal of Multilingualism*, 10(3), 225–35.

Ben-Rafael, E., Shohamy, E., Amara, M. H., & Trumper-Hecht, N. (2006). Linguistic landscape as symbolic construction of the public space: The case of Israel. *International Journal of Multilingualism*, 3(1), 7–30.

Blackwood, R., & Macalister, J. (Eds.). (2020a). *Multilingual Memories: Monuments, Museums and the Linguistic Landscape*. London: Bloomsbury.

Blackwood, R., & Macalister, J. (2020b). Introduction. In R. Blackwood & J. Macalister (Eds.), *Multilingual Memories: Monuments, Museums and the Linguistic Landscape* (pp. 1–9). London: Bloomsbury.

Blommaert, J. (2013). *Ethnography, Superdiversity and Linguistic Landscapes: Chronicles of Complexity*. Bristol/Buffalo/Toronto: Multilingual Matters.

Blommaert, J., & De Fina A. (2015). Chronotopic identities: On the timespace organization of who we are. *Tilburg Papers in Culture Studies*, 153.

Brandão, L. A. (2006). Chronotope. *Theory, Culture, Society*, 23(2–3), 133–4.

Cadier, L., & Mar-Molinero, C. (2012). Language policies and linguistic superdiversity in contemporary urban societies: The case of the City of Southampton, UK. *Current Issues in Language Planning*, 13(3), 149–65.

Cadier, L., & Mar-Molinero, C. (2014). Negotiating networks of communication in a superdiverse environment: Urban multilingualism in the City of Southampton. *Multilingua*, 33(5–6), 505–24.

Candlin, F. (2012). Independent museums, heritage, and the shape of Museum Studies. *Museum and Society*, 10(1), 28–41.

Clifford, J. (1997) *Routes: Travel and Translation in the Late Twentieth Century.* Cambridge, MA: Harvard University Press.

Cooke, S., & McLean, F. (2002). Our common inheritance? Narratives of self and other in the Museum of Scotland. In D. C. Harvey, R. Jones, N. McInroy, & C. Milligan (Eds.), *Celtic Geographies: Old Culture, New Times* (pp. 109–22). London and New York: Routledge.

Department for Education. (2013). Statutory guidance: National curriculum in England: Citizenship programmes of study for key stages 3 and 4. Retrieved from https://www.gov.uk/government/publications/national-curriculum-in-england-citizenship-programmes-of-study/national-curriculum-in-england-citizenship-programmes-of-study-for-key-stages-3-and-4 (accessed August 18, 2019).

Deutsche Welle. (2019). D-Day 75th anniversary celebration in Portsmouth. Retrieved from https://www.dw.com/en/d-day-75th-anniversary-celebration-in-portsmouth/g-49066007 (accessed August 16, 2019).

Fielder, G. E., & Catalano, E. (2017). Othering others: Right-wing populism in UK media discourse on "new" immigration. In J. Chovanec & K. Molek-Kozakowska (Eds.), *Representing the Other in European Media Discourses* (pp. 207–34). Amsterdam: John Benjamins.

Garvin, R. T., & Onodera, Y. (2020). Multiple "ways of telling" in the LL at the Second World War Japanese American Internment Camp Memorial Cemetery in Rowher, Arkansas. In R. Blackwood & J. Macalister (Eds.), *Multilingual Memories: Monuments, Museums and the Linguistic Landscape* (pp. 135–60). London: Bloomsbury.

Golding, V. (2009). *Learning at the Museum Frontiers: Identity, Race and Power.* Farnham: Ashgate.

Guibernau, M. (2007). *The Identity of Nations.* Cambridge: Polity.

Hampshire County Council. (n.d.). Mid-year population estimates by district, gender and single year of age 2017. Retrieved from https://www.hants.gov.uk/landplanningandenvironment/facts-figures/population/estimates-forecasts (accessed August 16, 2019).

Hooper-Greenhill, E. (2000). *Museums and the Interpretation of Visual Culture.* London and New York: Routledge.

Hurdley, R. (2006). Dismantling mantelpieces: Narrating identities and materializing culture in the home. *Sociology*, 40(4), 717–33.

Kallen, J. (2009). Tourism and representation in the Irish linguistic landscape. In E. Shohamy & D. Gorter (Eds.), *Linguistic Landscape: Expanding the Scenery* (pp. 270–83). New York and London: Routledge.

Kelly-Holmes, H., & Pietikäinen, S. (2016). Language: A challenging resource in a museum of Sámi culture. *Scandinavian Journal of Hospitality and Tourism*, 16(1), 24–41.

KhosraviNik, M. (2014). Immigration discourses and critical discourse analysis: Dynamics of world events and immigration representations in the British press. In C.

Hart & P. Cap (Eds.), *Contemporary Critical Discourse Studies* (pp. 501–19). London and New York: Bloomsbury.

Krausova, A., & Vargas-Silva, C. (2014). England: Census profile. *Migration Observatory at the University of Oxford*. Retrieved from https://migrationobservatory.ox.ac.uk/wp-content/uploads/2016/04/CensusProfile-England.pdf (accessed August 16, 2019).

Loester, B. (2016). Where (and when)'s your heritage? A comparison of linguistic landscapes in Winchester and Southampton. Paper presented at the *Sociolinguistics Symposium 21*, University of Murcia June 16, 2016.

Moore, N. (2007). Valorizing urban heritage? Redevelopment in a changing city. In N. Moore & Y. Whelan (Eds.), *Heritage, Memory and the Politics of Identity. New Perspectives on the Cultural Landscape* (pp. 95–108). Aldershot: Ashgate.

Museums Association. (1998). FAQs: What is a museum? Retrieved from https://www.museumsassociation.org/about/frequently-asked-questions (accessed December 27, 2019).

Newman, A., & McLean, F. (2002). Architectures of inclusion: Museums, galleries and inclusive communities. In R. Sandell (Ed.), *Museums, Society, Inequality* (pp. 56–68). London and New York: Routledge.

O'Keeffe, T. (2007). Landscape and memory: Historiography, theory, methodology. In N. Moore & Y. Whelan (Eds.), *Heritage, Memory and the Politics of Identity. New Perspectives on the Cultural Landscape* (pp. 3–18). Aldershot: Ashgate.

Pahl, K. (2012). Every object tells a story: Intergenerational stories and objects in the homes of Pakistani heritage families in South Yorkshire, UK. *Home Cultures*, 9(3), 303–28.

Pahl, K., & Rowsell, J. (2010). *Artifactual Literacies: Every Object Tells a Story*. New York: Teachers College Press.

Pratt, M. L. (1992). *Imperial Eyes: Travel Writing and Transculturation*. London: Routledge.

Ravelli, L. J. (1996). Making language accessible: Successful text writing for museum visitors. *Linguistics and Education*, 8, 367–87.

Sandell, R. (2002). Museums and the combating of social inequality: Roles, responsibilities, resistance. In R. Sandell (Ed.), *Museums, Society, Inequality* (pp. 3–23). London: Routledge.

Sandell, R. (2005). Constructing and communicating equality: The social agency of museum space. In S. Macleod (Ed.), *Reshaping Museum Space: Architecture, Design, Exhibitions* (pp. 185–200). London and New York: Routledge.

Sandell, R. (2007). *Museums, Prejudice and the Reframing of Difference*. London and New York: Routledge.

Scollon, R., & Scollon, S. W. (2003). *Discourses in Place: Language in the Material World*. London and New York: Routledge.

SeaCity Museum. (2019a). SeaCity Museum. Retrieved from www.seacitymuseum.co.uk (accessed August 20, 2019).

SeaCity Museum. (2019b). Southampton Stories. Retrieved from www.seacitymuseum.co.uk/southampton-stories (accessed December 23, 2019).

Shohamy, E., & Waksman, S. (2011). Building the nation, writing the past: History and textuality at the *Ha'apala* Memorial in Tel Aviv-Jaffa. In A. Jaworski & C. Thurlow (Eds.), *Semiotic Landscapes: Language, Image, Space* (pp. 241–55). London: Continuum.

Shohamy, E., & Waksman, S. (2012). Talking back to the Tel Aviv Centennial: LL responses to top-down agendas. In C. Hélot, M. Barni, R. Janssens, & C. Bagna (Eds.),

Linguistic Landscapes, Multilingualism and Social Change (pp. 109–25). Frankfurt am Main: Peter Lang.

Southampton City Council. (n.d.a). Previous elections and results. Retrieved from https://www.southampton.gov.uk/council-democracy/voting-and-elections/elections-and-referenda/previous-elections-results.aspx (accessed August 16, 2019).

Southampton City Council. (n.d.b). 2011 census documents: 2011 census briefing: Profile of Southampton wards. Retrieved from http://www.southampton.gov.uk/council-democracy/council-data/statistics/2011-census-documents.aspx (accessed August 16, 2019).

Southampton City Council. (n.d.c). 2011 census documents: 2011 census briefing: 2011 Ethnicity, religion and origins. Retrieved from http://www.southampton.gov.uk/council-democracy/council-data/statistics/2011-census-documents.aspx (accessed August 16, 2019).

Southampton City Council (2016a). 2016 EU referendum S.E. region. Retrieved from https://www.southampton.gov.uk/policies/doct_tcm63-389207.pdf (accessed August 16, 2019).

Southampton City Council (2016b). 2016 EU referendum Southampton area. Retrieved from https://www.southampton.gov.uk/policies/declaration%20of%20count%20totals_tcm63-389208.pdf (accessed August 16, 2019).

Szekeres, V. (2002). Representing diversity and challenging racism: The Migration Museum. In R. Sandell (Ed.), *Museums, Society, Inequality* (pp. 142–52). London and New York: Routledge.

Valentine, G., & McDonald, I. (2004). *Understanding Prejudice: Attitudes towards Minorities*. London: Stonewall. Retrieved from https://www.stonewall.org.uk/resources/understanding-prejudice-2004 (accessed August 16, 2019).

van Dijk, T. A. (2018). Discourse and migration. In R. Zapata-Barrero & E. Yalaz (Eds.), *Qualitative Research in European Migration Studies* (pp. 227–45). Cham: Springer.

Vaughan, M. (2012). Review: Artifactual literacies: Every object tells a story. *Community Development*, 43(5), 684–5.

Vertovec, S. (2007). Super-diversity and its implications. *Ethnic and Racial Studies*, 30(6), 1024–54.

Xiao, R., & Lee, C. (2019). English in the linguistic landscape of the Palace Museum: A field-based sociolinguistic approach. *Social Semiotics*, published online December 2, 2019. doi: 10.1080/10350330.2019.16975

Part Three

LLs as Activist Education

8

Exploring Multimodal Story Houses in the Indigenous Paiwan-Rukai Post-Disaster Reconstruction

Chun-Mei Chen

Introduction

This chapter explores multimodal story houses in multilingual contexts of an indigenous post-disaster reconstruction for Paiwan and Budai Rukai aborigines. Paiwan and Budai Rukai are Austronesian languages spoken in Southern Taiwan. Typhoon Morakot hit Taiwan in August 2009, with more than 2,500 mm of precipitation in three days, resulting in catastrophic damage, such as massive mudslides and severe flooding, to certain Paiwan and Rukai mountainous villages in Pingtung County. The Paiwan residents in the Makazayazaya and Tavalan tribes and the Rukai residents in the Kucapungane tribe lost their original homelands and their farms. The Morakot Post-Disaster Reconstruction Special Act was passed by the Taiwan government and was effective for five years. Makazayaza, Tavalan, and Kucapungane indigenous people, who have different ethnic backgrounds and languages, were brought together in a new permanent settlement in 2010 after the Morakot typhoon disaster. The land for the settlement and reconstruction was provided by the government, and the housing plan for the relocation was financially supported by World Vision organization. Two years after the Morakot typhoon disaster, permanent housing was built and indigenous languages and cultures were transformed in the reconstruction community. Rinari, meaning "going together to the blessed place" in the Paiwan language, which includes 483 households from Paiwan (132 households from Makazayazaya and 174 from Tavalan tribes) and Budai Rukai (177 from Kucapungane tribe) disaster-affected indigenous regions, is one of the post-disaster reconstructions funded by the nongovernmental organization. This area hosts one official dominant language (Mandarin), two indigenous languages (Paiwan and Budai Rukai), two national languages (Taiwanese and Hakka), and several other languages, such as English, triggered by tourism or pop culture. Evergreen Lily Elementary School, located in the reconstruction community, was founded in 2011 by the government and financially supported by the Chang Yung-Fa Foundation. This experimental elementary school ensured the community children's right to education in Rinari. The reconstruction community underwent social change wrought by post-disaster recovery.

Several issues regarding housing and spaces have been raised during the process of reconstruction. The stone slab roofing was not compatible with the resettlement housing. The density of the housing and spatial allocation did not reflect the original societal hierarchy of the indigenous people. Tensions and negotiations with the governmental regime were inevitable. "What we can offer in the reconstruction is the physical frame, and the residents have to take actions to fill their houses," explained the chief architect of the permanent housing. Losing their slate houses, the indigenous residents in Rinari did not have enough land for farming or hunting and realized the importance of actively participating in the reconstruction plan with the local government. The Indigenous Tourism Affiliation, launched by the tribal cadre members of the community approximately four years after the typhoon disaster, proposed the vital voice that indigenous culture and well-being were not separable, with each providing support for the development of the other. Indigenous residents could not go back to their homeland, and they faced the problems of livelihood and the sustainability of their ancestral culture and languages in the post-reconstruction community. Keeping a state of positive emotions with life satisfaction could reduce the emigration of young generations to other urban areas. Their permanent housing became the space for their physical settlement, cultural fulfilment, and positive functioning of their ancestral voice. A story display of their indigenous cultures and languages in their houses served as a starting point for their children and visitors to become more enlightened regarding their social purpose. The aborigines were aware of their culture and their new relationships with the reconstruction community. Housing with longer-term socioeconomic values and environmental adaptions in the community of practice could support their livelihood, ethnic identity, and indigenous culture. The aborigines decorated their houses for private use and community centers with various indigenous semiotic resources and genres. With the aid and training from the Indigenous Tourism Affiliation of the community, some house owners joined the partnership for the homestay plan, which usually consisted of indigenous field trips and was complemented by verbal arts of ancestry stories elicited by elder members or native tour guides. Housing with indigenous materials or linguistic artifacts with educational functions in this specific reconstruction context are called "story houses" in this study. In Rinari, story houses were designed by the disaster-affected aborigines with visual, verbal, and contextual practices in a complex multilingual setting after the typhoon disaster. Story houses are lodgings for indigenous individuals who were displaced by the typhoon disaster and are homestay spaces for tourists. The Tourism Affiliation in Rinari became the first indigenous organization to promote homestay tourism after the typhoon disaster in Taiwan. Story houses are for lodging, services, trading, heritage treasures, communicative practices, and beyond-classroom learning. This chapter investigates the linguistic landscape of story houses and the surrounding neighborhoods in the Rinari community in Pingtung County, Southern Taiwan. The historical perspective in this analysis is crucial, as indigenous residents and their story houses are seen as projecting a future and cannot be analyzed without reference to the past. These story houses, acting as linguistic landscapes in the reconstruction community, are the product of the actions and practices of the language norms, individual experiences, and attitudes of the indigenous residents.

Linguistic landscape studies focus on examining the processes that have given a particular linguistic landscape its particular characteristics (Coupland, 2010; Shohamy & Gorter, 2009). The exploration performed in the present study takes the visibility and modality of the language processes in the space of story houses as foci. With the diverse ethnolinguistic background of the residents in the post-disaster reconstruction community, social dynamics may shape the linguistic landscape in the multilingual setting. Both the Paiwan and Budai Rukai languages are taught in the elementary school of the community. The indigenous culture is introduced in Mandarin in the school. Due to the impact of the Mandarin language and the settlement, the indigenous residents observed the abandonment of their indigenous languages among many children and the migration of young generations to cities to pursue work.

Most signs in the story houses are multilingual, with indigenous languages being displayed in some places. This exploration emphasizes experiential and project-based learning through action and an awareness of the indigenous environments. The reconstruction community highlights concrete experiences that indicate that learning models should include contextualizing indigenous languages in real-world purposes. The present study adopted an ethnographic observation with the intention of determining how discourses are visible in the landscape. Among the speakers in Rinari, the roles of the indigenous languages vary, and visual tradition has transformed into various modalities in the reconstruction. A sign, a mural, or a storytelling voice in story houses could highlight the meaning-making mechanism of the social change in the linguistic landscape semiotic ensemble. Multimodal story houses represent the complex nexus of multilingualism in this study. In the practices of language learning, few texts were produced in either Paiwan or Budai Rukai, making visual images appropriate meaning-making resources for learning the indigenous languages.

This chapter addresses the question of how visual, verbal, and contextual modalities of languages are used in the story house landscapes, with the identification of the traces of historical, economic, ecological, and social processes in these landscapes. A nexus analytical approach was adopted to examine the interrelated linguistic landscape issues of Rinari. How indigenous languages are used in the modalities of the story house landscapes will be addressed, and the historical traces in these story houses will be identified. What happened to the indigenous languages in these landscapes will be explored and contextualized in an educational setting. In addition to exploring the story house landscapes, this chapter also examines how these linguistic and cultural resources can be preserved and revitalized in the sustainable multilingual context. Finally, the interrelated aspects of linguistic resources and language education are discussed. The multimodal analyses offer insights into multilingual studies on story houses in this field and their application to experiential learning. The linguistic landscape in this indigenous community can provide a different perspective on language education. These multimodal houses will be used as a nexus in the linguistic landscape study of their dynamics of community resilience, and the goal of the nexus analysis is to focus on the language education role of these houses. This study contributes to the ongoing discussion on linguistic landscape research and language education beyond the language classroom.

Linguistic Landscape Framework and Education

The linguistic landscape refers to the display of words and images in a public space (Shohamy & Gorter, 2009). Spaces in the community such as streets, parks, or public institutions were considered "public spaces" (Ben-Rafael, 2009). In the study by Landry and Bourhis (1997), the languages used for public road signs, street names, place names, commercial shop signs, and public signs on government buildings were included in the domain of the linguistic landscape research. A useful frame for analyzing the visual production of meaning is provided in the notion of visual grammar in the spatial organization of texts (Kress & van Leeuwen, 1996, 1998). All signs take their meaning from when, where, and how they are placed (Scollon & Scollon, 2003). To make sense of the linguistic landscape of the indigenous community, the social and cultural contexts in which the story houses were placed must be understood. Spolsky and Cooper's (1991) study provides criteria to establish the taxonomies of language signs. This study follows their taxonomies of function and use of signs, the language used for signs, and the number of languages. Visual signs in story houses enable the researcher to evaluate social change over time in the reconstruction, and by looking at those signs they become embedded in the "aggregates of discourse" (Scollon & Scollon, 2003). The preference for one particular code can be inferred from its position relative to the nondominant code (Scollon & Scollon, 2003), which was also delineated in the multimodal linguistic landscape study of Malinowski (2009). Conversely, the symbolic function of signs refers to the perception that members of a language group have the value and status of their languages (Landry & Bourhis, 1997; Spolsky & Cooper, 1991). The spatial ordering of languages carries not only visual information but also an ideological meaning. To interpret the relationship between languages in multilingual signage, Backhaus (2006, 2007) introduces another perspective to the interpretation of multilingual signs, identifying code preference through the order and size of text from different languages. Studies on the linguistic landscape suggest that the preferred code is placed at the top, left, or center of the sign, while the marginalized code is placed on the bottom, right, or in the margins (Scollon & Scollon, 2003: 120). The semiotic perspectives are useful in deconstructing the language choice and placement in multilingual signage, and the visual data in Curtin's (2009) study also provide examples of languages on display. Signs in the reconstruction are linguistic artifacts that were made by the indigenous residents or the local government. Interpretations of the signs in story houses point to the transformation of social change in the post-disaster context.

The recent language ecology approach calls upon researchers to pay attention to multilingualism and the relationships between languages and the social contexts of languages (Hornberger, 2002; Hornberger & Hult, 2008). Hult (2009) argues that the union of two emerging methodologies for researching language in society, linguistic landscape analysis (Gorter, 2006) and nexus analysis (Scollon & Scollon, 2004), are well suited to the aims of an ecological approach to study multilingualism. Both linguistic landscape analysis and nexus analysis contribute to the ecology of language. Linguistic landscape analysis emphasizes visually situated language in public spaces. Nexus analysis, an ethnographic sociolinguistic approach, focuses on the relationships between language use and the social actions of the individuals who construct linguistic landscapes. Hult (2009) has shown that nexus analysis complements linguistic landscape analysis by providing a systematic way of interpreting data on the distribution of languages in public spaces. Nexus analysis provides a framework for the linkage of social actions and circulating discourses. Combining linguistic landscape analysis and nexus analysis creates possibilities for making discursive connections between the actions of individuals and the society within a multilingual space. It is evident that attention should be paid to the historical forces that shape the built environment and the use of language in an indigenous community, especially micro-level contexts. To study the post-disaster reconstruction community in a multilingual context, nexus analysis helps to elaborate various aspects of the linguistic landscape. The visual signs and verbal texts, as well as the contextual activities, in story houses are spaces for displaying language rights and also reflect regulations of the relationship between the languages and the environment.

Literacy skills can be developed in the indigenous community, but the story house landscape provides an additional opportunity to experience nonlinear multimodal texts in the public space (Cenoz & Gorter, 2008). Research on the linguistic landscape has focused on semiotic messages and social connotations (Landry & Bourhis, 1997; Shohamy, 2006). The presence or absence of languages in public spaces communicates the power or significance of the languages. Under the intriguing context of promoting indigenous tourism as a form of community resilience after the disaster, an iconic association carries a direct and natural link between form and meaning (Curtin, 2009: 225). Iconicity refers to the relationship between "a sign and its object in which the sign recapitulates the object in some way" (Mannheim, 2000: 107). Observations of the symbolic message allude to "the semiotic property of pointing to other things" (Kallen, 2009: 273). The signs and icons in story houses, along with other linguistic resources, can provide opportunities for indigenous children and language learners to acquire literacy skills by considering the inputs in the story houses as part of the semiotic resources in the linguistic landscape. The exploration seeks to identify the features of signs, murals, and discursive connections with the community residents to interpret their meaning in place and their application to educational contexts.

The multilingual education model is also important for the present study. Cenoz (2009) analyzed the sociolinguistic contexts of the degree of multilingualism in the subjects and languages taught and of the characteristics of the community members, linguistic landscape, and linguistic distances among the community and target languages. In terms of educational theory, experiential learning (cf. Eyring, 1991) provides learners with concrete experiences and physical links with the target subject or topics. Educational inputs should be provided in a variety of experiences. It is widely agreed that involving learners in physical actions leads them to utilize language skills and cultural knowledge. The use of local environmental facts for indigenous language education would be carried out with goals of speaking resident's rights and sustaining their livelihood in a reconstruction community in the social contexts of two Paiwan tribes and one Budai Rukai indigenous tribe living in the same environment and speaking Mandarin as the dominant language.

Story houses in the indigenous reconstruction are related to language endangerment and revitalization in the context of post-disaster resettlement. Sixteen indigenous languages are recognized by the Council of the Indigenous Peoples in Taiwan. Budai Rukai is an endangered language that is known by fewer than 3,000 people. Although the Paiwan language is not endangered, approximately half of the Paiwan people do not speak their ancestral language, especially in urban areas. The present study on post-disaster reconstruction investigates languages in story houses in a long-standing cultural and linguistic contact zone. The two Paiwan tribes and one Budai Rukai tribe in Rinari share cultural similarities, but they speak different indigenous languages. Chen (2011) reported that Budai Rukai speakers who had frequent contact with the Paiwan speakers tended to produce Paiwan stress patterns in their Rukai speech. Geographical adjacency is the primary factor for the phonological similarities. Most Budai Rukai speakers are bilingual or trilingual, speaking Mandarin or Paiwan as a second or third language. In traditional Paiwan and Budai Rukai villages, oral tradition and verbal arts give priority to linguistic resources. Although the Taiwan government proposed the "Development of National Languages Act" to promote language equality in 2019, Mandarin is the dominant language in schools. Kucapungane, the Rukai tribe that resettled in Rinari, has resided in its original homeland for more than 300 years. The government language equality act also suggested that revitalization action had not been performed to protect the linguistic heritage of indigenous people in the past. Outside of Rinari, the Paiwan and Budai Rukai languages are marginally visible in the Taiwanese linguistic landscape. With story houses as the nexus for experiential learning in a post-disaster context, this study considers historical events as a link through which indigenous residents might have more opportunities to take social actions and speak for their own rights as they participate in the post-disaster reconstruction. Linguistic landscape research performed in this context will reflect sociolinguistic change and discursive connections. The present study, therefore, adopted a discourse ethnographic approach to analyze story houses in multilingual landscapes.

Methodology in the Reconstruction Community

Nexus analysis was conducted at the micro level, with the multimodal elements in story houses serving as a social action performed by indigenous residents as social actors. Social action is considered to be any action performed by a social actor through the use of cultural mediational means (Scollon & Scollon, 2001, 2004). After identifying a social action, the analysis proceeds to mapping the cycles of the people, places, discourses, objects, and concepts that circulate through the moment when the social action takes place (Scollon & Scollon, 2004: 159). All social action is seen as inherently mediated by both social and semiotic tools ranging from language to material objects (Scollon & Scollon, 2001).

By focusing on the actions of the indigenous residents and historical processes, nexus analysis provides an ethnographic and discourse analytical approach to linguistic landscape studies (Hult, 2009: 90). For language learning, few written texts have been produced in either Paiwan or Budai Rukai, making visual images and verbal texts appropriate meaning-making resources for learning these languages. The linguistic landscape is seen as a dynamic multilingual space in the reconstruction community, in which various processes affect the value and function of a particular language. Strategic uses of the linguistic and semiotic resources of story houses create a linguistic landscape for the Rinari, for language rights purposes, for tourism, and for their sustainability.

The researcher worked on a language documentation project with speakers from the Paiwan Makazayazaya and Rukai Kucapungane tribes in their homelands since 2004. I have conducted extensive fieldwork in traditional Paiwan and Rukai villages in the area surrounding Rinari. The representative informants were relocated in Rinari after the disaster. Although few studies have been conducted in this community, native speakers of Paiwan and Rukai worked with the researcher to identify the key issues of story houses. The researcher visited Rinari and its neighborhood in 2014, 2016, 2017, and 2019; took detailed notes on the images, design, and languages of the story houses; and collected verbal traditions and texts. Prior to the field trips to Rinari, 68 local news stories and 155 minutes of documentaries about Rinari were collected from the Taiwan Indigenous TV channel founded by the Indigenous Peoples Cultural Foundation. Interviews with eighteen Paiwan and twenty Rukai residents were conducted in the community by the researcher during the fieldwork. The residents were inquired about their homeland villages, date of arrival in the reconstruction community, motivation for the design of their houses, provenance of the internal and external images or signs of their houses, education, professional career, and attitudes toward their languages and culture. The languages used and the kinds of information conveyed in the public story houses and neighborhood were collected from indigenous staff and guides. After collecting and reviewing the data, semiotic resources, such as the languages (Mandarin, Paiwan, Budai Rukai, and English) used on signs and murals, types of symbolic meanings in communication and multimodal representations of the story houses, were categorized in spatiotemporal order. The methodological strategy is to identify the most significant elements in each story house for further analysis. The salient elements in each selected story house served as the nexus of the other elements for social actions.

This study uses the design and display of story houses as a nexus of language policy, experiential learning of the indigenous languages, and literacy practices. Indigenous residents or the owners of story houses selected the various resources to express their own ethnic purposes. I paid attention to the language choice and genre modification in the representations of story houses. I collected data from story houses regarding language-related human actions to comprehensively explore the indigenous post-disaster community. Navigation of the linguistic landscape goes beyond the signs in the houses, which regulate the production and circulation of the space. Languages prevail in various spatial and temporal contexts.

In addition to navigating the nexus of practice, the researcher engaged in the practice through participating in the journey promoted by the local tourism association to further map the semiotic resources circulating the houses. Exploration of the nexus of practice in story houses will be chronologically presented here, focusing on the relevant discourses and educational purposes of the linguistic landscape. The themes of houses that are central for learning were selected in the community. The slate story house in the playground of the Evergreen Lily Elementary School is meaningful from the perspective of the Paiwan or Rukai language and culture under the post-disaster context. Spaces for inhabitants, such as the Rukai chieftain's house, allowed the researcher to examine various genres of semiotic resources. The Quinoa story house is a designated building for the local government and a landmark with an indigenous visual display in this area. The distribution of the houses under scrutiny is illustrated in Figure 8.1, which can be found on the book's website.

Using the nexus analytical framework, the themes and genres in these houses were identified. The analysis of the practice is presented in the following section, starting from story houses in an educational context beyond the language classroom and progressing to the residential story houses of the Rukai shoes-off tribe by participating in the landscape, followed by a return to the public institution space of the Quinoa story house and workshop houses in an experiential learning journey.

Multimodal Story Houses in Multilingual Contexts

This section presents multimodal story houses in the multilingual contexts of Rinari. The exploration of experiential and project-based learning took place in both public institutional houses and spaces for inhabitants through the action and awareness of the indigenous environments. Themes for learning in the slate story house and the surrounding house module in the playground offer lessons for culture, ecology, and language education in visual and contextual modalities. Concrete experiences in the landscape of the Rukai shoes-off tribe contextualize indigenous languages in real-world purposes through practicing Rukai history, culture, and verbal arts in story houses. The visual space of the Quinoa story house and the adjacent workshop houses reflected the social actions of the indigenous residents through cultural, economic, and language education connections with the authority. The modalities of the story houses in the exploration are shown in Figure 8.2 (refer to the book's website).

In the following section, I present the exploration of the slate story house in the playground, engage with the Rukai shoes-off tribe houses, and then navigate the experiential learning in the Quinoa story house. I also expand the journey to the adjacent workshop houses in the process of reconstructing cultural and educational bridges.

Slate Story House in the Playground

The slate house presenting the story of millets beyond the language classroom forms the nexus of the linguistic landscape analysis in the context of post-disaster recovery. Residents in Rinari lost their slate houses in their homelands. With support from the local government, their hopes for tribal sustainability were transformed into the slate story house in the educational space.

Beyond the sports field of the Pingtung Evergreen Lily Elementary School near the playground is a story house module for schoolchildren to act as indigenous farmers and hunters. Near the wooden bridge-like path is a millet story house (shown in Figure 8.3) made of slates where there are tools, utensils, and materials for making and storing traditional food; this area is also called the cultural discovery section of the playground. Indigenous children learn to grow food and store millet, quinoa and taro, as well as how to use a bow and arrow to catch prey. Through experiences and discovery, indigenous children learn about the characteristics of a farmer or hunter. "They took what they needed from nature and gave something back to the land," said the indigenous schoolteacher who designed the activities in the playground. These activities were their ecology of life.

Older Paiwan and Rukai speakers are invited to tell stories in either indigenous languages or in Mandarin to the children in the story houses. The use of Mandarin is to facilitate the understanding of the indigenous utensils in the post-disaster reconstruction. The taro-roasting kiln made of stone was particularly important for indigenous people to dry and store taros in traditional villages, and the story of the kiln was told in Mandarin. Stone slate culture has formed an essential component of their life. Through listening to the stories, indigenous children learned their material culture and related indigenous vocabulary in an integrated module.

A Mandarin sign is positioned at the entrance of the millet story house, reflecting the dominant status of the instructional language for indigenous cultural education in the community. After entering the slate house, a large portion of the illustrations of ingredients and methods is presented in Mandarin. The use of the Paiwan and Rukai indigenous languages varies from child to child in Rinari. According to the school educators, the school invited Paiwan and Rukai farmers to teach indigenous children how to grow crops. The millet story house offers an authentic site for children to recognize food production methods. Other houses surrounding the slate house, including "*tapau*" (or "*tapav*" referring to "working cottage" or "farmer's hut" in the Paiwan language, shown in Figure 8.3), mobile classrooms of "*vuvu*" ("female elder" in the Paiwan language), and other module houses in the playground, provide spaces for children to interact with their Paiwan or Rukai elders and learn their mother languages, an appreciation for nature and the land, and perceptions of life. Three languages of welcome are presented on the sign of a bamboo house illustrating categories of carved lines at the front door: "歡迎光臨" in Mandarin, "*maelanenga*" in Rukai, and "*davaidavai*" in Paiwan, as shown in Figure 8.3. The display of the indigenous languages also speaks for the resident's right and stance in the educational context. Surviving in the resettlement after the disaster without assistance from outsiders was almost impossible. The use of Mandarin on the signs of the houses also promotes indigenous tourism as a dynamic of community resilience. As shown in the second layer of Figure 8.3, four languages are carved on the illustration board, including Mandarin, English, Paiwan, and Rukai. The multilingual sign of "the breathing slate house" emphasizes the educational purpose of demonstrating the indigenous "house" to outsiders. The indigenous languages on the signs circulate the experiential practices of slates and the resident's appreciation to build and live in their

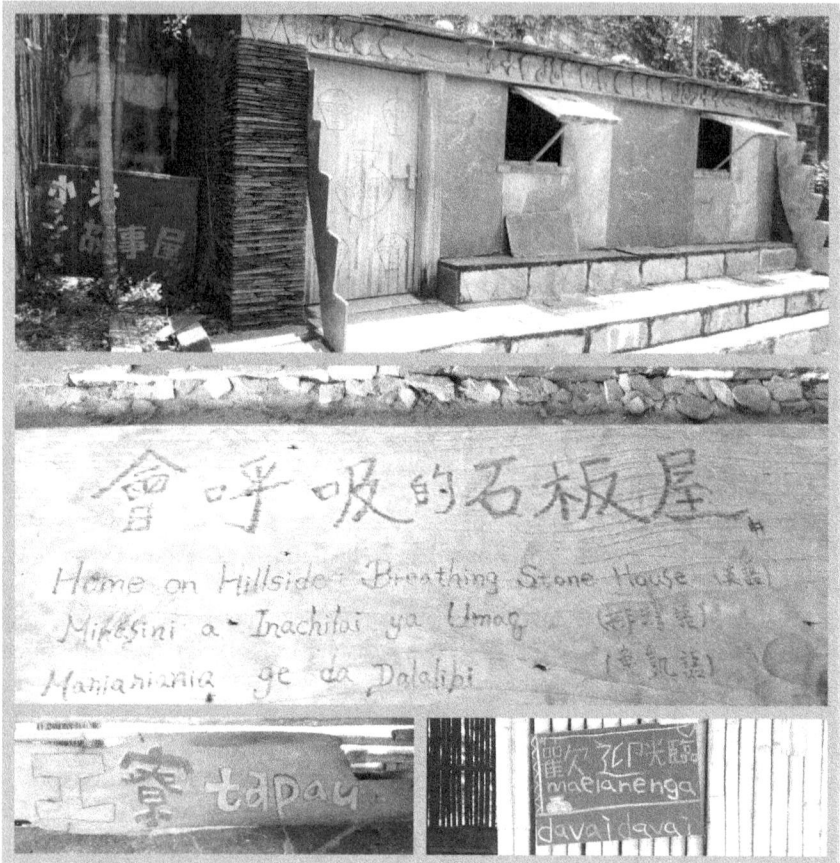

Figure 8.3 Slate story house and multilingual signs in the playground

traditional houses. Visitors are also invited to perceive the visual and verbal inputs and immerse themselves in the learning trip.

The open spaces of the houses in the playground are ideal sites for children to learn traditional farming and hunting skills for their livelihood, as well as their ancestral languages, surrounded by their land and nature in visual and contextual modalities. The residents were not allocated lands for farming or hunting in the resettlement. Children learn how to use materials, such as bamboo, to make arts and crafts and buildings, as the learning process of their heritage culture after the disaster. One bamboo structure, with a sign of "穀倉" ("granary") in Mandarin and "*kubav*" in the Paiwan language, that is used to store quinoa, millet, and other grains in traditional villages, demonstrates the experiential learning practices of the children. The granary house is an important material structure for the Paiwan tribe. Another module house in the playground is a traditional hunter's hut with a sign in both Mandarin and the Paiwan language that serves as a place for storing prey or resting after hunting. The house buildings make use of traditional materials and construction methods. Exploring the connections between these landscapes and the indigenous resident's well-being is transformational for heritage culture conservation and indigenous language learning. From these houses in the playground, it can be seen that educational discourses on the linguistic landscape treat multilingual signs in the playground as both instrumental objects and symbolic spaces. The learning system of the slate story house with a discursive discourse of the linguistic landscape is summarized in Figure 8.4 (found on the companion website).

The historical traces of recovery processes in this discursively constructed space are presented by various educational actors. The physical slate house identified what happened to the Paiwan and Rukai homelands. Oral stories represent a cross-section of the materials surrounding the story houses as a complement to the visual information in the linguistic landscape. Language learners in a field trip are faced with indigenous texts in the playground, but they need cultural contexts to be facilitators during the practices. Multilingual signs in a landscape are "aggregates of discourse" (Scollon & Scollon, 2003) in language learning. Exposure to the indigenous language can take place in different ways outside the classroom. The slate story house in the playground constitutes an illustration of language ideology because it shows that social actors promote the nature and functions of the indigenous culture and language. The educational display of the indigenous identity has an impact when various forms of linguistic practices by Paiwan and Rukai elders and children are embedded in the recovery process. The indigenous languages become a vehicle for social accommodation in mapping the circumstances of actions. The story houses in the playground are very practical educational tools in the post-disaster reconstruction community. The slate story house forms a nexus in the playground, and there are historical recovery arrangements in the linguistic landscape, such as the millet story house, working cottage, and granary module houses. Indigenous children own their spaces for learning languages and culture, and the multilingual languages on the signs are products of the direct and indirect participation of outsiders.

Rukai Shoes-Off Tribal Houses and the Chieftain's House

The Rukai Kucapungane tribe resettled in Rinari after the typhoon disaster. Their old settlement of Kucapungane was recognized by the World Monuments Fund (WMF) and listed by the 2016 World Monument Watch as one of fifty at-risk cultural treasures in the world. Their rich cultural resources and ancestral language were relocated in Rukai shoes-off tribal houses and the chieftain's house in the reconstruction community. The following linguistic landscape was navigated through an ethnographic participant observation of the researcher.

At the entrance of Lane #17, footprints paralleling the Rukai word "*Saabaw*" on the ground welcome their visitors. "Saabaw" in Rukai means "hello, we welcome you to become our family members and friends." According to the Rukai residents, they are very hospitable, so-called "*pasudalu*" in the Rukai language. Because of the disaster, they left their homeland Kucapungane, and they could no longer see their traditional landscapes, such as their sacred mountains, streams, and forests. Many elders lived alone and missed their family members who passed away in the typhoon disaster.

Figure 8.5 Rukai shoes-off tribal houses, murals, and the chieftain's house

The Rukai community development association initiated the homestay projects in 2011 for visitors to learn and respect their culture and, simultaneously, to accompany their Rukai elders and families. Seeing rows of shoes at the front doors of the houses indicates to visitors a particular set of social actors that they will learn. The ritualized statements of "please leave your shoes here" should be followed before entering shoes-off tribal houses to respect the Rukai house owners. Semiotic objects in these landscapes communicate messages in relation to the social action.

As shown in Figure 8.5, near the footprints is a circular sign with Rukai "*Saabaw*" ("welcome") and drawings of the hundred-pace snake. Next to the circular sign is a map of the Rukai shoes-off tribal houses. The names of commercial stores and traditional workshops are displayed on the map in the Mandarin, the Rukai language, and English (such as "pizza"). The Mandarin name of the workshop "法法樣" (pronounced "fǎfǎyàng" in Mandarin) is translated from the sounds of the Paiwan word "*vavayan*" (referring to "woman" or "female"), and the horizontal street name in Chinese characters is translated from the sounds of the Rukai word "*Kucapungane*." The multilingual signs reflected the linguistic interplay among the Paiwan and Rukai residents, as well as their visitors. The store name "*AKAME*" on the sign means "to roast" in the Rukai language, and the place serves roasted food. The decorated guesthouses were designed by Rukai residents with signs referring to the commercial or lodging functions of the houses.

The Rukai residents called their original Kucapungane village "the homeland of the cloud leopard." It was stated that the first ancestor of the Kucapungane tribe, called Puraruyan, hunted with a cloud leopard in sacred mountains and found the place suitable for living. The ancestor led the tribal people to the Kucapungane village, and the place thereafter became the "the homeland of the cloud leopard." The sacred leopard is depicted on the mural of the story house.

The Rukai shoes-off tribal houses are composed of traditional-style story houses, including the House of the Millet, House of the Athlete, House of the Hunter, House of the Shellflower Stalk Weaver, House of the Sun, and the chieftain's house. The names of the houses represent the specialities or characteristics of the owners. For instance, the Millet house owner specializes in planting millet, and the Hunter house owner is good at catching prey. The Rukai name of the female owner of the "House of the Sun" is "*cemedjas*" (meaning "the sun"), and the residents in the community call her "the princess of the Sun." The murals of each house also correspond to the specialities of the owners. The lily flowers in the Rukai culture denote social order and morality, as introduced by a tour guide. The right to wear lily flowers in one's headdress is only granted to outstanding hunters and to women with virtue. The indigenous identity is exhibited on the murals of their story houses.

Traditional Rukai tribes maintained a social hierarchy according to the tour guide. Certain patterns carved on their houses could only be used by the nobility, such as lily and pottery vessel patterns. Examples of the story houses are illustrated in Figure 8.5. The carved Chinese characters "魯凱族大頭目" on the stud denote "the Rukai chieftain." The Rukai residents called their chieftain the "king," "*tjalialjalay*" in the Rukai language. The sculpture and the decoration of the houses are indexical to the Rukai tribal history, societal organization, and traditional culture after resettlement in Rinari.

The cultural and linguistic projects in the shoes-off tribe begin with a blessing ceremony in the Rukai chieftain's story house. In a typical learning journey, visitors are asked to touch the pottery vessel, receiving good luck and a blessing. The chieftain elaborates on his headdress in the Rukai language, which is translated by a Rukai tour guide into Mandarin, as shown in (1). His verbal arts also deliver respectful attitudes toward nature in the Rukai culture.

(1) Verbal arts of the Rukai chieftain

Our Rukai headdress is made of natural materials. The decoration is not luxurious, compared with a Chinese emperor's crown. The feather of an eagle represents a royal status and nobility because the eagle is the king of the birds. The eagle flies to claim his domain. The claw of the eagle represented the power (narration in January 2016).

The verbal arts of the chieftain with the traditional costume and headdress can be used as teaching and learning materials beyond the language classroom. Visitors perceive the Rukai words with the ancestral rhythm in the space of a house with visual illustrations, practicing imagery and verbal coding approaches in language learning. The story house of the chieftain allows visitors to be exposed to the sound of words and to practice them. Interactive activities are integrated into the dual encoding learning methods, and learners are immersed in the Rukai language and culture. The chieftain's house is a modality of literacy. The languages carry not only visual and verbal information but also ideological meaning. The linguistic landscape in this context increased the availability of learning input, which is appropriate for the acquisition of phonological and pragmatic competence, as well as cultural knowledge.

The researcher participated in the tour of the shoes-off tribal houses. Rukai youths were practicing their verbal language and cultural knowledge as the social actors. They delivered lily flower coronets to visitors, indicating that they were becoming their family members. Rukai elders performed their traditional rhythm to express their thoughts and reflections. One single rhythm could be performed with different Rukai content words and expressions. One "*ina*" ("mother"), a female owner of a story house, sang the traditional Rukai rhythm, with the Rukai text "do not change your heart and concern for our tribe." She also wore a colored glass bead necklace, indicating in the Rukai language that the necklace was bestowed by her mother as a dowry. Aesthetic perceptions with verbal arts were simultaneously practiced in the story house.

Many female owners of the story houses were weavers and presented their traditional art forms. Rukai women were weaving when they explained artifacts in the Rukai language. The house owner of the "Shellflower Stalk Weaver" is able to weave a basket in a day. It takes patience and persistence to weave baskets and other utensils from shellflower stalk. Visitors observed traditional handicrafts and shellflower stalk weaving, learning their weaving skills and languages.

One Rukai resident depicted the old village and trials on the interior side of the door in his story house, reconstructing an ideological path from the present to the past. The front door of the house represented a gate. According to his story, it took five to six hours to travel from the gate to the oldest village, with a rest area called "*tinevai*" in the Rukai language. The stone slate alcove along the trial in the mural was a secret mailbox for lovers to store love letters. Looking at the murals, his strong emotion toward his homeland was released. He reconstructed a hope from the past to the present in his story house. Historical traces of these landscapes were presented through visual images and verbal stories in combination with the post-disaster homestay project in the recovery context. Learners were invited to participate in the sets of social actors to practice the Rukai language and culture. These Rukai linguistic and cultural resources were transformed into the multimodal story houses in the resettlement.

Experiential Learning in the Quinoa Story House and Workshop Houses

An official Quinoa story house was launched by the Pingtung government in 2017 to promote indigenous products and the economy, as well as an indigenous landmark in the area. The spatial organization of the house forms a nexus for experiential learning of the indigenous community. Adjacent to the tourist center of Rinari, the Quinoa story house exhibits a variety of traditional crops and cultural materials of the indigenous community. The Paiwan word "*djulis*" (meaning "quinoa") is embedded in the English sign of the story house, shown as "PINGTUNG *DJULIS* STORY HOUSE" in Figure 8.6, paralleling the Chinese characters "屏東紅藜故事館" at the entrance. The name of quinoa in the Rukai language is "*baae*" (in contrast to "*djulis*" in Paiwan). The Paiwan language in the story house is locally contextualized, and the choice of languages used in the story house reflects the ecology of the indigenous languages, with two Paiwan tribes and one Rukai tribe in the Rinari community.

Social actors in the establishment of the house are on display from signs to murals. The local government provided financial support and developmental projects, and the local residents were the major designers of the physical story house. Quinoa alcohol products, surrounded by other traditional crops in the adjacent indigenous community, together with the exterior murals of the ancestral spirits of the story house, form the ethnic indexical link to the community members, even those without language proficiency in the indigenous languages. The space for the first floor is for exhibitions, while the space of the second floor is for stores and workshops of the

Figure 8.6 Quinoa story house and the "Silent Protest"

indigenous commodities. Spirituality in these public institutional houses displayed the blessing from the indigenous ancestors in the reconstruction.

Touching the quinoa sampling, listening to the quinoa story, reading the production process, and reviewing the recovery images of the indigenous community after the disaster are educational activities that provide visitors with actual situated lessons in the linguistic landscape. The Paiwan legend of quinoa was delivered by the story house guide in Mandarin and translated by the researcher as shown in (2).

(2) *Paiwan legend of the quinoa*

Once upon a time, a poor indigenous grandmother and her little girl did not have costumes to attend their tribal festival. The girl walked sadly along the skyline of the quinoa farm. Suddenly, a rainbow bridge appeared in the sky, and the green quinoa plant turned into a colorful quinoa. The grandmother and the girl used this colorful material and weaved their head garlands. With these pretty quinoa decorations, they were able to attend the festival. From then on, it was said that quinoa originated from a rainbow. The indigenous ancestors passed quinoa on, and the plant became one of the traditional grains of the indigenous people.

Visiting the quinoa farms adjacent to Rinari, the authentic indigenous landscape is integrated into the verbal story delivered by the indigenous tour guide in the authority language. The quinoa materials circulated in the story house have a strong link with the indigenous culture and customs. Relevant plant words in Paiwan are included in the situated learning. The house has become the nexus of the community, demonstrating the indigenous identity and cultural treasure. The social actors behind the spatial organization of the house narrate their cultural and economic processes, as well as their history and languages in visual images and stories. The discursively constructed space and stories are complemented by the indigenous voice in the house. The visual space and the verbal tradition of the story house reflect human actions, and the actions impact the indigenous residents of the community.

Flanking the Quinoa story house is the space for an indigenous kitchen, handicraft workshops, and extension exhibition area for artworks. The exterior murals of the story house displayed a creative caricature produced by a Rukai artist and approved by the authority. The visual illustrations of the ancestral spirits were inspired by Rukai verbal legends and fairy tales, according to the artist. The hundred-pace snake, regarded as a mascot by the Rukai and Paiwan people, is depicted on the pillar, carrying a link with the sacred and respectful indigenous culture.

The mural named "Silent Protest" on the story house, shown in Figure 8.6, is a display of the circumstance under the development of tourism. According to the artist, the Rukai elders were too courteous to express their anger when their houses were invaded by uninvited tourists. Instead of complaining about the disorders of tourists, they had no choice but to keep silent. The eyes of the cloud leopard, a symbol of Rukai societal dignity, were depicted without mouths, contrasting with the pipe and rising smoke. The mural foregrounds demonstrate the interplay between the social actions of the Rukai elders and semiotic meaning-making resources, disclosing their ethnicity and attitudes.

The Paiwan language on the exterior sign, the visual illustrations of the Rukai ancestral spirits and the mascot, and the verbal story of the red quinoa in Mandarin construct the multilingual and multimodal linguistic space of the story house. This ordering of linguistic resources speaks to the negotiation among the Mandarin, Paiwan, and English languages. Signs produced by organizations, particularly relevant to the promotion for tourism, are displayed in Mandarin and English for guidance. The use of the majority language inside and outside of the story house was influenced both by policies and by literacy skills (cf. Spolsky, 2009). The indigenous language on the sign and the linguistic environment of the Quinoa story house offer a site to examine language identity and the hierarchical order in a multilingual situation. The use of indigenous design indexes the integration processes of local resources and identity. The social actors behind the signs and murals were the Paiwan and Rukai members of the local tourism organization and association that actively participated in the recovery plan with the local government. They worked within an accepted framework to construct their cultural identity and ethnic esteem. The local government relied on indigenous resources for commodification and advertisement, and the display of the indigenous languages was negotiated and embedded in the semiofficial space. In terms of the nexus analysis, the languages and symbols in the story house mediated social actions in the reconstruction community.

There are a variety of workshops around the tourist center. The workshops are run by local artists, weavers, and carvers from Paiwan and Rukai tribes. Visitors are invited to enter the houses to experience indigenous works as well as to interact with residents. The themes of the houses vary from the gathering of food to accessories for ceremonies, as well as verbal legends. There are exhibition panels in Mandarin around the houses that provide information for guidance. The houses are surrounded by mountains, offering experiential learning for ecotourism activities. Decorated with Paiwan or Rukai tribe motifs, the houses not only preserve agricultural products but also promote handicrafts and traditional arts. Some indigenous artists are considered national treasures for the quality of their painting or embroidery. There is a good selection of works, including beads, woven textiles, woven shellflower stalk baskets, and wood carvings. Visitors can learn about indigenous cuisines and food culture through engaging in cooking lessons and the physical house landscape. Large tables in the kitchen honor the sharing economy of the traditional Paiwan society. The spatial arrangements of the workshops are also platforms for teaching and learning indigenous arts and culture. Exploring houses in relation to culture provides clues to the meaning encoded in the generated spatial forms. The workshop houses not only reflect sociocultural concerns but also shape their social actions in the landscape.

The indigenous language spelling or orthography on display did not always correspond to a verbal tradition, but the sounds or symbols of the languages delivered their cultural identity. Two murals in the workshop houses disclosed the indigenous identity, culture, and respectful attitudes toward the sun and nature, as shown in Figure 8.7 (refer to accompanying website). Both murals depict indigenous figures in the Paiwan and English languages in different sizes. The literal translation of English explained the indigenous lifestyles and motivated visitors to participate in the landscape.

In a multimodal approach to literacy, interpretations of any particular language are not complete without the consideration of socioeconomic factors in a recovery context. The use of the Paiwan language in murals indexes the house as an indigenous space and speaks for linguistic rights. The murals are also contextualized, as they create a symbolic connection between the residents and the visitors. The Paiwan sentence of "look at the sunshine" carries the optimistic attitudes of the residents in the post-disaster recovery process. The "*tjamaku*" (meaning "tobacco leaf") was planted around Paiwan slate houses in the homelands before the disaster, according to one of the shop owners. The handmade pipe was important in Paiwan culture and used to express emotions. To "smoke slowly" was the social action of the Paiwan elders; by doing so, visitors entered the indigenous space. The practice of literacy in this context is multimodal (Leander & Lewis, 2007). The images and languages are embedded in the landscape and are processed at the same time as the reconstruction of cultural and educational bridges. Experiential learning in this landscape is a holistic process of adaptation to the indigenous culture, semiotic resources, and linguistic creativity.

Discussion and Conclusion

This chapter explored the role that can be played by story houses in language and cultural education by examining their use in the indigenous community as a source of linguistic input and for the learning of indigenous cultural knowledge. This chapter also analyzed the linguistic landscape in post-disaster reconstruction as multimodal and multilingual as well as their symbolic functions. There is a spirit of recovery in the Paiwan-Rukai reconstruction community, as exemplified in homes, workshops, educational sites for indigenous languages, and culture. Most elders in Rinari speak their indigenous languages, while the children know little of them. The most practical educational tool for preserving their indigenous culture is through teaching and practicing their languages. The intended audience of the story houses consists of both members of the community and tourists. Deliberate fashioning of the linguistic landscape in the recovery context supports cultural sustainability and speaks for their rights. Exploration of the multimodal story houses provides contextual opportunities for indigenous children and visitors to learn and experience their culture and languages.

The slate story house in the playground, Rukai shoes-off tribal houses, the chieftain's house, and the Quinoa story house, and the workshop houses, are ideal sites for local children and visitors to interact with indigenous elders, bilingual and multilingual teachers and guides. The educational activities in these public houses provide visitors with actual situated lessons in the linguistic landscape. Through the visual, verbal, and contextual modalities of learning in the Rukai shoes-off tribal houses and the chieftain's house, the children can acquire their ancestral languages and respect the wisdom of their ancestors. Indigenous history, culture, and verbal arts can be learned, and language education can be processed through awareness and action.

The presence of the indigenous languages in the story houses "sends direct and indirect messages with regard to the centrality versus the marginality of certain languages in society" (Shohamy, 2006: 110). The visual signs, images, and verbal arts can be explicit displays of the indigenous identity, and the use of Paiwan, Rukai, Mandarin, and English in the linguistic landscape enables us to evaluate the social change in the post-disaster recovery. The presence of the Paiwan and Budai Rukai languages indicates the sustainability of the indigenous languages in spaces for organization and inhabitants. In these story houses, languages are symbolic and in contact with other modes of representation.

Based on the visual murals and images in these multimodal story houses, together with the verbal complement, the linguistic landscape on its own in Rinari can be used as teaching material for the development of pragmatic competence. The verbal arts and indigenous texts in the story houses are authentic inputs beyond the language classroom. The use of the indigenous languages varies among residents in Rinari, and visual and verbal tradition gives priority to linguistic resources. With the themes and instances of the story houses as learning resources, each language learner can conduct linguistic projects in the indigenous environments, engage in the landscape, and shape the expression in activities. The multimodal story houses in the reconstruction community highlight concrete experiences in real-world purposes. The multimodal practices of the visual signs, images, and verbal texts in the story houses illustrate how the indigenous readers in the Rinari community explore languages and cross-cultural borders.

The story houses in the post-disaster reconstruction were regarded as symbolic and informational sites where localized actions on indigenous language, culture, and identity are practiced. By identifying story houses as a nexus of practice, the present study mapped the link between language use, revitalization of the Paiwan and Budai Rukai languages, and multilingualism through these semiotic systems. The multimodal presentations of the story houses in educational contexts are connected to the post-disaster recovery, interplay discourse, and meaning-making resources in the post-disaster reconstruction community.

There are many story houses in Rinari for indigenous language education. This exploration suggests possible interpretations from a reader's perspective. Indigenous children can choose a genre, theme, and contextual materials for their integrated learning. Field trips can help visitors understand the language learning situation, including the multimodal story houses with which they make connections between cultural materials and human actions. Through the learning journey in multimodal story houses, indigenous residents practice their values and identity in the reconstruction community. Story houses as linguistic landscapes in the post-disaster reconstruction point to the speech community in various modalities. The visual and verbal aspects of languages and the sociolinguistic repertoire are mediated by the local government through the process of negotiation and the promotion of indigenous products, by the local resident's attitudes, and by the ideologies shared by the community. The present study examines how Paiwan and Budai Rukai aborigines in Rinari cooperated with local policy and designed their own story houses to express their language norms, individual experiences, and attitudes in both public spaces, such as the Quinoa story house, and ethnic spaces, such as Rukai shoes-off tribal houses.

The findings of this exploration indicate that each story house has its own strategies for revealing the indigenous ethnicity and attitudes by making choices regarding the use of semiotic resources to construct identities. Nevertheless, multiple discourses are operating in this situation. Oral stories share the strategies of distributing the material culture of the physical houses as a complement to the linguistic landscape in this indigenous community. Through linguistic creativity and the combination of indigenous languages and cultures in multimodal practices, the occurrence of different linguistic forms, signs, and modalities provides empirical evidence for the ethnolinguistic vitality of the Paiwan and Budai Rukai language groups. This study contributes to the linguistic landscape literature on indigenous discourse by showing how a multimodal analysis can offer insights into learning beyond the language classroom.

References

Backhaus, P. (2006). Multilingualism in Tokyo: A look into the linguistic landscape. In D. Gorter (Ed.), *Linguistic Landscape: A New Approach to Multilingualism* (pp. 52–66). Clevedon: Multilingual Matters.

Backhaus, P. (2007). *Linguistic Landscapes. A Comparative Study of Urban Multilingualism in Tokyo*. Clevedon: Multilingual Matters.

Ben-Rafael, E. (2009). A sociological approach to the study of linguistic landscape. In E. Shohamy & D. Gorter (Eds.), *Linguistic Landscape: Expanding the Scenery* (pp. 40–54). New York & London: Routledge.

Cenoz, J. (2009). *Towards Multilingual Education: Basque Educational Research from an International Perspective*. Bristol: Multilingual Matters Ltd.

Cenoz, J., & Gorter, D. (2008). The linguistic landscape as an additional source of input in second language acquisition. *International Review of Applied Linguistics in Language Teaching* (IRAL), 46, 267–87.

Chen, C.-M. (2011). Phonetic evidence for the contact-induced prosody in Budai Rukai. *Concentric: Studies in Linguistics*, 35(2), 123–54.

Coupland, N. (2010). Welsh linguistic landscapes "from above" and "from below." In A. Jaworski & C. Thurlow (Eds.), *Semiotic Landscapes* (pp. 77–101). London: Continuum.

Curtin, M. (2009). Languages on display: Indexical signs, identities and the linguistic landscape of Taipei. In E. Shohamy & D. Gorter (Eds.), *Linguistic Landscape: Expanding the Scenery* (pp. 221–37). New York and London: Routledge.

Eyring, J. (1991). Experiential language learning. In M. Celce-Murcia (Ed.), *Teaching English as a Second Language* (pp. 346–59). New York: Newbury House.

Gorter, D. (2006). The study of the linguistic landscape as a new approach to multilingualism. *International Journal of Multilingualism*, 3(1), 1–6.

Hornberger, N. H. (2002). Multilingual language policies and the continua of biliteracy: An ecological approach. *Language Policy*, 1(1), 27–51.

Hornberger, N. H., & Hult, F. M. (2008). Ecological language education policy. In B. Spolsky and F. M. Hult (Eds.), *Handbook of Educational Linguistics* (pp. 280–96). Malden, MA: Blackwell.

Hult, F. M. (2009). Language ecology and linguistic landscape analysis. In E. Shohamy & D. Gorter (Eds.), *Linguistic Landscape: Expanding the Scenery* (pp. 88–104). London: Routledge.

Kallen, J. (2009). Tourism and representation in the Irish linguistic landscape. In E. Shohamy & D. Gorter (Eds.), *Linguistic Landscape: Expanding the Scenery* (pp. 270–83). New York and London: Routledge.

Kress, G., & van Leeuwen, T. (1996). *Reading Images: The Grammar of Visual Design*. London: Routledge.

Kress, G., & van Leeuwen, T. (1998). Front pages: (The critical) analysis of newspaper layout. In A. Bell & P. Garrett (Eds.), *Approaches to Media Discourse* (pp. 186–219). Oxford: Blackwell.

Landry, R., & Bourhis, R. Y. (1997). Linguistic landscape and ethnolinguistic vitality: An empirical study. *Journal of Language and Social Psychology*, 16, 23–49.

Leander, K., & Lewis, C. (2007). Literacy and internet technologies. In Brian V. Street & N. Hornberger (Eds.), *Encyclopaedia of Language and Education*, (Vol. 2, pp. 53–70). New York: Springer.

Malinowski, D. (2009). Authorship in the linguistic landscape: A multimodal, performative view. In E. Shohamy & D. Gorter (Eds.), *Linguistic Landscape: Expanding the Scenery* (pp. 107–25). New York and London: Routledge.

Mannheim, B. (2000). Iconicity. *Journal of Linguistic Anthropology*, 9(1–2), 107–10.

Scollon, R., & Scollon, S. (2001). *Intercultural Communication: A Discourse Approach*, 2nd ed. Malden, Oxford & Carlton: Blackwell.

Scollon, R., & Scollon, S. (2003). *Discourse in Place: Language in the Material World*. London and New York: Routledge.

Scollon, R., & Scollon, S. (2004). *Nexus Analysis: Discourse and the Emerging Internet*. London: Routledge.

Shohamy, E. (2006). *Language Policy: Hidden Agendas and New Approaches*. New York: Routledge.

Shohamy, E., & Gorter, D. (2009). *Linguistic Landscape: Expanding the Scenery*. London: Routledge.

Spolsky, B. (2009). Prologomena to a sociolinguistic theory of public signage. In E. Shohamy & D. Gorter (Eds.), *Linguistic Landscape: Expanding the Scenery* (pp. 25–39). New York & London: Routledge.

Spolsky, B., & Cooper, R. L. (1991). *The Languages of Jerusalem*. Oxford: Clarendon Press.

9

Activist Teaching through the Linguistic Landscape in Göttingen and Lviv

Corinne A. Seals and Greg Niedt

Introduction: Activism in and through the LL

Education through the linguistic landscape is not only a matter of bringing students from a classroom into the wild; the linguistic landscape also serves as a vehicle for educating passersby every day. Additionally, this education of the public through the LL can be via both official and unofficial signs, but the latter receives comparatively less attention in LL research. The current project is interested in looking at how the public are educated about contemporary topics of interest through the LL by activists in two locations: Göttingen, Germany, and Lviv, Ukraine. We ask, "How do activists utilize the linguistic landscape to educate the public in both locations, and what (if anything) is unique to each city?"

When activists communicate through the linguistic landscape, they are drawing upon the power of *dialogism* (Bakhtin, 1984, 1992). Dialogism is the notion that all texts and textual performances (be they written, spoken, presented through images, bodily performance, or otherwise) are both responding to voices and ideas that came before, as well as anticipating responses that may come next. Additionally, it is notable that all linguistic landscapes, including those created and utilized by activists, are *polyphonic* (Bakhtin, 1984), meaning that many voices and ideas, both past and present, contribute to the meaning that they carry and convey. Because of this, all linguistic landscape texts are also *heteroglossic* (Bakhtin, 1984), meaning that they echo the voices and ideas that preceded them and informed their creation. Activists are able to draw upon the inherent dialogism, polyphony, and heteroglossia of the linguistic landscape purposefully to create a dialogue of resistance (Coulmas, 2009; Hanauer, 2011, 2012; Pennycook, 2009; Scollon & Scollon, 2003; Seals, 2012, 2015).

Dialogues of resistance, in the form of linguistic landscapes, have become an area of major interest for linguistic landscapes scholars in the last decade. For example, some researchers have chosen to examine activism in the linguistic landscape through an examination of graffiti. Pennycook (2009) argued that graffiti is a form of transgressive semiotics, which then inspired additional studies in the linguistic landscapes of graffiti. Hanauer (2011) examined how graffiti functioned as political discourse in Abu Dis, a Palestinian village bordering Jerusalem, and Rubdy (2015) examined how commemoration graffiti helped people reach deeper understandings following the 26/11 Mumbai terror attacks. Recently, Machetti and Pizzorusso (2020) traced the way we talk about graffiti in linguistic landscapes and looked at similarities and differences between modern street art and that which existed several hundred years ago.

In addition to graffiti, the linguistic landscapes of protests have also been investigated. In some cases, specific local sites have been investigated, emphasizing the importance of interpreting the linguistic landscape through knowledge of local context. These studies include protests in Tahrir Square (Aboelezz, 2016), Algiers (Messekher, 2015), Tunisia (Shiri, 2015), the paper cities of Hong Kong (Anfinson, 2020), candlelight protests of South Korea (Lee, 2018), the city of Pittsburgh in the United States (Hanauer, 2012), and Washington, DC (Seals, 2012). Large, international activist movements have also been a focus of attention for linguistic landscapes research. For example, Barni and Bagna (2016) and Seals (2012, 2015, 2017) examined the international immigration reform marches and how the linguistic landscapes contributed to giving a voice to an often silenced population. Also, Hanauer (2015), Seals (2015, 2017), and Steinberg (2016) looked into the different functions and achievements of the multi-site Occupy movement in bringing about change by altering the way people perceive and participate in activism.

While there has even recently been a study of the linguistic landscapes of activist demonstrations at an educational institution (Cerimaj, Milani, & Kitis, 2020), there is no known research specifically looking at how activism in the general linguistic landscape is used *as* an educational vehicle to teach the public about social issues. This, therefore, is the focus of the current chapter. The research we present here adds to the growing body of studies on utilizing the linguistic landscape for teaching purposes (e.g., Chesnut, Lee, & Shulte, 2013; Malinowski, 2015; Sayer, 2010). However, like the other chapters in the current volume, we push this conceptualization further by looking at how teaching occurs in linguistic landscapes "in the wild" of public spaces every day.

In the sections that follow, we introduce you to the contextual background of the two cities which take center stage in this chapter: Göttingen, Germany, and Lviv, Ukraine. We then present our methods of data collection as well as data analysis, including places where the two authors used similar methods and where we diverged. Following this, we focus on three main areas of findings: spray-painted graffiti of the type popular globally, vinyl stickers of the type popular in urban centers, and elements of the linguistic landscape in each place that are city specific and draw upon each city's history. We then end this chapter by returning the focus to how the linguistic landscape serves as a global and local tool for activist teaching.

Contextual Background

Göttingen, Germany

Located in the southeast corner of Lower Saxony and near the heart of the reunified German state, Göttingen's history extends back to at least the medieval era, when it was a prominent town and member of the Hanseatic League. The Georg-August University, founded in 1737, became one of the top destinations for scholars in mathematics and the natural sciences, counting several Nobel laureates among its ranks (Imhoof, 2013; Rupke, 2002). Despite the vibrant intellectual life of the city, it remained conservative overall due to its well-established and moneyed middle class; this enabled Germany's interwar nativism to blossom, as in many other small cities, into Nazism (Imhoof, 2013). Göttingen escaped heavy bombing in the Second World War, allowing its university became the first to resume operation after the war; the renowned Max Planck Society was founded there soon afterward, renewing interest in Göttingen as a center of academic culture. This period was marked by a dissonant political reality: an increasingly progressive and "self-denazifying" professoriate (Weisbrod, 2003) contrasted with the growing tension along the border with East Germany, only a few kilometers away (Ewald, 2019; Schaefer, 2018). The city continued to globalize through the university, bringing in a greater diversity of ideas and a leftward slant to political thought in the city, with notable contributions including the Göttingen Manifesto against nuclear weapons, authored by some of the university's leading physicists (including Werner Heisenberg).

In some ways, Göttingen continues to be a city of contradictions. The university thrives, bringing in large numbers of student activists and anarchists, with the squats and meeting houses along the aptly named Rote Straße ("Red Street") serving as a focal point of anarcho-communism. Yet the mansions and affluent neighborhoods along the eastern edge of the city are a reminder of the old money that has remained entrenched in the region for decades. Another recent bellwether of political friction is the refugee crisis that has taken prominence in German politics since 2015. Under the government's resettlement plan, the state of Lower Saxony was assigned roughly 10% of incoming refugees from Syria and its environs (Katz, Noring, & Garrelts, 2016), many of whom have settled in and around Göttingen. Despite the state's low rate of deportations (Laubenthal, 2015) and liberal education access for new arrivals (Morris-Lange & Brands, 2016), there was a corresponding increase in violence against refugees (Schumacher, 2016), culminating in some towns beginning to refuse them housing and services.

While Germany continues to grapple with the crisis' ramifications, a synchronic view of Göttingen's current linguistic and semiotic landscape shows features that reflect all of these elements extending through history and across the political spectrum. The preserved antiquity of the university's buildings and monuments, as well as older businesses in the pedestrian zones downtown, maintain an old German aesthetic. But it is not uncommon to hear a bit of Turkish or Arabic in the street or to see Thai or Vietnamese on a posted flyer, indicators of the immigration pulses that have occurred in recent decades. And although the architecture is scrupulously maintained, there are sections downtown—notably along Rote Straße again—covered in stickers, banners, flyers, and other media that feature a wide array of political slogans and symbols. The dynamic historical and political backdrop to these traces of activism in the landscape, along with its relatively small size, makes Göttingen an intriguing microcosm to investigate.

Lviv, Ukraine

Lviv is the hub of culture, education, religion, and politics in Western Ukraine and was historically the capital of this region. It is the largest city in the region and has the seventh largest population of any city in Ukraine (Figol, Kubijovyč, & Zhukovsky, 2016). Because of its geographical location, cultural importance, and influence in regional trade, Lviv has had (and continues to have) major influence in the Galicia region and has served a strategic role in negotiations between Eastern and Western Europe (Fäßler, Held, & Sawitzki, 1993; Isaievych & Lytvyn, 1996; Hrystak, 2000). During the Second World War, it was the home of the Ukrainian Resistance Movement (Hrystak, 2000), a role that continues to influence the identities of many who reside there today (Seals, 2019). Additionally, there are currently twenty-six institutions of higher learning in the city, which mark it as a major center of Ukrainian science and arts as well (Figol, Kubijovyč, & Zhukovsky, 2016). Because of its history and location, Lviv has been highly influenced by both Western and Eastern Europe (Fäßler, Held, & Sawitzki, 1993; Isaievych & Lytvyn, 1996; Hrystak, 2000) and is one of the centers for pro-European Union protests and rallies (Tsentr Doslidzhennya Suspil'stva, 2014). Most recently, when Ukraine debated submitting a bid to join the European Union in 2013, Lviv was one of the largest centers of activist movement, along with the Ukrainian capital city Kyiv.

The official language of Ukraine is Ukrainian, and the country has been actively instituting Ukrainization policies since its independence in 1991, in an effort to reverse Soviet Russification policies and reclaim Ukrainian as a nationally used language. The Ukrainian language, and bilingualism in Ukrainian and Russian, is now widespread throughout the country. A large-scale survey conducted by Ukrainian linguist Masenko (2009) found that when Ukrainians were asked about their "mother tongue," 55.5% of respondents said Ukrainian, 32.0% said Russian, and 11.1% said they were natively bilingual in Ukrainian and Russian. However, the number of people who claim Ukrainian as their preferred language is significantly higher in Western Ukraine than in other parts of the country. In Western oblasts (the term used for administrative regions in certain states of the former Soviet Union), residents are instructed in the Ukrainian language as much as 99.9% of the time, while this number dips to as little as 2% of the time in some southeastern oblasts (Bilaniuk & Melnyk, 2008: 79).

Furthermore, due to historical and current sociopolitical tensions between Ukraine and Russia (and formerly the Soviet Union), language of choice and use in Ukraine often carries significant weight (Bilaniuk, 2005; Csernicskó, 2017; Himka, 2015; Kohut, 2011; Seals, 2019). Language politics have been utilized by politicians to sway public opinion one way or another (Csernicskó, 2017; Osnach, 2015), such as the example of a billboard campaign during the 2007 parliamentary elections, which read, "Вода. Дороги. Язык. [Water. Roads. Language.]", a list of essentials that highlights the political centrality of language to the debate (Kovalçhuk, 2009). These language politics were also a major part of the Euromaidan protests in Ukraine 2013–14, during which time Ukrainians protested against alignment with Russia and in favor of joining the European Union (cf. Csernicskó, 2017; Seals, 2019). As reported by Csernicskó (2017), language choice and use was so contentious that people were recorded as calling

Ukrainians who spoke Russian "traitors" (p. 123). This historical and sociopolitical background provides the context in which the Lviv linguistic landscape data are analyzed.

Methods

Both researchers used similar methodologies for collecting and analyzing the data. In terms of data collection, both researchers undertook linguistic landscape data collection within an ethnographic framework. The researchers were familiar with the history (past and recent) of the respective sites and were staying in each respective city for an extended period of time in the second half of 2017. Understanding past history and recent events is crucial for being able to interpret the findings in a contextually appropriate diachronic way (Abdelhay, Ahmed, & Mohamed, 2016; O'Connor & Zentz, 2016; Pavlenko, 2010). Therefore, both researchers actively engaged with current events in each city and country, as well as regularly talking with locals about current and past events that have/had importance for each city. For example, in Lviv, locals drew attention to the importance of Lviv's shared history with other parts of Western Ukraine and parts of Eastern Poland, as well as the strong support found within the city for joining the European Union. In Göttingen, they reminisced about the legacy of student protests dating back to the 1970s, as well as life on the border with East Germany, while describing the remnants of the Cold War infrastructure there. They also shared pointed information about which businesses in town were seen as Nazi collaborators during the Second World War and told stories about the different anarchist squats on the edge of the city center.

When collecting the data, the first author (in Lviv) made use of the same experiential data collection techniques as described in Seals (2017). That is, she walked around the city taking constant photos and videos at eye level in an attempt to capture her own visual experience of "walking the city" (Trumper-Hecht, 2010). This resulted in a total of 104 photographs and 15 minutes of video recording. All images and video data were coded according to the following:

- language(s) present,
- layout of language(s),
- perceived intended audience,
- author/artist of message (if information is available),
- official/unofficial status (e.g., government-approved sign vs. graffiti),
- type(s) of message(s) being conveyed (e.g., informational, directional, political, etc.),
- tone(s) of message(s) being conveyed (e.g., humorous, serious, frustrated, informative, etc.),
- location of message (lamppost, ground, historical building wall, window, car, etc.),
- any interaction(s) with other aspects of the linguistic landscape,
- modality/ies, and
- any contextually specific aspects of note.

Based on the frequency and co-occurrence of coded items, themes emerged from the data. These themes, such as "activist graffiti," became the basis of the findings.

Additionally, the photographs were presented to approximately forty students and staff members at Kyiv National Linguistic University and approximately fifty students and staff members at University of Warsaw for a workshop in each place at the end of 2017 on linguistic landscapes. Participants of both workshops were asked to analyze the photographs and report their observations and findings verbally to the researcher and other participants at the end of the workshop. The observations from both workshops served as additional contextual data for the analysis of the linguistic landscape of Lviv,[1] as well as providing researcher triangulation.

For the second author's data collection (in Göttingen), the walking approach was also used over the course of several months, with hundreds of photographs taken and notated for their location, context, and content. At the most concentrated point of grassroots signage, along Lange-Geismar-Straße and Mauerstraße, the second author walked up and down the streets, mapping and counting/categorizing types of every visible text created by an independent, unofficial actor (e.g., sticker, flyer, graffiti, etc.). As an indicator of the density in this area, they counted the number of discrete surfaces used for bottom-up signage along these four blocks: ninety-eight drainpipes, twenty-four streetlamps, twenty-five street signs, and forty-five other infrastructural features (e.g., electrical junction boxes, bicycle racks, posts, etc.). Out of this total, only twelve drainpipes, six street signs, and three other surfaces had *no* texts affixed to them; every street lamp in the survey had at least one. In many cases, surfaces were entirely covered with stickers and the like. The author then analyzed the data with a combination of content analysis and semiotics, as informed by Scollon and Scollon's (2003) schema of *discourses in place*. Each surface is considered for the meaning it brings to the location, in addition to the medium of the sign, and its content, forming a layered discursive whole that, in the aggregate, presents an impression to occupants of what the city's landscape is like. These data were presented in a workshop session at the Max Planck Institute for Religious and Ethnic Diversity in November 2017.

Following each independent analysis, the authors discussed similarities and differences found in the linguistic landscapes of Göttingen and Lviv. Both authors were struck by the amount of activism present in the linguistic landscapes of each place, as well as the inclusion of contextually specific history into these activist messages. Additionally, the authors were intrigued by the use of activist messages in the linguistic landscape to engage and teach passersby about past and current concerns for each city. Based on this co-analysis of themes found in both the Göttingen and Lviv data, the following salient themes emerged in conjunction with activist teaching in the linguistic landscape and thus become the focus of our findings: (1) the somewhat global tactic of utilizing spray-painted graffiti and Banksy-style spray-painted stencils to provide short commentary about social issues; (2) vinyl stickers on walls and lampposts of the type common in urban centers to relay short directed slogans and statements; and (3) an activist contribution to the LL reflective of each city's own history and populace. Namely, the Göttingen activists used flags and banners with tailored messages of social change, while Lviv activists painted poetic murals drawing upon historical poetry by pro-Ukrainian literary activists. These findings are discussed in turn below.

Findings

Spray-Painted Graffiti and Bansky-Style Stencils

Göttingen

Much of the graffiti in Göttingen is what one would typically see in any urban area: a combination of tags, activist slogans (including the occasional use of other languages such as "FUCK COPS" emblazoned in a pedestrian tunnel near the train station), and artwork. However, more elaborate stencils and complex texts occasionally appear in the landscape, providing richer material to analyze. The example we have chosen here reflects this latter tendency.

The observer's eye is immediately caught by two features: the large amount of text and the stencil of a young girl with her face obscured and holding a burning object, perhaps a Molotov cocktail ready to throw. The photographic level of detail, coupled with the subversion of expectations about the subject of the image, is indicative of street art undergoing the "Banksy effect," an homage to that artist's style and sociopolitical commentary that has become internationally popular among activists (DeTurk, 2015). The splash of color from the flame stands out, along with the stark use of red and black against the pale cement wall. In accordance with theories about the impact of multimodality (Jewitt et al., 2016), the contrast is itself meaningful, as it demands attention and triggers cultural associations: red for anger and passion, and red and black together as symbols of anti-fascism.

On either side of the girl, two texts elaborate on her message. The left side is rendered as a speech balloon; she is stating, with Z's in place of S's, "STOPPT ZEXIZMUZ RAZZIZMUZ ... POLIZEIGEWALT! [STOP SEXISM RACISM ... POLICE BRUTALITY!]."[2] A bit further in the mini-manifesto, the text becomes multilingual, with the words "NO JUSTICE NO PEACE" appearing. She finishes with "VERTEIDIGEN!," a call to stand up. On the right side, the text "VOM 30.6.17 BIS ZUM [FROM 30 JUNE 2017 UNTIL ...]" is followed by the hammer-and-sickle symbol of communism. This references the date of the summer protest when the graffiti was created and the unknown time in the future when the artist's political ideology will take hold.

In the photo, two windows are visible above the framing texts, indicating the height at which this sign was placed; the girl is roughly life-sized and only slightly elevated off the ground. The building itself is a residential one in the city center and was populated at the time with many student activists. However, without that foreknowledge, a passerby might see this as a violation of private property—until they saw that in many of the windows, there were banners displaying similar texts and flyers covering the back entrance. The semiotic transformation of place occurring here is twofold. A simple, relatively featureless wall becomes a gallery, and the neutrality of an anonymous building is recoded as politically left-leaning. Among the many reasons for putting texts into public view, this one simultaneously raises visibility for the producer's message, claims space, and memorializes its own creation, becoming announcement, speech act, and monument all at once.

184 Linguistic Landscapes Beyond the Language Classroom

Figure 9.1 Graffiti on the walls of Göttingen (left) and Lviv (right)

Lviv

Like Göttingen, much of the graffiti found in Lviv is also the type found in urban centers around the world. Tagging with artistic signatures as well as quickly painted messages of varying types are found on most streets around the city, particularly noticeable in the city center where it stands in stark contrast to the historic buildings, some of which are several hundred years old. Additionally, much of the graffiti in Lviv is dialogic in character, with individuals modifying and responding to earlier messages tagged in the same place, thereby creating a visible longitudinal running record of discourses.

Interestingly, it is also not uncommon to find quotations from famous individuals (particularly including those in Ukrainian and/or English) as part of the graffiti landscape. One such example appears on the right of Figure 9.1. On one of the walls in Lviv's city center, the linguistic landscape is focused on a tagged quote by prolific Ukrainian writer, translator, and researcher Yuri Pokalchuk. The text of the quote is translated into English below:

To love as to breathe
Simply to live
Beyond the rules
And the universe
Simply to love
This means to live.

—Y. Pokalchuk

The quote itself is an artistic elaboration upon the statement "love is life."[3] This is not surprising, as Pokalchuk was known for writing about love and was also known for being quite expressive in his work and life (Volyn, 2019). However, the fact that a graffiti artist has chosen this message to adorn the side of a building in the city center also means that it is a message meant to be read and to resonate with passersby. Additionally, the message is written in Ukrainian and features a writer largely known only in Ukrainian- and Spanish-speaking countries (Volyn, 2019). Therefore, the intended audience is Ukrainians (including residents of the city), and not likely tourists. This message of love being life, then, is a message for Ukrainians from another speaker of Ukrainian, which can also be understood as a call for brotherhood and peace.

By signing Pokalchuk's name at the end of the quote, the graffiti artist also accomplishes several more things. First, this brings a sense of legitimacy as well as adding further edginess to the graffiti, as these words come from a respected cult Ukrainian writer. Second, "ownership" of the words, and peripherally responsibility for the graffiti, falls to the famous writer instead of the graffiti artist. This alleviates the sense of trespassing made by the graffiti and instead asks passersby to focus on the message. Third, the text is heteroglossic, as Pokalchuk's voice is brought to the forefront through his words and through the attribution of his name. This is meaningful because it then associates this piece of graffiti with the memories people have of Pokalchuk (he died of cancer in 2008) and of the high energy he was known to have. The words thus take on an emotional, living message, adding to the culture on display in the linguistic landscape. Finally, the graffiti artist draws attention to Pokalchuk so that anyone unfamiliar with his work but intrigued by his words will be able to learn more about him. For example, the first author did not actually know about Pokalchuk before stumbling upon this piece in the streets of Lviv. However, after finding it, she learned much about this writer of seventeen books who spoke eleven languages and performed his work to the musical backing of a band (Volyn, 2019). Therefore, the goal of many in Lviv to keep Ukrainian language, culture, and history alive found its mark through this piece of graffiti in the city streets.

Vinyl Stickers

Göttingen

As types of media go, stickers are a popular choice for activists, as they are easily and cheaply reproducible, more durable and colorful than paper, harder to remove from surfaces, and often anonymous (Vigsø, 2010). Like graffiti, they are popular in cities around the world, though in some locales more than others. Downtown Göttingen is no exception; they were by far the most common format in which activist messaging was presented, both in the city's commercial district at large and in the more focused blocks where the second author conducted the exhaustive count of marked surfaces.

The example given here comes from a municipal street sign in the downtown's pedestrian-only core, quite close to the town hall and the iconic "Gänseliesel" statue. The sign is an official placard from the EU, whose translation states, "The 'Development of Weender Straße, Markt and Kornmarkt' Project [referring to the main shopping streets] was supported by means of the European fund for regional development." On the right is a logo with the words "Europa fördert Niedersachsen," meaning "Europe supports Lower Saxony." The positioning of the sign above eye level, its high production value, and its metal construction all suggest a level of economic capital behind its manufacture, indexing the authority of the figure(s) who created it. Most top-down signs follow this same pattern, with the material semiotics imbricating additional meaning into the actual content.

On the left side, however, the European Union flag has been covered by a sticker, placed by an enterprising (and presumably agile) individual or group. The sticker reads, "ÜBERALL POLIZEI, NIRGENDWO GERECHTIGKEIT [POLICE EVERYWHERE, JUSTICE NOWHERE]." Underneath, it states, "Wir lassen uns nichts mehr von Loch gefallen [We're not putting up with anything anymore]." While the original sign features images, they are stylized logos; the sticker uses a blue-tinted photo as its backdrop, depicting a line of riot police. The fact that the sticker almost completely covers the flag's circlet of stars, and blends in to the dark blue background, allows it to go almost unnoticed at first, until the observer pauses and looks again. Perhaps this more subtle placement (not to mention the fact that it is difficult to reach without a ladder) allows the activist message to remain a part of public LL for a longer period of time. Graffiti's drawback is that it is so immediately noticeable, and widely considered a public nuisance, that any message it conveys will be both overshadowed by the practice itself and quickly earmarked for removal. A sticker that indexes the same political stance, however, is almost polite and unobtrusive in its simplicity, at least until one is faced with the task of trying to scrape it off.

Regardless, there is a similar intention behind both forms of media: the insertion of a call to action into the landscape, as integrated as the surfaces onto which they are affixed. And the same themes repeat throughout the left-wing messaging that one

Figure 9.2 Some of many stickers found in the streets of Göttingen (left) and Lviv (right)

sees throughout Göttingen: raising awareness about systemic social injustice, resisting police and the carceral state, imploring readers to be environmentally conscious (with callbacks to the German nuclear protests of the 1970s and 1980s), and so on.

Lviv

Lviv also had a plethora of stickers on public surfaces throughout the city at the time of data collection. In the case of the sticker above that we focus on for Lviv (above, right), the social issue being addressed is that of pension reform. Pension reform has been a major issue of social and political discussion in Ukraine during the past three years, with divided opinions. The pension reform proposed in 2017 by the Ukrainian parliament involved raising the number of years of required service in the workforce before an individual could access a governmental pension. This effectively meant that the age at which people could access their pension would also go up. Additionally, the proposal for this reform stated that the years of service would also continue to raise every few years. However in January 2020, the Constitutional Court of Ukraine declared that such a change in requirements for accessing a pension was unconstitutional for several categories of workers, including those who work in hard labor or dangerous conditions.

As the above photo was taken toward the end of 2017, the debates around the proposed pension reform were in full swing. The sticker states, "It's not permissible to raise the age of retirement nor seniority [years of service]."[4] This statement carries with it the echoes of voices and ideas that came before, both in terms of the members of parliament who proposed the reform and the many people who have contributed their own voices to the debate.

For those who might not know what is being referred to or who want to learn more, a website for the group is printed at the bottom: nationalcorps.org. This website belongs to National Corps—one of the smaller political parties of Ukraine (winning 2% of the popular vote in Ukraine's 2019 parliamentary elections), which is based in Lviv. National Corps is a Ukrainian far-right party, inspired by the more right-leaning ideas of the Ukrainian Resistance Movement. Yet it is important to not forget that while we often think of left-leaning individuals or groups when discussing activism, right-leaning individuals or groups can and do also take part in activism and activist teaching, as is the case here. When accessing National Corps' website (as listed on the sticker), there are a plethora of news items and blogs seeking to "educate" the public in social and political issues from the group's perspective.

Interestingly, a passerby has attempted to remove the sticker from the light pole. As seen in the photo, the part most successfully removed is that with the web address, which is also the part showing the right-leaning authors of this message. If one is not familiar with the sticker in its entirety, the remaining message is one advocating against raising the age and service requirements for pensioners, while removing any association with National Corps. Therefore, this act of partial removal carries with it its own message of resistance to right-leaning politics, while not necessarily acting against the message of rejecting the proposed age and years of service increase for pensioners. This then allows the message to support more general social concerns, such as workers' rights and the rights of the elderly, making it resonate across international activist voices.

Providing a Voice to Local History

In addition to considering trends common across the activist LL of both cities (and indeed how these reflect global urban trends), we must also consider the local. In the sections below, we focus on the instances of activist teaching in the linguistic landscape that are reflective of each city's respective local history.

Flags in Göttingen

The flag or banner as a medium features several semiotic advantages for the display of activist messaging. While they do not have the lasting durability of stone or metal, they are much more resistant than paper or cardboard; they display a medium amount of authority that stems from the relative effort that goes into their creation. Beyond their color and image content, they are eye-catching by virtue of their size and constant mobility in the wind. As an added bonus, they are portable and can be easily rehung in different spaces. Finally, flags at the national or regional level are emblematic of political structures that can easily be indexed and altered to produce recognizable satire or commentary (e.g., US flags that are given rainbow stripes for Gay Pride celebrations).

As stated earlier, Rote Straße in Göttingen has a particularly strong tradition of activist and anarchist occupation. A stretch of historical houses along the route was scheduled for demolition in the 1970s, but plans were scrapped when the residents refused to leave, banding together to create a collective that has occupied the street ever since. While the buildings are now in a state of disrepair, they remain a local symbol and model for communal living for similar housing projects elsewhere in the city (RSG, n.d.). During the second author's time in Göttingen, the street itself was undergoing construction work, creating some tension between these residents and the city. Banners were hung featuring slogans like "ROTE STRASSE BLEIBT [RED STREET REMAINS]," also seen on stickers and flyers around the city, and "WIR BLEIBEN ALLE! [WE ARE ALL STAYING!]." Occasional protests, and gatherings like "Strassenfest," highlighted the unique history and culture of the street. Even the local café, Dabis, became part of the narrative, with its own beloved banner stating "Keine Kulturkampf ohne Kaffeedampf [No culture war without coffee steam]."

The left of the photo below shows the central building of the housing collective, with a high density of signage—and in particular flags—on its façade. In the top-floor windows, the red-and-black flags reference the Antifa (anti-fascist) movement, while below them is draped a banner that calls for "FREIHEIT FÜR ALLE [FREEDOM FOR ALL]" against a background of silhouetted prisoners. On the right side, a young woman makes a peace sign in front of a red star, symbol of communist ideology; below her, between the center windows, hang pennants with red stars on green and yellow backgrounds. Just above the main door, the comparatively plain "HANDY BLEIBT [CELLPHONE REMAINS]" banner indexes both the language of the street that centers around the German verb *bleiben* and the iconicity of wireless media via the antenna symbol. (The sentence underneath asserts that their media will not be banned.) Finally, the main door is papered with black-on-red flyers that say, "ANTIFA AREA"; these can also be found throughout the city, as paper is perhaps the most reproducible medium of all. Other flyers commemorate past and future actions in the city, while even at this tight resolution, the image clearly shows a vast array of stickers on the doorways and a bit of graffiti on its foundation.

The contrast between the older building surface and the modern materials draped on it, with their contemporary messaging, is similar to the graffiti example given above. At a broader level of discourse, one could read the material symbolism as the new and radical challenging the old and conservative, or the mutable flags overlaying the unchanging stone. Drilling down, these dichotomies reflect the politics of the nation, the state of Lower Saxony, and the city of Göttingen itself; at the most geographically confined level of discourse, they are a celebration of the specific politics of this one street. How much education the viewer receives is dependent on how much knowledge they have about each of these discursive layers, but regardless, the flags and flyers—like the other messaging posted by activists around the city—transmit information about that political struggle itself and the delineation of space between the parties involved.

Poetry in Lviv

As previously mentioned, Lviv is known as the cultural and educational capital of Ukraine. It has also historically been the home to the Ukrainian Resistance Movement. As such, many Ukrainians who are living in Lviv feel a strongly positive Ukrainian identity and take part in efforts to preserve and promote Ukrainian culture and language. While some attempts at this take a more right-leaning approach (such as

Figure 9.3 Local flags hung from buildings in Göttingen and poetry mural in Lviv

National Corps, discussed above), most other groups have a much more left-leaning style. One group of local activists who have been taking part in cultural and linguistic efforts since 2006 is the NGO "Granite." Granite states that their mission is "to work for the good of the country," and they do this through lectures, master classes, volunteering at orphanages, "Вірші на стінах" (poetry murals), and "патріотичні графіті" (patriotic graffiti).[5] Poetry murals are particularly interesting and fit well within the culture and history of Lviv, given their multiple layers of artistic application. Additionally, murals are considered by many across societies to be artistically pleasing and are therefore more likely to withstand the test of time than is graffiti (whether or not the murals are formally sanctioned by local government).

One of the poetry murals that Granite had finished shortly before data collection was that shown on the right of Figure 9.3. The artistry of the mural is immediately noticeable, as it has been placed inside a historical alcove, therein "framing" the mural as one would see in a gallery. This adds to the sense of institutional legitimacy (connecting with the idea of a gallery) and also creates a semiotic bridge between the historical building and the new mural on its façade. Written originally by Lesya Ukrainka in 1897, the poem above can be translated into the following in English:[6]

Do not reproach the word I gave
And in reply to this difficult resolution
You gave a sharp twig of thorns,
Without fear I wove it into a crown.
Sharper became my crown of thorns ...
No matter, I knew you! And yet, as I accepted
From you came a weapon that shone silver,
I took a ruthless blade in my heart.
Now I regret neither pain nor blood,
I am ready to accept, along with pain, and thorns
For idle dreams, for sacred dreams
Pure brotherhood and love.

The above poem connects with several social issues as well as educating the public in several ways. First, the message of the poem has to do with betrayal that is accepted in the name of brotherhood and love. This message echoes discourses of betrayal of Ukrainians by Russians via the war taking place in Eastern Ukraine between Ukrainians and Russian-supported pro-Russian separatists (see Seals, 2019, for a full discussion of this and further discursive examples from interviews). This message is therefore polyphonous in the many voices it carries with it and heteroglossic in that it is drawing upon this recent event to imbue the poem with an additional layer of meaning. Additionally, the message of brotherhood and love is one that has been a major focus of activist dialogues in Ukraine, many of which the first author saw in Western Ukraine when she was there in 2017. Therefore, this is also consistent with the region and responds dialogically both to those in favor of and against such an approach to society.

Educationally, Granite embraced Lviv's cultural capital status to familiarize passersby with one of Lesya Ukrainka's lesser-known poems. Additionally, while

Ukrainka is a well-known Ukrainian poet, she is not known to all, and efforts have been made in recent years in Ukraine and in diaspora communities to further raise awareness of her life and work. Finally, an additional clue to Granite's educational intention can be found in the comments section on one of their Facebook posts relating to this poetry mural, where a member of Granite asked who is ready to take on the challenge of this poem.[7] As this poem is from 1897, it features a much older variety of Ukrainian that is considered by many in modern-day Ukraine to be difficult to read and to understand (both aurally and visually) (cf. Del'Gaudio, 2018; Seals, 2014, 2019). By encouraging people to engage with an older form of the Ukrainian language, Granite is furthering their mission of cultural and linguistic preservation and education.

Concluding Discussion

Göttingen and Lviv each have their own unique histories which have influenced the cultures, politics, and landscapes of each place; this coexists with their shared identity as Central/Eastern European cities both affected by the Second World War. There are also trends found in the LL of both cities that reflect their status as long-established urban spaces. While some of these latter commonalities can be found in urban centers around the world (such as the frequent presence of graffiti and vinyl stickers to convey sentiments and messages to the public), we discuss here that it is not enough to simply look at each city as an urban center. To truly understand the LL of each place, we must also consider where the local becomes visible, and we must use our contextual knowledge of each place to interpret the associated meanings of the local alongside the global.

Furthermore, as we have shown throughout this chapter, both the global and the local elements of the LL allow activists to educate passersby about contemporary social and political issues. This education may be directed to locals of the region (such as the messages written exclusively in German or Ukrainian, respectively) and/or may draw on recognizable semiotic resources that can be decoded by non-locals as well, such as the use of multimodality (e.g., the Bansky-style images, bright colors, and gallery format), or largely universal textual characters might be used (such as internet addresses, as discussed with Figure 9.2).

Additionally, the structures of dialogism, polyphony, and heteroglossia play a major role in the attempt to educate passersby. Activist messages in the LL largely rely on the power of drawing upon multiple voices and discourses, as they have limited space in which to engage the public and make an impact. For example, the messages displayed in Figure 9.3 require that viewers/readers know the underlying context of the messages being conveyed, which also requires a knowledge of local/regional history and events. However, if the viewers/readers do have this knowledge, then an entire extensive conversation is accessed through these relatively small parts of the LL. Alternatively, if the viewers/readers are unfamiliar with the necessary context, these aspects of the LL provide talking points from which people can access further information by asking locals. Therefore, these elements of the LL provide entry portals into the rich totality of local/regional history, politics, and social concerns.

This chapter has provided a brief contribution to research examining how activist teaching of the public occurs in and through the LL. Our hope is that this heretofore sparse area of research will become of interest to many, lighting sparks of interest that will lead to a much greater understanding of ways that activists can and do educate others.

Notes

1. Linguistic landscapes data from Lviv, Kyiv, Warsaw, and Krakow were discussed in these workshops, but only the Lviv data are being discussed in the current chapter.
2. Ukrainian translations are by the first author; German translations are by the second author.
3. Thank you to Tetyana Sanders for consultation on this quotation.
4. Translation by first author.
5. "Granite's mission statement." https://www.facebook.com/pg/mo.granit/about/?ref=page_internal
6. Translation by the first author.
7. No link is given in order to protect the anonymity of the poster and responders.

References

Abdelhay, A., Ahmed, M., & Mohamed, E. (2016). The semiotic landscaping of heritage: Al-Mantiqa al-Tarikhiyya in Jeddah. *Linguistic Landscape*, 2(1), 52–79.

Aboelezz, M. (2016). The geosemiotics of Tahrir Square: A study of the relationship between discourse and space. In L. Martin Rojo (Ed.), *Occupy: The Spatial Dynamics of Discourse in Global Protest Movements* (pp. 23–46). Philadelphia: John Benjamins.

Anfinson, A. (2020). Hong Kong's Paper Cities: Heterotopia and the semiotic landscape of civil disobedience. In D. Malinowski & S. Tufi (Eds.), *Reterritorializing Linguistic Landscapes: Questioning Boundaries and Opening Spaces* (pp. 137–59). London: Bloomsbury.

Bakhtin, M. (1984). *Problems of Dostoevsky's Poetics*. Minneapolis, MN: University of Minnesota Press.

Bakhtin, M. (1992). *The Dialogic Imagination: Four Essays*. Austin, TX: University of Austin Press.

Barni, M., & Bagna, C. (2016). 1 March—'A day without immigrants': The urban linguistic landscape of the immigrants' protest. In R. Blackwood, E. Lanza, & H. Woldemariam (Eds.), *Negotiating and Contesting Identities in Linguistic Landscapes* (pp. 55–70). London: Bloomsbury.

Bilaniuk, L. (2005). *Contested Tongues: Language Politics and Cultural Correction in Ukraine*. Ithaca, NY: Cornell University Press.

Bilaniuk, L., & Melnyk, S. (2008). A tense and shifting balance: Bilingualism and education in Ukraine. In A. Pavlenko (Ed.), *Multilingualism in Post-Soviet Countries* (pp. 66–98). Buffalo, NY: Multilingual Matters.

Cerimaj, N., Milani, T. M., & Kitis, E. D. (2020). The semiotics of spatial turbulence: Re/deterritorializing Israel-Palatine at a South African University. In D. Malinowski & S. Tufi (Eds.), *Reterritorializing Linguistic Landscapes: Questioning Boundaries and Opening Spaces* (pp. 96–116). London: Bloomsbury.

Chesnut, M., Lee, V., Schulte, J. (2013). The language lessons around us: Undergraduate English pedagogy and linguistic landscape research. *English Teaching*, 12(2), 102-20.
Coulmas, F. (2009). Linguistic landscaping and the seed of the public sphere. In E. Shohamy & D. Gorter (Eds.), *Linguistic Landscape: Expanding the Scenery* (pp. 13-24). New York: Routledge.
Csernicskó, I. (2017). Language policy in Ukraine: The burdens of the past and the possibilities of the future. In S. E. Pfenninger & J. Navracsics (Eds.), *Future Research Directions for Applied Linguistics* (pp. 120-48). Bristol: Multilingual Matters.
DeTurk, S. (2015). The "Banksy Effect" and street art in the Middle East. *Street Art and Urban Creativity Scientific Journal*, 1(2), 22-30.
Del' Gaudio, S. (2018). *An Introduction to Ukrainian Dialectology*. Frankfurt: Peter Lang.
Ewald, W. (October 25, 2019). Göttingen, 1987. *The Pennsylvania Gazette*. Retrieved from https://thepenngazette.com/gottingen-1987/.
Fäßler, P., Held, T., & D. Sawitzki (Eds.). (1993). *Lemberg, Lwów, Lviv. Eine Stadt im Schnittpunkt europäischer Kulturen*. Köln: Böhlau.
Figol, A., Kubijovyč, V., & A. Zhukovsky. (2016). Lviv. *Енциклопедія України в Інтернеті*. http://www.encyclopediaofukraine.com/display.asp?linkpath=pages%5CL%5CV%5CLviv.htm
Hanauer, D. (2011). The discursive construction of the separation wall at Abu Dis: Graffiti as political discourse. *Journal of Language and Politics*, 10(3), 301-21.
Hanauer, D. I. (2012). Transitory linguistic landscapes as political discourse: Signage at three demonstrations in Pittsburgh, USA. In C. Helot, M. Barni, R. Janssens, & C. Bagna (Eds.), *Linguistic Landscapes, Multilingualism, and Social Change* (pp. 139-54). New York: Peter Lang.
Hanauer, D. I. (2015). Occupy Baltimore: A linguistic landscape analysis of participatory social contestation in an American city. In R. Rubdy & S. Ben Said (Eds.), *Conflict, Exclusion and Dissent in the Linguistic Landscape* (pp. 207-22). New York: Palgrave Macmillan.
Himka, J. P. (2015). The History behind the regional conflict in Ukraine. *Kritika: Explorations in Russian and Eurasian History*, 16(1), 129-36.
Hrytsak, Y. (2000). Lviv: A city in the crosscurrents of culture. *Harvard Ukrainian Studies*, 24, 47-73.
Imhoof, D. (2013). *Becoming a Nazi Town: Culture and Politics in Göttingen between the World Wars*. Ann Arbor, MI: University of Michigan Press.
Isaievych, F. S., & M. Lytvyn (Eds.). (1996). *L'viv. Istorychni narysy*. Lviv: Instytut ukraynoznavstva.
Jewitt, C., Bezemer, J., & O'Halloran, K. (2016). *Introducing Multimodality*. New York: Routledge.
Katz, B. Noring, L., & Garrelts, N. (2016). *Cities and Refugees: The German Experience*. Washington, DC: The Brookings Institution.
Kohut, Z. E. (2011). *Making Ukraine: Studies on Political Culture, Historical Narrative, and Identity*. Toronto, Canada: Canadian Institute of Ukrainian Studies Press.
Kovalchuk, I. (November 23, 2009). Мовознавець і соціолінгвіст Лариса Масенко: «В Україні має бути українська мова». *Друг Читача* https://vsiknygy.net.ua/interview/4713/
Laubenthal, B. (2015). *Refugees Welcome? Federalism and Asylum Policies in Germany*. Fieri Working Papers.
Lee, S. (2018). The role of social media in protest participation: Case of candle light vigil in South Korea. *International Journal of Communication*, 12, 1523-40.

Machetti, S., & Pizzorusso, C. (2020). From graffiti to street art and back: Connections between past and present. In D. Malinowski & S. Tufi (Eds.), *Reterritorializing Linguistic Landscapes: Questioning Boundaries and Opening Spaces* (pp. 160–76). London: Bloomsbury.

Malinowski, D. (2015). Opening spaces of learning in the linguistic landscape. *Linguistic Landscape*, 1(1–2), 95–113.

Masenko, L. T. (2009). Language situation in Ukraine: Sociolinguistic analysis. In J. Besters-Dilger (Ed.), *Language Policy and Language Situation in Ukraine: Analysis and Recommendations* (pp. 101–38). Frankfurt: Peter Lang.

Messekher, H. (2015). A linguistic landscape analysis of the socio-political demonstrations of Algiers: A politicized landscape. In R. Rubdy & S. Ben Said (Eds.), *Conflict, Exclusion and Dissent in the Linguistic Landscape* (pp. 260–79). New York: Palgrave Macmillan.

Morris-Lange, S., & Brands, F. (2016). German universities open doors to refugees: Access barriers remain. *International Higher Education*, 84, 11–12.

O'Connor, B. H., & Zentz, L. (2016). Theorizing mobility in semiotic landscapes: Evidence from South Texas and Central Java. *Linguistic Landscape*, 2(1), 26–51.

Osnach, S. (2015). Мовна складова гібридної війни. *Пормал мовноїполітики*, June 13. http://language-policy.info/2015/06/serhij-osnach-movna-skladova-hibrydnoji-vijny/

Pavlenko, A. (2010). Linguistic landscape of Kyiv, Ukraine: A diachronic study. In E. Shohamy, E. Ben-Rafael, & M. Barni (Eds.), *Linguistic Landscape in the City* (pp. 133–52). Bristol: Multilingual Matters.

Pennycook, A. (2009). Linguistic landscapes and the transgressive semiotics of graffiti. In E. Shohamy & D. Gorter (Eds.), *Linguistic Landscape: Expanding the Scenery* (pp. 302–12). New York: Routledge.

RSG [Rote Strasse Göttingen]. (n.d.). Über uns. Retrieved from https://redstreet.noblogs.org/ueber-uns/.

Rubdy, R. (2015). A multimodal analysis of the graffiti commemorating the 26/11 Mumbai terror attacks: Constructing self-understandings of a senseless violence. In R. Rubdy & S. Ben Said (Eds.), *Conflict, Exclusion and Dissent in the Linguistic Landscape* (pp. 280–303). New York: Palgrave Macmillan.

Rupke, N. (2002). The Göttingen location. In N. Rupke (Ed.), *Göttingen and the Development of the Natural Sciences*. Göttingen: Wallstein Verlag.

Sayer, P. (2010). Using the linguistic landscape as a pedagogical resource. *ELT Journal* 64(2), 143–54.

Schaefer, S. (2018). At the frontlines of the Cold War: Border-guarding and the practices of German division. *Journal of Modern European History*, 16(1), 105–25.

Schumacher, E. (January 29, 2016). Report: Five times more attacks on refugee homes in Germany in 2015. *Deutsche Welle*. Retrieved from https://www.dw.com/en/report-five-times-more-attacks-on-refugee-homes-in-germany-in-2015/a-19011109.

Scollon, R., & S. W. Scollon. (2003). *Discourses in Place: Language in the Material World*. London: Routledge.

Seals, C. A. (2012). Creating a landscape of dissent in Washington, DC. In C. Helot, M. Barni, R. Janssens, & C. Bagna (Eds.), *Linguistic Landscapes, Multilingualism, and Social Change* (pp. 127–38). New York: Peter Lang.

Seals, C. A. (2014). *Heritage Voices: Language: Ukrainian*. Washington, DC: Alliance for the Advancement of Heritage Languages, Center for Applied Linguistics.

Seals, C. A. (2015). Overcoming Erasure: Reappropriation of space in the linguistic landscape of mass-scale protests. In R. Rubdy & S. Ben Said (Eds.), *Conflict, Exclusion and Dissent in the Linguistic Landscape* (pp. 223–8). New York: Palgrave Macmillan.

Seals, C. A. (2017). Analyzing the linguistic landscape of mass-scale events. *Linguistic Landscape*, 3(3), 267–85.

Seals, C. A. (2019). *Choosing a Mother Tongue: The Politics of Language and Identity in Ukraine*. Bristol: Multilingual Matters.

Shiri, S. (2015). Co-constructing dissent in the transient linguistic landscape: Multilingual protest signs of the Tunisian revolution. In R. Rubdy & S. Ben Said (Eds.), *Conflict, Exclusion and Dissent in the Linguistic Landscape* (pp. 239–59). New York: Palgrave Macmillan.

Steinberg, R. L. (2016). The Occupy Assembly: Discursive experiments in direct democracy. In L. Martin Rojo (Ed.), *Occupy: The Spatial Dynamics of Discourse in Global Protest Movements* (pp. 127–56). Philadelphia: John Benjamins.

Trumper-Hecht, N. (2010). Linguistic landscape in mixed cities in Israel from the perspective of "walkers": The case of Arabic. In E. Shohamy, E. Ben-Rafael, & M. Barni (Eds.), *Linguistic Landscape in the City* (pp. 235–51). Bristol: Multilingual Matters.

Tsentr Doslidzhennya Suspil'stva. (September 2014). *Чи назріває новий Майдан? Результати моніторингу протестів, репресій та поступок за серпень 2014 року*. Київ: Центром дослідження суспільства. https://cedos.org.ua/system/attachments/files/000/000/056/original/CSR_-_August_-_11_Sep_2014.pdf?1410775900

Vigsø, O. (2010). Extremist stickers: Epideictic rhetoric, political marketing, and tribal demarcation. *Journal of Visual Literacy*, 29(1), 28–46.

Volyn. (June 8, 2019). Юрко Покальчук: «Я вивертаю те, що кожен має «на споді». https://www.volyn.com.ua//news/129319-iurko-pokalchuk-ia-vyvertaiu-te-shcho-kozhen-maie-na-spodi

Weisbrod, B. (2003). The moratorium of the mandarins and the self-denazification of German Academe: A view from Göttingen. *Contemporary European History*, 12(1), 47–69.

10

Educating the Public? Affective and Epistemic Stances as Approaches to Campaigning during Ireland's Eighth Amendment Referendum

Louis Strange

Introduction

Political campaigns in the Republic of Ireland (henceforth "Ireland") play out on posters, billboards, stickers, and graffiti. In spite of the advent of online political campaigning, campaign organizations and political parties continue to spend millions communicating their message through physical signage. The linguistic landscape (LL) thus affords key insights into the discursive tactics used by such groups to argue their case.

This is particularly true of the 2018 referendum on whether to repeal the Eighth Amendment of the Irish Constitution, which enacted an almost total ban on abortion in the state. The referendum campaign was characterized by fierce debate between those in favor of liberalizing Ireland's abortion laws (i.e., repealing the Eighth Amendment) and those against. In the weeks before the vote, the issue dominated the linguistic landscape across the country, as campaign posters, leaflets, and badges were produced in a bid to persuade voters. Abortion was for many years—and arguably still is—a taboo subject in Ireland. As such, it has seldom been discussed in the public sphere—at least, until 2018. It might be expected that this would be an opportunity to disseminate information on abortion to the public as part of a voter education campaign (of sorts), particularly for those seeking to overturn the constitutional ban and destigmatize the issue. However, this is not necessarily how the campaign played out in the LL.

The concepts of epistemic and affective stances can help us theorize an educational approach—or lack thereof—to campaigning in the referendum's LL. Epistemic stance refers to how knowledge or certainty regarding a statement is represented, whereas affective stances represent emotional or affective states (Jaffe, 2009; Kiesling, 2018). I argue that those signs taking an epistemic stance adopted an educational approach to campaigning: disseminating information to the public requires signaling your degree of certainty regarding that information or authority to communicate it. An alternative approach relied on taking an affective stance, which meant setting a tone or creating a feeling around the campaign, appealing primarily to voters' emotions.

In this chapter, I will analyze stance in the linguistic landscape from a multimodal perspective, in line with Scollon and Scollon's (2003) geosemiotic framework. Drawing on a dataset including both fixed and mobile LL items (campaign posters and leaflets), in addition to interviews carried out with campaigners, I argue that the distinction between epistemic and affective stances is a useful heuristic for understanding the discursive tactics employed by different groups in the referendum campaign's LL.

First, I will give a brief overview of the background to the referendum campaign and outline my understanding of stance in the context of education and LL research, before moving on to an analysis of interview data to demonstrate the relevance of epistemic and affective stance types to the referendum campaign's LL. I will then analyze the LL data in terms of the different discursive tactics of those campaigning on either side of the debate, how stance is constructed using both linguistic and multimodal resources, variation between (and within) groups on the same side of the debate, and finally, how different stance types are used in different types of LL items.

Background to Abortion in Ireland

Abortion has been criminalized in Ireland since the Offences against the Person Act 1861. Following a 1983 referendum, an amendment acknowledging the equal right to life of "the unborn" and "the mother" was added to the Constitution of Ireland.[1] The "Eighth Amendment"—as Article 40.3.3° came to be known—effectively banned abortion in the state.[2] Over 170,000 women and pregnant people traveled to England between 1980 and 2018 to obtain a termination, with 2,879 doing so in 2018 alone, while thousands more each year ordered safe but illegal abortion pills online (Aiken, Gomperts, & Trussell, 2017; Department of Health & Social Care, 2019; IFPA, n.d.).[3] In 2012, seventeen-week pregnant Savita Halappanavar died from septicemia at University Hospital Galway after being denied a termination; her death prompted a renewed push for legalization of abortion in Ireland and she became a symbol of the abortion rights movement. In response to Halappanavar's death, legislation (the Protection of Life during Pregnancy Act 2013) was passed allowing for terminations to be carried out in very limited circumstances, yet the constitutional question remained unresolved and this movement gained momentum. The annual March for Choice held in September 2017 was attended by 40,000 people, up from 5,000 in 2014 (Holland, 2014; RTÉ, 2017). That same month, Taoiseach (Irish prime minister) Leo Varadkar announced that a referendum on the issue was planned for May or June the following year ("Vote on abortion laws among seven planned referendums," 2017). In March 2018, a Referendum Commission was established to oversee campaigning and the Referendum Bill passed through the Oireachtas (parliament of the Republic of Ireland), setting the date for the referendum as May 25, 2018. Early March to late May 2018 saw the most intense period of campaigning. The final result of the referendum was 66.4 percent in favor of repealing the Eighth Amendment ("Yes"), 33.6 percent against ("No") (Referendum Commission, 2018).

It is important to highlight the scale of campaigning in the LL leading up to the vote, when campaign posters lined the streets of practically every town and city in Ireland. Together for Yes, the umbrella organization representing a coalition of groups backing a "Yes" vote to repeal the Eighth Amendment, crowdfunded over €500,000 in a matter of days to fund their poster campaign; with each poster costing €10, this translates into more than 50,000 posters (Hosford, 2018). Rival campaign group Save the 8th, opposed to abortion and campaigning for a "No" vote in the referendum, raised €400,000 (Hosford, 2018). The fact that two campaign groups alone—albeit major ones—would have produced potentially hundreds of thousands of campaign posters indicates the impact on the LL which the campaign had. Yet only 10 percent of voters claimed that campaign posters influenced their vote in the referendum (RTÉ & Behaviour & Attitudes Exit Poll, 2018). In fact, a poll in the lead-up to the referendum indicated that a strong majority (74 percent) of the public were in favor of banning posters altogether (Ní Aodha, 2018). That said, the analysis presented here is not primarily concerned with the impact of the linguistic landscape on voting patterns, as the question of the efficacy of campaign posters is beyond the scope of this chapter. Instead, I focus on the discursive tactics used to convince voters. From this perspective, the LL can provide valuable insights into the specific ways in which voters are "interpellated" (Milani, 2014).

In terms of existing research on abortion and education in Ireland, McDonald et al. (2020) have argued that door-to-door canvassing during the referendum campaign can be viewed as a form of "feminist pedagogy," whereby both campaigners and the voting public who they spoke to on the doors were engaged in a process of learning. NicGhabhann (2018) offers an overview of various creative strategies (including public performance, direct action, and signage) used by pro-repeal groups between 2015 and 2017, arguing that the campaign for abortion rights should be understood as part of the rich Irish tradition of political satire. This chapter, focusing on signage from both pro- and anti-repeal groups during the weeks before the vote in 2018, aims to provide a new perspective on the referendum campaign which might complement this research.

Stance, Education, and Linguistic Landscape Research

In its simplest terms, stancetaking means "taking up a position with respect to the form or the content of one's utterance" (Jaffe, 2009: 3). Stancetaking can be further broken down into affective and epistemic stance types: affective stances "represent emotional states of the speaker," while epistemic stances "convey speakers' degree of certainty about their propositions" (Jaffe, 2009: 7).[4] However, several authors have questioned the utility of the concepts of affective and epistemic stance. Du Bois (2007) points out the theoretical limitations of elaborating a (potentially ever-expanding) typology of different stance types. Stance is more than just a question of epistemic and affective stance(s): for example, interpersonal stance is often included alongside epistemic and affective stances in a tripartite distinction (Kiesling, 2018). In fact, Kiesling (2018: 197) admits to being "sceptical of the notion of affect as useful for analysis" of linguistic form altogether, locating stancetaking in the "text" and affect in "actual individuals" so that "stancetaking is an imaginary that stimulates authentic affective responses in all language users" (2018: 200). Preferring the term "investment" to "affect," Kiesling argues that an "affect of emotionlessness or, in [his] terms, lack of investment" (2018: 205) contributes to the construction of a persona of masculine ease among members of an American fraternity. But in the context of as highly charged and politically significant a debate as that surrounding the issue of abortion, it often makes little sense to distinguish between LL items on the basis of investment. To characterize campaign posters demanding your vote as lacking in investment offers less explanatory power than an analysis according to *how* they employ this investment, particularly when groups and individuals have invested time, effort, and often significant financial resources into producing signage. While we might distinguish between graffiti and professionally produced signage (such as official campaign posters) on the basis of the resources implicated in their production, even graffiti indexes at least a base level of investment. Therefore, I retain the distinction between affective and epistemic stance as a useful one in the context of the referendum campaign.

This binary distinction is not unproblematic, though. Lempert (2008: 570) proposes the terms "propositional" and "interactional" stance, which may be roughly equated to epistemic and affective stance, respectively, arguing that there is a "movement" from the former into the latter (in other words, it is by taking a stance with regard to the claims being made by an utterance that interactional work is carried out). Affective and epistemic stances are therefore not necessarily mutually exclusive categories. For example, Jaffe (2009: 7) contrasts the functions of affective stance, used to "lay claim to particular identities and statuses as well as evaluate others' claims and statuses," with those of epistemic stance, which "serves to establish the relative authority of interactants, and to situate the sources of that authority in a wider sociocultural field." It is not difficult to imagine the functions of laying claim to identities and establishing authority as merging into one another, particularly if an identity is based on authority. Thus, it is often untenable to strictly separate affective and epistemic stance and isolate their respective functions. Nor should we conceptualize affective and epistemic stance as two opposing poles of a single scale: Du Bois (2007) notes that speakers can position themselves along both affective and epistemic scales by communicating greater or lesser emotional investment or certainty with regard to their talk. Fundamentally, while it may not be possible (or, indeed, desirable) to draw a hard-and-fast line between these two stance types, affective and epistemic stance may be viewed as a useful heuristic or tool for identifying two broadly distinct approaches to campaigning in the LL.

There has been relatively little theoretical engagement with stance in the LL literature. Screti (2018) demonstrates how orthographic choices in Galician signage index particular "glottopolitical stances," language ideologies linked to specific political positions. While this chapter will also address the interplay of stance, linguistic (or, more broadly, semiotic) resources, and political positions, I argue that there is not necessarily a fixed relationship between linguistic form (in this case, stance type) and a given political position, thus allowing for two different groups to adopt broadly similar positions on the issue of abortion (for example, both campaigning for a "Yes" vote) while differing when it comes to the type of stance which they adopt. Although Wee's (2016) approach to "affective regimes" in the LL brings affect into LL research without (explicitly) framing it in terms of stance, it is lurking under the surface in the characterization of affect as "a broader notion—an evaluative orientation that may or may not be identifiable via culture-specific and conventionalized emotion labels—that subsumes [emotion]" (Wee, 2016: 107). Affective regimes are conceptually useful not only in stressing that affect is a broader concept than emotion but also in thinking beyond the affective stance of an individual sign and considering the general tone being set by signage in space during the referendum campaign. While Ng (2019) focuses on how affect is used as part of corporate branding in a higher education setting, an approach to affect "as enacted in and through linguistic, visual and spatial modalities" (Ng, 2019: 122) highlights the importance of multimodal resources in constructing an identity based on affect in the semiotic/linguistic landscape, whether in the context of branding or political campaigns.

I argue that the discursive tactics of signage during the referendum campaign can be understood through the prism of education: some LL items attempted to "educate" the public by communicating information on abortion through signage, for example by presenting statistics or facts in an effort to convince voters; others sought to set a tone, appealing to affect rather than providing information.[5] The first approach relies on adopting a stance of epistemic authority—being in possession of knowledge to be disseminated to the public—whereas the second makes no claims vis-à-vis its propositional content. As signaled above, I do not mean to suggest that there is a strict separation between epistemic and affective stance; indeed, in many cases those LL items which seek to inform may do so while simultaneously appealing to emotion. Additionally, a given sign may incorporate more than one type of stance: for example, a poster or leaflet may contain multiple texts or, from a multimodal perspective, a variety of modes such as text, image, and color, all working to produce stance. I therefore take epistemic and affective stances to be broadly distinct types of stance which serve as useful tools for theorizing an educational approach to campaigning in the LL.

Data and Methods

A sign was included in this study if it met the criterion of "relating to the referendum campaign." Although most signs explicitly advocated either a "Yes" or a "No" vote, this broader definition allowed for LL items undeniably commenting on the issues involved in the referendum, albeit without necessarily "picking a side" (for example, LL items satirizing other campaign posters). I adopt Backhaus's (2007: 66) definition of a sign as "any piece of written text within a spatially definable frame." To illustrate how stance type varies according to the medium of an LL item, I follow Sebba (2010) in including both fixed and non-fixed (or "mobile") signage: this means LL items such as campaign posters and (non-mobile) stickers, but also badges, placards, wearable items, and "ephemera" such as leaflets. In this chapter, I will restrict the focus to campaign posters and leaflets; however, it is worth noting that this chapter presents only a fraction of the diversity of stances, materials, and media on display during the campaign.

Primary data collection was carried out in multiple locations in Ireland (Dublin, Dingle, Tralee, Boyle, Sligo) during the week preceding the vote (May 18–25, 2018). These locations were selected so as to cover both urban and rural settings, varying in terms of socioeconomic status and covering a wide geographic spread, including the Gaeltacht.[6] Throughout the campaign, images of signage were also collected by informants within my own social network (in addition to the locations mentioned above, this included signage from Cork, Limerick, and Greystones). Overall, the dataset for this study consisted of a set of 748 LL items, mostly campaign posters, plus a set of 14 leaflets, produced by a range of groups, which were collected during the same period of fieldwork. Following LL data collection, semi-structured interviews were carried out with members of campaign groups, covering a variety of topics related to interviewees' experiences of the referendum campaign and its LL. These interviews aimed to understand the choices made by sign-makers from an emic perspective in order to use categories of analysis relevant for campaigners when analyzing the LL data collected.

The first stage of data analysis consisted of a qualitative content analysis of interview data to uncover the socially meaningful categories for those involved in campaigning. This allowed for those themes relevant to education and to epistemic and affective stance types to be pulled out of the interview data and guide the analysis of LL data. A qualitative, multimodal analysis of the LL data was then carried out, employing Scollon and Scollon's (2003) geosemiotic framework. Geosemiotics is divided into three systems: the interaction order (the format and nature of social interaction, which in the context of this chapter means how the public engages with LL items), visual semiotics (the visually salient characteristics of signage), and place semiotics (the relevance of where in the world signage is located). Scollon and Scollon (2003) stress the multimodal nature of communication, going beyond linguistic resources alone. Unlike Kress and Van Leeuwen (1996), upon whom they base much of their own framework, Scollon and Scollon (2003) elaborate a more contextually oriented approach to communication in public space, not only through their attention to "place semiotics" but their emphasis on the need for ethnographic insights to understand what—if any—meaning these semiotic systems may have for particular communities of practice. I now turn to an analysis of interviews carried out with campaigners to demonstrate the relevance of both an educational perspective on the referendum campaign's LL and a multimodal approach.

Interview Analysis

When asked about the function and efficacy of signage, interviewees often framed these issues in terms of the use of information and educating the public. "No" campaigner Kayla stated that in their own sign-making practices, the focus was on an "educational viewpoint."[7] Mentioning that the "No" campaign was accused of presenting inaccurate information on its posters, they stated that "it was completely fact-checked, the stats were underneath it," reiterating that the posters "were all really to educate people, to really inform people." This is a point made by another "No" campaigner, Conor, for whom "perhaps the most striking thing about the rhetoric of the referendum was the language of truth and lies." They cited (what they perceived as) accusations of "lies" and "scaremongering" leveled at the "No" side, denying that the "No" side were more dishonest than the "Yes" side and, likewise, stressing that any material produced by their own group was fact-checked. This would suggest a preoccupation among "No" campaigners regarding the perception of their campaign material as accurate and thus not lacking in epistemic authority. Echoing this, "Yes" campaigner Catherine "could see the 'No' posters having more of an impact than the 'Yes' ones […], the more fact-based ones I could imagine having an impact, the statistics." In fact, Catherine even stated that they "[didn't] think anyone's mind was changed by a 'Yes' poster" and that Together for Yes "should have been a bit stronger on the facts and statistics," recalling that "any time I was on the doors [i.e. canvassing], people were starved of factual information." By contrast, "No" campaigner Elizabeth argued that "the 'No' side were on the back foot as they were trying to get information out there—people don't want that, they don't want information, nor do they want footnotes, which is a shame because you'd like to think you're in a world where people really love chewing on information." While these conflicting views demonstrate the difficulty of analyzing the effectiveness of different tactics in terms of convincing voters, they both identify the "No" side's discursive tactics as being based on the dissemination of information, facts, and statistics—in other words, an "educational approach"—which was absent from "Yes" posters.

Interviewees also spoke about the medium and design of LL items in the campaign in ways relevant to questions of education and stance type. Whether to adopt an educational approach and include more information depends on the medium of a LL item, according to Elizabeth: "People have limited attention span for banners, but people want information and expect text in leaflets." Elizabeth also believed that "the unity of the 'Yes' side was overwhelmingly powerful" in spite—or because—of there being "no footnotes, no science on any of it," and that although it was not possible to include footnotes on a badge or too much information on a banner, badges were nevertheless the most effective LL item in terms of convincing voters. "Yes" campaigner Andrew also questioned the effectiveness of posters because they "necessarily lack nuance," instead arguing that "door-to-door [canvassing] can change a lot more minds and thrash out the issue." Both Elizabeth and Andrew appear to identify differences in the effectiveness of different media based on their affordances (i.e., expectations of differing information loads depending on the type of LL item). Andrew also suggested that the design of Together for Yes posters played a role in managing or moderating affect: "[Y]ou almost had to put aside your emotions, [it's] about having a positive and warm but also grown-up attitude, reflected in the poster not being too busy and the font being quite clean." The balance between, on the one hand, "putting aside your emotions" and a "grown-up attitude" (Andrew also referred to "an adult tone" later in the interview) and, on the other hand, "positive and warm," serves as a reminder that affect is not reducible to emotion, but a distinct concept (Wee, 2016). The argument here is not necessarily that posters can be distinguished on the basis that some used more "emotion" than others, but that their discursive tactics relied on the careful management of affective tone, rather than trying to disseminate information to voters.

This positivity and warmth were interpreted differently by other campaigners, however. Kayla, for example, commented that "it was just really abortion rights from the other ['Yes'] side, it wasn't really specific" and found the "Yes" posters "quite bland, they were very fluffy, they were, I guess, quite feel good: 'care', 'compassion', the colouring." The "blandness" of "Yes" posters was a recurring theme, even among "Yes" campaigners. For Catherine, "the 'Yes' side went overboard on 'caring' and 'compassion'—it lost all meaning [...] every soundbite, every poster, every leaflet had it, I think it became tired really fast, it was like the 'strong and stable' thing [...], it just lost something."[8] Lily, a "Yes" campaigner whose group was not officially affiliated with the Together for Yes campaign, pointed to the "anodyne, middle-of-the-road use of language" by Together for Yes to appeal to a broad spectrum of Irish society, contrasting this with their own group's role, which was "to open up those itchy questions" (for example, making specific reference to the Catholic Church during the campaign). In particular, they cited the comments of TD Ruth Coppinger on the centralized campaign "blanding out the issue."[9] Where others criticized the "blandness" of the Together for Yes campaign, Andrew argued that when it came to signage the "main thing was simplicity, positivity," "never to think negatively, never to over-complicate things," and that Together for Yes posters were "very same, all the time, because you can't get this, this, this and this coming at you from different [angles]." On the other hand, the "No" side "had a real wide spread of posters, of images [...], I don't know if that felt like a bombardment, I don't know if it was good, if it was effective, I don't know."

Irrespective of individual evaluations of the effectiveness of campaign tactics, all interviewees identified differences in campaign tactics between the "Yes" and "No" sides, which can be characterized as either a more direct, information-based and educational approach or a less specific (perhaps "bland"), more tonally oriented approach; these can in turn be equated with epistemic and affective stance, respectively. Interviewees also implicitly acknowledged the role of multimodal resources in constructing these stances, as well as the factor of different media. The broad bimodal categorization of "No" signs with epistemic stance and "Yes" with affective stance is, of course, overly simplistic. However, although analyzing the referendum campaign's LL through the prism of a "Yes" vs. "No" binary is reductive and ignores significant variation among groups on the same side of the debate, interviewees' comments nonetheless suggest that the distinction between affective and epistemic stance is a relevant and useful heuristic for analyzing the LL of the referendum campaign, to which I now turn.

"Yes" vs. "No": Different Sides of the Debate, Different Types of Stance

It is not trivial that a debate about abortion—historically treated as a "private" issue—was conducted very publicly in the LL. For this reason, Scollon and Scollon's (2003) distinction between "public" and "private" spaces is relevant here. Without taking into account the public nature of the language use during the referendum, we risk neglecting the importance of *where* the debate is taking place, in addition to *how* it is taking place (i.e., stance type). Ailbhe Smyth—feminist academic and co-director of the Together for Yes campaign, hailed as one of the architects of the "Yes" campaign's victory—has previously written about breaking the public silence on such a taboo issue: "We have already started to speak plainly about the facts that matter, and the realities of our lives. We will not stop until we are free to make decisions about our reproductive lives for ourselves" (A. Smyth, 2015: 118). The issue of information on abortion comes with significant baggage in an Irish context. Following the introduction of the Eighth Amendment in 1983, information on abortion was suppressed in Ireland, to the extent that magazines and telephone directories which included information on services available in Britain were removed from libraries (L. Smyth, 2005: 11). It was not until a 1992 referendum that a further amendment guaranteeing the right to information on abortion was added to the constitution.[10]

Therefore, it might be expected that those campaigning to repeal the Eighth Amendment would seek to break the taboo by talking about "the facts that matter" in the LL, in a push to destigmatize the issue through a voter education campaign. On the other hand, Smyth (1992: 20) previously characterized the Irish electorate as "always susceptible to emotional manipulation by Pro-Life discourse and still capable of being swayed by the subtly intimidatory tactics of the Catholic Church." Following this line of reasoning, there would be an expectation that the "No" campaign's tactics in 2018 would revolve around appeals to emotion, with the "Yes" side's discourse characterized by use of epistemic stance and that of the "No" side by affective stance. However, this is not borne out by the data.

Figure 10.1 shows two campaign posters which illustrate typical use(s) of stance types by different campaign groups. Figure 10.1a (top) was produced by Together for Yes and invokes "[c]are" as a reason to "VOTE Yes." On the other hand, Figure 10.1b (bottom), produced by the Love Both campaign, urges voters to "Vote NO," including a quote from GP Siobhán Crowley. Figure 10.1b offers a statement which can be evaluated in terms of its truth conditions: in asserting that "[a] baby's heartbeat starts at 22 days," the poster takes a specific type of stance on the issue of abortion—one based in knowledge, presenting its own relationship to that knowledge as one of certainty. This educational approach is a common tactic among posters campaigning for a "No" vote, often using statistics or facts, yet in other cases adopting a broader stance of being "in the know"; see Table 10.1 for examples of such messages on "No" posters. These messages reveal the underlying relationship between epistemic stance and an educational approach to campaigning in the LL: an epistemic stance of certainty assumes having knowledge which the reader does not, and by extension, the need to disseminate such information to the reader.[11]

By contrast, Figure 10.1a does not offer anything which can be evaluated in terms of truth-conditional meaning. Instead of attempting to educate the public, "Yes" signage typically sought to set the tone of the debate and appeal to emotion or create an "affective regime" (Wee, 2016). Interviewees picked up on the fact that many "Yes" posters (from a variety of groups) drew from a pool of emotive buzzwords, including "care," "love," "compassion," "respect," "dignity," and "trust"; see Table 10.2 for examples of such

Figure 10.1 Donnybrook Road, Dublin

messages on "Yes" posters. However, it is difficult to maintain that "Please don't stop [a baby's heartbeat]" in Figure 10.1b does not register anywhere on the affective scale. Therefore, while I claim that it is possible to broadly distinguish between epistemic and affective stance as ways of understanding the different campaign tactics adopted in the referendum LL, this is not to say that a given poster can be unequivocally sorted into one category or the other; to do so would ignore the complexity of the data.

Educating the Public?

Table 10.1 Epistemic stance(s) in "No" poster messages[12]

Campaign group	Campaign poster message
Save the 8th	In England 1 IN 5 babies are aborted
Save the 8th	In Britain, 97% of abortions are on healthy babies
Save the 8th	preborn babies will have NO rights
Save the 8th	In Britain 90% of babies diagnosed with Down's Syndrome are aborted
Save the 8th	"The State will fund abortions"—Simon Harris. Your taxes should fund healthcare, <u>not</u> abortion.
LOVE BOTH	I am 9 weeks old/I can yawn and kick/Don't repeal me
LOVE BOTH	A baby's heartbeat starts at 22 days. Please don't stop it.
LOVE BOTH	REPEAL MEANS UNRESTRICTED ABORTION UP TO 12 WEEKS
LOVE BOTH	If you saw an abortion you would vote NO
People Power	Abortion stops a heartbeat!
Anonymous	FACT: ABORTION INCREASES BREAST CANCER RISK & DEATHS/ FAKESTREAM MEDIA DENY AND WOMEN DIE ….

Table 10.2 Affective stance(s) in "Yes" poster messages

Campaign Group	Campaign Poster Message
Amnesty International	FOR COMPASSION AND RESPECT
Amnesty International	FOR EQUALITY AND DIGNITY
Green Party	Your sister/Your friend/Your daughter/TRUST HER/VOTE YES
Labour Party	FOR COMPASSION IN A CRISIS
Sinn Féin	SHOW COMPASSION
Sinn Féin	CARE/COMPASSION/TRUST
Social Democrats	Yes for Dignity/Yes for Compassion/Yes for Health
Together for Yes	A woman you love might need your Yes

Multimodality: Linguistic and Other Semiotic Resources

As Jaworski and Thurlow (2009: 220) point out, "stancetaking tends to be subtle and is premised on inference rather than assertion of evaluation." The stances in these campaign posters are not explicitly marked by phrases such as "I'm glad" or "I don't know" (Du Bois, 2007: 143). Instead, epistemic stance is produced by the implications of making concrete claims for a given poster's relationship to its own "talk": rather than explicitly stating "I know that …," the fact of making a falsifiable claim in itself constitutes a form of stancetaking. Stance, then, can be indexed by means other than explicit phrases. Expanding on this idea, we can investigate whether taking an epistemic stance, for example, can be achieved via both linguistic and nonlinguistic resources. It is worthwhile bearing in mind that epistemic stance "serves to establish the relative authority of interactants" (Jaffe, 2009: 7) in a situation. While there are clearly differences between stancetaking in the LL and in face-to-face interaction, it is nevertheless possible to identify ways in which signs establish their own authority for the benefit of, or in relation to, a reader. Figure 10.1b states its credentials clearly, including the title (and name) of a medical professional—"GP Siobhán Crowley"— to index authority. Tracing the provenance of the knowledge solidifies the basis for claiming it as fact and makes more explicit the certainty with which the statement is made. However, we can go beyond the text and ask what role other modes play in indexing authority in this poster. Scollon and Scollon (2003: 96) analyze how participants in an image "establish relationships with viewers of the image." The "demand gaze" (Scollon & Scollon, 2003: 96) of the interactive participant in the Love Both poster engages the viewer in social interaction, with the function of challenging or "interpellating" (Milani, 2014) the viewer. This interpellation is lent authority by the inclusion in the image of the GP's stethoscope, indexing authority in much the same way as the name "Siobhán Crowley" is prefaced by the qualification "GP." Other posters may use the same tactic—a woman's face interpellating the viewer—without necessarily using this resource to take an epistemic stance. These include other Love Both posters as well as "Yes" posters which adopt an affective stance approach. However, it is the contextually dependent relationship between the text and the interactive participant in Figure 10.1b which makes the image relevant to epistemic stance, whereas in another poster a similar image might be used to index affective stance.

This brings up the question of what role multimodal resources play in the construction of affective stance. Returning to Figure 10.1a, here too there is an interaction between text and multimodal resources, particularly color. Several interviewees mentioned the importance of "coming together" as a key theme in the Together for Yes campaign: Andrew framed this in terms of imagery and coloring, which communicated the message that "while we might have different opinions […] we can all unite under this needing to be repealed." In a similar vein, Catherine characterized the Together for Yes campaign messaging as: "'we're all in this together, let's vote for choice', in a nice, huggy way." This is reflected in the multicolored speech bubbles in Figure 10.1a, representing a coalition of disparate elements coming together, in dialogue with one another. Scollon and Scollon's (2003) framework for analysis of color draws on Kress and Van Leeuwen's (1996) approach to modality, using concepts such as color saturation, differentiation, etc.; Kress and Van Leeuwen further elaborated on color as a semiotic mode in greater detail elsewhere (Kress & Van Leeuwen, 2002). The use of pastel colors—pale green, pink, and orange—shows low levels of saturation, reducing the "emotive temperature" (Kress & Van Leeuwen, 2002: 356) of the poster and indexing a softer, less-intense stance. The use of several, overlapping colors indicates high levels of differentiation, "the use of a maximally varied palette" (Kress & Van Leeuwen, 2002: 357), indexing the diversity and "coming together" alluded to by interviewees. Significantly, one interviewee who was involved in the Together for Yes campaign, Catríona, noted the importance of such "differentiation" in terms of color, in that it was important to avoid excessive use of pink or blue, which might be interpreted as gender markers. The color design of the Together for Yes posters therefore aimed to moderate the affective temperature of their message, setting a warmer, softer tone, which might appeal to a broader tranche of the public, while using multimodal resources to align with the poster's text. Rather than attempting to educate the public, Together for Yes posters used both linguistic and multimodal resources to communicate something more intangible: the ethos of the campaign or "what the campaign is about."

Heterogeneity: Variation between (and within) Groups

Figures 10.1a and 10.1b are representative of the discursive tactics employed by two of the most influential groups in the referendum campaign. While an affective stance approach was the norm among groups campaigning to repeal the Eighth Amendment, feminist campaign group ROSA (supporting a "Yes" vote) bucked the trend by adopting an educational approach. ROSA produced posters offering statistics relevant to the debate on abortion ("1 in 3 will face a crisis pregnancy"), detailing facts about abortion in other countries ("NETHERLANDS/one of the lowest abortion rates/✓ right to choose/✓ accessible contraception/✓ sex education"), and one including a quote from the father of Savita Halappanavar urging Irish people to repeal the Eighth Amendment (referencing the *Irish Times* as the source of the quote, along with the date of publication); see Figure 10.2. One interviewee, Lily, commented that, unlike other "Yes" posters, the ROSA posters "weren't shying away from the issue," which aligned with Lily's own group's aims of "opening up the itchy questions." This would suggest that the epistemic stance adopted toward information on abortion (as well as on sexual health and education) marked ROSA out as taking an educational approach uncharacteristic among "Yes" posters.

Of course, not all ROSA posters took such a stance. ROSA posters reading "STOP SHAMING WOMEN!" can be considered educational only in the broadest sense of the word (for example, in attempting to change the attitudes or behavior of those reading the poster); they do not seek to inform the public or provide voters with new information. For interviewee Andrew, ROSA posters featuring Savita Halappanavar represented a "definite shift in tone, different from the rest of the official campaign," but not because of the educational aspect, instead because they were "more emotive." In Figure 10.2, then, it could be argued that we are dealing with *both* affective and epistemic stance in a single LL item: the use of the quotation (including the source, significantly) indexes a claim regarding knowledge (i.e., knowing what Savita Halappanavar's father thinks about the referendum), whereas the use of Savita Halappanavar's face is better interpreted in terms of affective stance. The "demand gaze" (Kress & Van Leeuwen, 1996) in Figure 10.2 serves a similar function to that in Figure 10.1b, as it directly engages the viewer; unlike in Figure 10.1b, however, here it appeals to voters on the basis of the tragic death of Savita Halappanavar, rather than to back up the authority with which a statement is made, thus taking an affective stance rather than an epistemic one.

Not only is there variation between groups ostensibly on the same side of the debate, then, but different discursive tactics may be used in different posters produced by the same organization or even within a single LL item. Nevertheless, we can still find support for the claim that, generally speaking, "Yes" and "No" posters take affective and epistemic stances, respectively. In addition to "legitimate" campaign posters, mock (or "fake") posters, which satirically claimed that "5 IN 3/babies with 8 limbs/are aborted" and called on voters to "VOTE YAS" to "STOP THE SPREAD OF SPIDER BABIES," also appeared during the lead-up to the referendum.[13] Such posters satirized the Save the 8th campaign's use of facts (specifically, posters produced by Save the 8th carrying the message "In England 1 in 5 babies are aborted") by equating the hysterical tone of their own nonsensical claim with that of the Save the 8th posters. The background image of a screaming woman under the text on these mock posters invoked a "Won't somebody please think of the children?" stereotype privileging emotion over reason (Meany & Shuster, 2002: 65). They undermined the "No" campaign's claims to epistemic

Figure 10.2 Dorset Street, Dublin

authority, indexed by the use of statistics, by framing its use of information in terms of a hysterical tone of moral panic. This might be interpreted as a "meta-stance": such posters were caricaturing the epistemic stance taken by Save the 8th posters, thereby taking a stance *on* a stance type. This points to an implicit acknowledgment of the discursive tactics being used by the Save the 8th campaign, if not by the "No" campaign more generally.

Media: Variation According to Type of LL Item

Turning now to leaflets, the discursive tactics used by particular groups are different to those used in campaign posters. Compared to their campaign posters, Together for Yes leaflets adopted a more educational approach. Figure 10.3, a leaflet from the Together for Yes campaign, is structured as an FAQ with sections addressing certain key points in the debate, such as "What is the 8th Amendment?" or "12 weeks."[14] As argued above, using information in this way indexes a particular regime of knowledge and thus takes an epistemic stance on the issue of abortion. In providing the public with answers to common questions, this leaflet adopts an educational approach absent from Together for Yes campaign posters. This emphasis on knowledge and information is also found in leaflets produced by the Save the 8th campaign, with headings on the leaflets' front covers reading "The facts you need to KNOW" or "The more you KNOW about it, the more you'll vote NO to it." Opening the leaflets, the (capitalized) word "KNOW" is ubiquitous, contained in subheadings such as "What the government doesn't want you to KNOW …," "Irish medics KNOW abortion is not healthcare" and "Did you KNOW?," followed by facts and statistics. While this may be partly attributed to the homophony between "know" and "no," it also undoubtedly speaks to the concern with being "in the know" prevalent in much "No" messaging. On the basis of an analysis of leaflets, then, the distinction between the "Yes" and "No" campaigns' discursive tactics begins to break down.

Of course, this is not to say that leaflets are devoid of any affective stancetaking. For example, Figure 10.3's design is in keeping with that of Together for Yes campaign posters, including pastel-colored speech bubbles, which manage affective tone in much the same way as in Figure 10.1a. The testimonies at the bottom of each page offer insights into women's stories related to the Eighth Amendment and thus inform those who may not have had such experiences of the real-life effects of the Eighth Amendment. The leaflet thus takes an epistemic stance by indexing knowledge of the reality of abortion in Ireland, yet at the same time communicates the affective state(s) of these women regarding their personal experiences. It is therefore not possible to discount the affective work being carried out in Figure 10.3, even if the difference in approach between campaign posters and leaflets is clear.

Sebba (2010: 74) suggests that "non-fixed texts may be differentiated in terms of how prototypically 'public' they are (or are perceived to be) at different points in their trajectory." It is important to consider how readers engage with different LL items: although both posters and leaflets are destined for a public readership (rather than private correspondence), and in this sense are both public texts, posters may

Figure 10.3 Together for Yes leaflet

be viewed or read by many people at a given time, whereas leaflets are often read individually (or at most by perhaps two to three people at a time). The distribution of different stance types found in this data would suggest that it is generally deemed appropriate and possible to communicate more detailed information on the issue of abortion in leaflets, whereas different groups may diverge on whether they view an educational approach appropriate or effective in more public texts, such as campaign posters. This argument would align with recent research, which has argued that door-to-door canvassing during the referendum campaign can be thought of in educational terms (McDonald et al., 2020): stancetaking and education interact in different ways depending on the medium of communication (whether on the doors, in campaign posters, or in leaflets).

Conclusion

A complex picture of stance in the referendum campaign's LL emerges from this analysis. First, the distinction between epistemic and affective stances is shown to be relevant and conceptually useful as a heuristic for understanding how different discursive tactics are deployed by different campaign groups. These stances may rely primarily on linguistic resources, yet other semiotic resources often work in tandem with text, whether this takes the form of images of participants in a sign used to convey authority, or color to set the tone. While it is also broadly true that the "Yes" and "No" sides consistently adopt different tactics—predominantly taking affective and epistemic stances, respectively—at the level of individual groups such a simplistic, bimodal distinction does not hold, as some groups on the "Yes" side seek to educate via campaign posters or even use different tactics in different posters. However, this distinction between groups based on their position on abortion is less important when looking at leaflets. These mobile texts, destined for individual consumption rather than for a more public readership even if they are also "public texts" (Sebba, 2010), take an epistemic stance on the issue and focus on educating voters rather than appealing to emotion.

What does this analysis mean for theorizing education in the linguistic landscape? It suggests that the LL can potentially turn spaces—on a countrywide scale, if only for a limited period—into educational spaces. However, thinking about education in terms of stance reveals the partiality of education. Education is by no means a disinterested or non-partisan endeavor whereby information is benignly or transparently communicated to voters; it can be viewed as a tactic, one approach (among others) to campaigning mediated by a group's ideology and end goals, thus revealing the impartiality of education to be a myth. This brings issues of power and ideology to the fore when discussing education in the context of LL research.

Notes

1   Article 40.3.3° of the Constitution reads as follows: "The State acknowledges the right to life of the unborn and, with due regard to the equal right to life of the mother, guarantees in its laws to respect, and, as far as practicable, by its laws to defend and vindicate that right" (Article 40.3.3: Constitution of Ireland, 1937; last updated 2018).
2   Travel to Northern Ireland has not historically been an option: unlike the rest of the UK, at the time of the referendum in 2018 abortion was still illegal in Northern Ireland. However, abortion was decriminalized in Northern Ireland in October 2019, and at the time of writing there is an ongoing public consultation on the future framework for access to abortion services in the jurisdiction.
3   "Women and pregnant people" is the preferred terminology with regard to inclusivity, for example, as used by Fletcher (2018); see also Duffy (2018).
4   In the context of LL research, we can replace "speaker" with "sign" in these definitions.
5   I make no claims regarding the accuracy of any statements made in any sign (i.e., that what are presented as "facts" are indeed facts). I claim only that to present information as such is a rhetorical technique, which characterizes both an educational approach to the referendum campaign and a particular stance type (epistemic stance).
6   Gaeltachts are primarily Irish-speaking regions, mostly located in the west of Ireland.
7   All names of interviewees in this chapter are pseudonyms.

8. "Strong and stable" is a reference to former British Prime Minster Theresa May's (much derided) 2017 general election campaign slogan.
9. "TD" is an abbreviation of the Irish *Teachta Dála* "Dáil Deputy," a member of Dáil Éireann (the lower house of the Irish parliament).
10. Following the 1992 amendments, Article 40.3.3° of the Constitution included subsections reading as follows: "This subsection shall not limit freedom to travel between the State and another state. This subsection shall not limit freedom to obtain or make available, in the State, subject to such conditions as may be laid down by law, information relating to services lawfully available in another state" (Article 40.3.3: Constitution of Ireland, 1937; last updated 2018).
11. Although a full analysis of how readers take up these messages is beyond the scope of this chapter, interviewees voiced their awareness of the impact of posters on readers (including themselves), both through their discussions of signage, which they found inappropriate or offensive, as well as their experiences canvassing voters. For example, Catherine referenced a Save the 8th poster, which stated that "In England 1 in 5 babies are aborted," stating that "some peoples' minds were changed when they saw the '1 in 5' one, I know a lot of people started quoting that as if it was gospel."
12. The original formatting, punctuation, and capitalization of the messages presented in these tables are preserved as far as possible; however, this still cannot convey the nuances of meaning dependent on multimodal resources in LL items, which therefore require a more thorough multimodal analysis later in this chapter.
13. Please refer to the accompanying website to this volume for images of said posters.
14. The legislation to regulate abortion proposed by the government in the run-up to the referendum stipulated a time limit of twelve weeks of pregnancy regardless of reason given for the termination (after this limit, more stringent restrictions on abortion provision come into effect).

References

Aiken, A. R. A., Gomperts, R., & Trussell, J. (2017). Experiences and characteristics of women seeking and completing at-home medical termination of pregnancy through online telemedicine in Ireland and Northern Ireland: A population-based analysis. *BJOG: An International Journal of Obstetrics and Gynaecology*, 124(8), 1208–15.

Backhaus, P. (2007). *Linguistic Landscapes: A Comparative Study of Urban Multilingualism in Tokyo*. Clevedon: Multilingual Matters.

Constitution of Ireland. (1937). Retrieved from https://assets.gov.ie/6523/5d90822b41e945 32a63d955ca76fdc72.pdf

Department of Health & Social Care. (2019). *Abortion Statistics, England and Wales: 2018 Summary Information from the Abortion Notification Forms Returned to the Chief Medical Officers of England and Wales*. Retrieved from https://assets.publishing.service. gov.uk/government/uploads/system/uploads/attachment_data/file/808556/Abortion_ Statistics__England_and_Wales_2018__1_.pdf

Du Bois, J. (2007). The stance triangle. In R. Englebreston (Ed.), *Stancetaking in Discourse: Subjectivity, Evaluation, Interaction* (pp. 139–82). Amsterdam: John Benjamins.

Duffy, S. (2018). The Regulation of Termination of Pregnancies Bill 2018—an argument for "pregnant people" wording. Retrieved from https://sandraduffy.wordpress.

com/2018/07/18/the-regulation-of-termination-of-pregnancies-bill-2018-an-argument-for-pregnant-people-wording/ (accessed December 17, 2019).

Fletcher, R. (2018). #RepealedThe8th: Translating travesty, global conversation, and the Irish abortion referendum. *Feminist Legal Studies*, 26(3), 233–59.

Holland, K. (2014). March for choice attracts thousands in Dublin. *Irish Times*. Retrieved from https://www.irishtimes.com/news/social-affairs/march-for-choice-attracts-thousands-in-dublin-1.1944267

Hosford, P. (2018). Together for Yes crowdfunding appeal tops half a million euro. *Thejournal.Ie*. Retrieved from https://www.thejournal.ie/together-for-yes-crowdfunding-3957637-Apr2018/

IFPA. (n.d.). No title. Retrieved from https://www.ifpa.ie

Jaffe, A. (2009). Introduction: The sociolinguistics of stance. In A. Jaffe (Ed.), *Stance: Sociolinguistic Perspectives* (pp. 3–28). New York: Oxford University Press.

Jaworski, A., & Thurlow, C. (2009). Taking an elitist stance: Ideology and the discursive production of social distinction. In A. Jaffe (Ed.), *Stance: Sociolinguistic Perspectives* (pp. 195–226). New York: Oxford University Press.

Kiesling, S. F. (2018). Masculine stances and the linguistics of affect: On masculine ease. *Norma*, 13(3–4), 191–212. doi: /10.1080/18902138.2018.1431756

Kress, G., & Van Leeuwen, T. (1996). *Reading Images: The Grammar of Visual Design*. London: Routledge.

Kress, G., & Van Leeuwen, T. (2002). Colour as a semiotic mode: Notes for a grammar of colour. *Visual Communication*, 1(3), 343–68. doi: 10.1177/147035720200100306

Lempert, M. (2008). The poetics of stance: Text-metricality, epistemicity, interaction. *Language in Society*, 37(4), 569–92. doi: 10.1017/S0047404508080779

McDonald, N., Antosik-Parsons, K., Till, K., Kearns, G., & Callan, J. (2020). Campaigning for choice: Canvassing as feminist pedagogy in Dublin Bay North. In K. Browne & S. Calkin (Eds.), *After the 8th* (p. 4). London: Zed Books.

Meany, J., & Shuster, K. (2002). *Art, Argument, and Advocacy: Mastering Parliamentary Debate*. New York: The International Debate Education Association.

Milani, T. (2014). Sexed signs—Queering the scenery. *International Journal of the Sociology of Language*, 228, 201–25. doi: 10.1515/ijsl-2014-0011

Ng, C. J. W. (2019). "You are your only limit": Appropriations and valorizations of affect in university branding. *Journal of Sociolinguistics*, 23(2), 121–39. doi: 10.1111/josl.12331

Ní Aodha, G. (2018). Most Irish people think referendum posters should be banned. *Thejournal.Ie*. Retrieved from https://www.thejournal.ie/referendum-posters-ban-4034334-May2018/

NicGhabhann, N. (2018). City walls, bathroom stalls and tweeting the Taoiseach: The aesthetics of protest and the campaign for abortion rights in the Republic of Ireland. *Continuum*, 32(5), 553–68. doi: 10.1080/10304312.2018.1468413

Referendum Commission. (2018). Referendum on the Thirty-sixth Amendment of the Constitution Bill 2018. Retrieved from http://www.referendum.ie/

RTÉ. (2017). Tens of thousands take part in March for Choice rally. Retrieved from https://www.rte.ie/news/ireland/2017/0930/908737-march-for-choice/

RTÉ & Behaviour & Attitudes Exit Poll. (2018). *Thirty-Sixth Amendment to the Constitution Exit Poll*. Retrieved from https://static.rasset.ie/documents/news/2018/05/rte-exit-poll-final-11pm.pdf

Scollon, R., & Scollon, S. W. (2003). *Discourses in Place: Language in the Material World*. London: Routledge.

Screti, F. (2018). Re-writing Galicia: Spelling and the construction of social space. *Journal of Sociolinguistics*, 22(5), 516–44. doi: 10.1111/josl.12306

Sebba, M. (2010). Discourses in transit. In A. Jaworski & C. Thurlow (Eds.), *Semiotic Landscapes: Language, Image, Space* (pp. 59–76). London: Continuum.

Smyth, A. (1992). A Sadistic farce: Women and abortion in the Republic of Ireland, 1992. In A. Smyth (Ed.), *The Abortion Papers Ireland* (pp. 7–24). Dublin: Attic Press.

Smyth, A. (2015). Telling the truth about women's lives. *Estudios Irlandeses*, 10, 115–18.

Smyth, L. (2005). *Abortion and Nation: The Politics of Reproduction in Contemporary Ireland*. Aldershot: Ashgate.

Vote on abortion laws among seven planned referendums. (2017). *RTÉ*. Retrieved from https://www.rte.ie/news/2017/0926/907522-cabinet_referendums/

Wee, L. (2016). Situating affect in linguistic landscapes. *Linguistic Landscape*, 2(2), 105–26.

11

Dynamic Walking Tour Methodology for LL Research: A Case Study in Jaffa

Amir Michalovich, Sarah Naaman, Moraia Trijnes, Iman Agbaria, and Elana Shohamy

Introduction

Linguistic landscape (LL) studies often utilize photos to document and categorize LL items in public spaces, frequently combining interviews with passersby or with policy makers. Yet such LL studies have been criticized for the static nature of the data, while newer studies introduce walking tours that call for more dynamic interactions with the LL and its documentations. These ethnographic methods utilize observations of people on the move as they interact with the public space, via interviews with locals and digital documentation, including videos (e.g., Garvin, 2010; Troyer & Szabó, 2017). The present study adds to this newer literature by offering a comprehensive framework for employing a dynamic walking tour methodology for LL research. We further highlight the educational opportunities inherent in this walking tour methodology.

The dynamic tour in this study is a reaction to a "static" documentation of the main street in Jaffa, a formerly Arab town that has been part of Tel Aviv for the past seventy-one years. Tel Aviv-Jaffa is a mixed Israeli city where Arabs reside alongside Jews, mostly in Jaffa. This static documentation pointed to the need for bringing Arabic back to public spaces. In order to gain a deeper understanding of this politically loaded site, we conducted a tour of the street with participants of an LL course at Tel Aviv University.

The data collection consisted of notes, images, audio and video recordings of observations, and interactions with local Arab residents of this main street in Jaffa. Inductive thematic analysis pointed to five features that distinguished the dynamic tour from the traditional "static" LL methodology: (1) a *heterogeneous research group,* consisting of local Arab residents of Jaffa and university students of mixed backgrounds, alongside local guides, who, as a group, contributed diverse perspectives and local access; (2) *transformability,* i.e., the potential for enacting change in the LL through meaningful interactions with locals (Szabó & Troyer, 2017); (3) *serendipity,* i.e., the flexible trajectory that deflects a uniform agenda and provides unexpected discoveries; (4) *immediacy,* i.e., the bodily presence in the moment, which facilitates reflection in action (Garvin, 2010); and (5) *emotional expression*, i.e., the tour enabled the display of emotions arising from in-situ interactions with the local residents. The study demonstrates the value of these features as they experientially highlight social injustices in Jaffa, such as gentrification and the deteriorating loss of the Arabic language. The study supports a methodological transition in LL studies from static to dynamic exploration of contested spaces and highlights its educational value.

The initial impetus for this study was, as previously mentioned, a standard LL documentation task given in a graduate-level LL course at Tel Aviv University, School of Education, the Program for Multilingual Education. Students were asked to document and present findings from their inquiries into local LLs. One of the students, a resident of Jaffa, presented findings showing lack of representation of Arabic in the local LL of Yefet Street, a central commercial street in Jaffa, in parallel to the dominance of Hebrew and English in the public space.

While in class, a discussion arose about the question of the extent to which increased activism could bring Arabic back to Yefet Street. This discussion highlighted the limitations of traditional LL documentation and analysis for understanding the complex issues and conflicts in Jaffa between Jews and Arabs. It culminated with a group decision to undertake a walking tour on Yefet Street, which would include interviews with passersby and shop owners, as well as documentation of those interactions with notes, images, and audio and video recordings.

Our case study analysis focuses on this excursion to Yefet Street, Jaffa, exploring the question: What are the affordances of a walking tour methodology for understanding the complexities of LL in a contested urban space?

As we will argue, our study adds to previous research by suggesting a comprehensive framework that incorporates these previously studied practices and shows the potential of an integrated and comprehensive methodological framework for a dynamic exploration of LL in public spaces. We further argue that the framework clarifies the educational opportunities made available by this dynamic walking tour methodology in the following ways: (1) it afforded an expansive inquiry based on dual insider and outsider perspectives as well as immediate, serendipitous interactions among a heterogeneous group of participants; (2) it nurtured an in-depth understanding of the complexities of LL in a contested urban space and how LL is a living construct in the lives of the neighborhood's inhabitants; and (3) it cultivated a desire for bringing about social change in the contested public space of Yefet Street, Jaffa.

Literature Review

Linguistic Landscapes in Mixed Cities

The term "mixed cities" refers to an urban space in which two ethnolinguistic communities reside equally abreast of one another (Monterescu, 2011a). In such spaces, there is often covert or overt contestation of the representation of the respective languages of each group in the shared urban space. Each group strives for maximum visibility and status of its language. In the case of Israel, Trumper-Hecht (2010) defines the term "mixed city" as "Israeli urban localities in which Arabs and Jews reside under the same municipal jurisdiction" (p. 235).

In the State of Israel, Hebrew and Arabic, the languages of the two ethnolinguistic groups (Jews and Arabs), shared official status until recently, when, under the Nation-State Bill of 2018, Arabic was declared a language with a special status, rather than the former official status it enjoyed. The new bill specifies that the regulation of Arabic use in or by state institutions will be set by law (Knesset, 2018). In practice, there had been a biased hierarchy favoring Hebrew long before the new bill (Trumper-Hecht, 2009), one which is arguably strengthened after the passing of the bill. As a result, especially in mixed cities, the LL has become a ground for both contestation and language activism, with the latter aiming to enhance the visibility of the minority language.

In cases like Israel, where one language dominates the other in practice, the reason is usually that the state promotes a "one-nation, one-language" policy (Moriarty, 2014) and uses LLs to preserve a particular system of national hegemony (Trumper-Hecht, 2009). In Israel, such policies have already emerged de facto but are now encouraged and receive support de jure, after the Nation-State Bill was passed.[1]

Both Arabs and Jews regard language as an essential tool for the construction and negotiation of group and national identity (Trumper-Hecht, 2010). The battle for linguistic representation in public spaces thus reflects the broader, national struggle between the two groups. Even when Arabic was an official language in the State of Israel, its lack of representation in public spaces eventually led to the Supreme Court ruling in 1999 (expanded upon below) that both Hebrew and Arabic must be presented on all official signs in Israeli mixed cities and major freeways, while private signs were left to individual preferences and were not to be governed by local or national regulations (Trumper-Hecht, 2010). Monterescu (2011a) claims that local residents prefer gaining recognition independently, rather than contesting their rights with national authorities, thus paving the way to language activism.

Interestingly, previous research suggests that Arab citizens in Israel tend to view bilingual representation in public spaces more positively than the Jewish population (Trumper-Hecht, 2010). This could be related to Moriarty's (2014) claim that local minorities tend to hold inclusive attitudes toward multilingual societies. In the case of the Arab population, the largest, indigenous minority in Israel, their acceptance of bilingual representation may also stem from a strong connection they identify between their language rights and other rights they deserve as a minority.

As briefly mentioned above, in 1999, a case was brought against Tel Aviv-Jaffa and other mixed Arab and Jewish Israeli cities, requesting that the municipality post all road signs in both Hebrew and Arabic on every street sign in every neighborhood throughout the city. The Supreme Court of Israel eventually ruled in favor of this request, declaring that "while Hebrew is Israel's first and most important language, Arabic's importance is far greater than that of any other language spoken by a major minority group" (Knesset, 2020). As a result of this ruling, it became mandatory (at least by law) for municipalities of mixed cities to have Arabic representation on all of their public signs.

This Supreme Court ruling of 1999 created a direct relation between individual rights, language representation, and collective, cultural rights (Trumper-Hecht, 2009). Therefore, Arab activists believe that visible representation in public spaces will improve the general status of Arab individuals within the State of Israel (Trumper-Hecht, 2009). In other words, influencing the linguistic landscapes impacts the rights and equality of ethnic communities.

Jaffa

Home to about 60,000 people (a third of whom are Arabs), Jaffa is an ancient port city that is nowadays considered the oldest quarter of Tel Aviv. The town's Arab population consists of roughly 7,000 Christians and around 13,000 Muslims. Until 1948, Jaffa was an Arab city, which included around 30% Jewish citizens. Since the establishment of the State of Israel, Jaffa's neighborhoods gradually merged with Tel Aviv and its municipality. In 1950, the name Jaffa was officially added to the name of the city of Tel Aviv in order to preserve Jaffa's historical value (Golan, 1995). By 1952, the entirety of Jaffa had geographically become a part of Tel Aviv, and today the demographics of what was once an Arab city have completely changed since: only 31% of its residents are Arabs (Monterescu, 2011a; Rudnitzky, 2018). Still, despite the complete reversal in population proportion between Arabs and Jews and the attempt to turn it into a Jewish city, Jaffa has not become a Jewish city in people's consciousness but remains Arab in the minds of both Arabs and Jews (Rabinowitz & Monterescu, 2007).

Since the incorporation of Jaffa within the Tel Aviv municipality, the relationship between locals and officials has been unstable (Monterescu, 2011b). This is manifested in the municipality's constant failure to present either a homogenous, ethnolinguistic urban space or, inversely, its failure to define distinct, separate ethnolinguistic spaces with clear boundaries for each of the two groups (Monterescu, 2010).

Additionally, the larger economic and housing market factors in the greater metropolitan area of Tel Aviv, Jaffa's multicultural appeal and historical value, as well as the proximity to Tel Aviv, have led to an increase in the area's popularity, especially since the 1990s. This has created an influx of middle- and upper-class Jewish residents (Monterescu, 2011b; LeVine, 2007) and is effectively causing gentrification and Judaization of Jaffa. When community leaders complained in the early 2000s that most young Arab couples could not afford to live in Jaffa because of the increasing prices of real estate due to the aforementioned influx, officials responded by explaining that "the market is the market" and that "selling some apartments more cheaply would hurt profits" (LeVine, 2007: 192). The gentrification process, which accompanied the Judaization process, has thus created a lack of available living spaces for Arabs, the native residents of Jaffa, who object to this process and demand fair housing solutions.

According to an internal survey conducted by the municipality of Tel Aviv-Jaffa published in 2013, of all nine neighborhoods and quarters of the city, Jaffa's residents belong to the lowest levels of the socioeconomic scale, scoring an average of 3.5 on a scale of 10, with the predominantly Arab neighborhoods of Jaffa scoring the lowest. Consequently, Jaffa suffers from a number of social issues, mainly high rates of drug-dealing and crime (Monterescu, 2015). In addition, social and political events often lead to confrontations between Jaffa's Arab residents and the authorities, making the tension between Arabs and Jews even higher.

The Jewish residents of Tel Aviv-Jaffa tend to hold a dichotomous view of the mixed city as a place of violence and danger but also one of artistic and multicultural qualities (Monterescu, 2011b). This dual perception of the predominantly Arab neighborhoods can explain why Jews do not feel completely comfortable to encroach upon them. In other words, Jews may hold a fear of the potential dangers or romanticize the added value of living in coexistence in a multicultural city, including the representation of Arabic in public space. In comparison, according to a study from the mid-2000s (Goldhaber, 2007), Arab residents may attribute more importance to the representation of Arabic in the public spaces where they retain dominance, as long as the Jews respect these invisible boundaries and do not encroach on them. Tensions between both groups of residents may rise and fall with the destruction or intrusion of neighborhoods (Goldhaber, 2007; Monterescu, 2011a), but the struggle over the LL in Jaffa is mainly a battle driven by social organizations and less by individuals (Monterescu, 2011b). Monterescu (2011b) further claims that by 2010 Jaffa had been effectively left without a clear, defined center, and thus each ethnolinguistic group had its own agenda and appeared to act according to its own ideals without any regard to the general, political sphere surrounding it.

Another issue that has come to light lately is the deterioration of the Arabic language among Arabs in Israel, Jaffa included. Although in Arab schools the language of instruction is Arabic, not all Arab children learn all subjects in Arabic. Some learn it as an additional language in schools where it is not the primary language of instruction, such as private schools or schools that belong to the Jewish educational system. Furthermore, since most courses in higher education are taught in Hebrew, with the majority of the texts in English, the academic need for Arabic among Arabs in Israel is virtually nonexistent. Thus, there seems to have been a noticeable decrease in motivation to study Arabic among Arab students, as there is no recognition or economic reward for being academically literate in the language within Israel (Abu Ghazaleh-Mahajneh, 2009; Shohamy & Abu Ghazaleh-Mahajneh, 2012)

The status of the Arabic language in Jaffa is further demonstrated through its LL. Previous research (Ben-Rafael et al., 2006) shows that Arabic is barely present in the streets of Jaffa. A study by Goldstein-Havazki (2011) found that very little use of Arabic was represented in the public space (82 signs), as opposed to higher frequencies of representation of Hebrew (461 signs) and English (147 signs).

Walking Tours in Jaffa

Previous studies have shown an inequitable image of the linguistic scenery of this multicultural city (e.g., Goldstein-Havazki, 2011). Limited studies based on walking tours were dedicated to LL in Jaffa, with the one conducted by Goldstein-Havazki (2011) serving as an important exception.

In the current study, we decided to focus on Yefet Street. As previously mentioned, the decision to explore the LL of Yefet Street derived from a heated discussion in the LL class, following a picture presentation by a resident of Jaffa. Full of historic buildings that house shops, cafés, restaurants, schools, and houses, Yefet Street is one of two main streets in Jaffa, connecting Tel Aviv to the city of Bat Yam. The street was previously known as Ajami Street, until the Tel Aviv-Jaffa municipality changed it to Yefet, after the son of Noah from the Bible (Japheth). This process was part of a larger initiative started by a municipal committee in the 1950s to rename streets after historical and biblical figures, many of whom are connected to Zionism and Judaism (Monterescu, 2017). Nowadays, Yefet Street is considered the central one in Jaffa for most of its Arab residents; the vast majority of nearly 100 businesses on the street are owned by Arabs. This makes it the perfect place to investigate the use of Arabic among Arabs and its importance in the public space of Jaffa.

Walking Tour Methodology

The walking tour methodology we used in this study, as detailed in Methodology section, was inspired by previous studies that incorporated various types of extended and dynamic engagements with participants beyond the limits of the interview, often situated in ethnographic approaches. To name a few, Anderson (2004) used a method of talking (interviewing) while walking, Kusenbach (2003) utilized the "go-along" method to inquire with participants while they were doing their mundane activities, and Lee and Ingold (2006) wrote extensively about walking as a research methodology. Pink (2015) also discussed the sensorial richness and potential for self-reflexivity in such research practices.

More specifically, Brown and Durrheim (2009) claim that an interactive participation on the part of the interviewer creates "a largely unrehearsed conversation, [and] a different form of (intersubjective) knowledge can be produced" (p. 911). Furthermore, they argue that mobile interviews provide opportunities for social facts such as discrimination and prejudice to be uncovered. We believe that the spontaneity of the interactions in the walking tour methodology allows for the emergence of social issues, which may otherwise remain less overt.

In LL studies, Garvin (2010) used what she called a "walking tour methodology," and Szabó and Troyer (2017) called their approach a "co-conducted walking tour." According to Garvin (2010), "a walking tour methodology [is] designed to investigate the dynamic processes of interaction and the co-construction of knowledge mediated and stimulated by the LL" (p. 255). Garvin also cites Pennycook (2009: 309) who emphasized that the "act of walking in the city is what brings to life spatial realization of place" (Garvin, 2010: 255). Szabó and Troyer (2017) claimed that guided walking tours that were co-constructed by researchers and participants in their study helped reveal how different school community members enacted agency in different school spaces, providing emic perspectives and narratives, and "an opportunity to transform the LL due to the interaction between researchers and participants" (p. 322). Finally, Garvin (2011) found the walking tour methodology in LL to be "a tool for exploring cognitive and emotional understandings played out in response to the LL" (p. 268). Such understandings of the potential of walking tours for transformative engagement with LL lead us to inquire about the role of emotion in such research practices.

Emotion in Relation to LL Studies

LL studies often assert that the LL is rarely impulsively or accidently created and that therefore by examining LLs we may obtain an insight into power relations and the sociolinguistic relationships within a linguistic community (Landry & Bourhis, 1997; Lefebvre, 1991). Because the LL is embedded with culture and values, it illuminates processes of human actions, which are enabled through the semiotic system we use (Scollon & Scollon, 2003). People form a personal relationship with semiotic systems. This relationship always results in some form of self-positioning and identity construction and negotiation in relation to the LL (Garvin, 2010; Said & Shegar, 2013). Such self-positioning, identity, and a personal relationship involve an enactment and display of emotions: one acts according to how one feels, which is related to how one perceives their surroundings.

In recent years we can indeed see a shift of focus in LL studies from examining the language on display in the LL itself to the impact the language has on its inhabitants (Shohamy & Gorter, 2008), and more and more studies have been examining the realm of emotions and feelings and linguistic landscape (Ben Rafael, 2009; Garvin, 2011; Leeman & Modan, 2009; Wee, 2016). While the review of the various definitions of terms such as "affect," "moods," "emotions," and "feelings"—often conflicting across academic disciplines—is beyond the scope of this study, we do find the concept of emotions as useful and therefore refer to a definition that we adhere to. Based upon the work of Antonio Damasio, Mark Johnson explains that "[e]motional response patterns are, literally, changes in our body state in response to previous changes in our body state caused by our interactions with our environment, and they usually precede any reflective thinking or conceptualization" (2018: 21). This definition is useful in that it highlights the role of the environment as a situated stimulus in the emotional responses of individuals.

In the field of LL, Wee (2016) adapted a distinction initially introduced by Arlie Hochschild (2012), according to which specific sites encompass expectations about what emotions can be felt or displayed. In essence, this distinction is useful for highlighting the emotions that are considered appropriate in a particular situation and the social expectations that regulate how these emotions should be overtly expressed. Wee (2016) concluded that each specific site has its own set of rules that govern the appropriate emotions to be experienced and the ways in which they can be expressed. As we will argue, this distinction is useful for explaining the relationship between people's reflections on their emotional experiences in the tour and the social expectations that these spaces evoke.

Contestation as well as negotiation of identity in the LL have each been researched extensively in recent years (e.g., Seals, 2015; Shohamy, 2006). Places of contestation and conflict, such as Jaffa, clearly disclose the role of the LL as an emotionally evocative place, reflecting the local population's quests for visibility, social justice, and economic and political survival, in the face of tensions between the hegemony and the dominance of capitalism and the grassroots reactions (Rubdy & Ben-Said, 2015). Arguably, language exclusions in public space are prone to have emotional reactions, for such exclusions may be the consequence of top-down policies, assigning prestige or stigma to particular languages, or the outcome of linguistic insecurities encountered as a result of dominant language ideologies, such as those mentioned in LL studies (e.g., Hicks, 2002). The fact that the Arabs in Jaffa have become a minority in the majority Hebrew-speaking culture, and the "unstable political situation imposed on [the Arabs in Israel], together with globalization processes and their consequences on Middle-Eastern politics, set[s] challenges for their complex identity repertoire" (Amara & Shnell, 2004: 175).

In Israel, where there is a clear prominence of Hebrew over Arabic, the identity of the Arab residents in Jaffa thus needs constant negotiation. "Having one's own language enshrined on most private and government signs should contribute to the feeling that the in-group language has value and status" (Landry & Bourhis, 1997: 27). When taking into account the identity repertoire of Arabs in Israel, we must consider the complexity of their self-positioning and their identities. The Arab population confronts specific aspects of identity, which may not be present among other Arab communities or countries. The question remains, whether the Arab population in Israel regards their relevant identities as a "source of richness instead of [an] emotional burden" (Amara & Shnell, 2004: 181).

Methodology

We conducted our excursion on Yefet Street as a case study to examine the affordances of a walking tour for understanding the complex issues embedded in the local LL of the contested urban space of Jaffa. As such, our study situates LL research, particularly walking tours, as an educational practice with the potential to provide learning opportunities.

Based on methodology utilized in previous LL studies, we incorporated: (1) interviews situated in the spaces that participants inhabit during their daily routines; (2) detailed and reflexive description of embodied experience in the field, including reflection on in-the-moment emotional responses to the LL; and (3) emic perspectives of participants enacting agency in the space as well as etic perspectives of visiting researchers.

Participants in the study comprised of three groups: (1) observer participants: seven Jewish nonresidents from the LL course, six students of the current LL course cohort, and one university professor; (2) participant observers: three local Arab residents of Jaffa, one from the current cohort of the LL course, and two from previous cohorts; and (3) six local residents of Jaffa. Pseudonyms were used instead of participant names in the excerpts below, except for two cases in which two authors—Elana and Iman—were mentioned.

Data consisted of nine reflexive field notes of participants from the current and previous LL cohorts, as well as thirty-one photos, three videos (approximately five minutes long), and four audio recordings (approximately half an hour long) of varied interactions (planned as well as spontaneous) with residents. Data analysis was conducted in ATLAS.ti 7.5 and consisted of inductive thematic coding by two of the authors who coded the data together (Boyatzis, 1998; Braun & Clarke, 2006), starting with noting issues (e.g., deterioration of Arabic), actions (e.g., activism), and emotions (e.g., frustration) that arose during interactions between the various participants. Moreover, photos were coded for the presence of languages on signs. Reflexive memos were written separately by the two coders to explore connections between codes pertaining to the presence of languages in various places along the street and the issues, actions and emotions arising from interactions of the participants in those places. The descriptive codes, along with initial insights from the reflexive memos, were then brought to a discussion with the rest of the authors. Following several group discussions, themes were abstracted that provided the framework for understanding the distinguishing features of the tour.

Findings and Discussion

Analysis of the data led to the identification of five distinguishing features of the walking tour (See Figure 11.1); we argue that these five features together produced a distinct dynamic quality for the tour. We further argue that this dynamic quality highlights the affordances of a walking tour for understanding the complex issues embedded in the local LL of the contested urban space in Jaffa. In the following sections, we provide data that demonstrate each of the interlocking five features that make up this dynamic quality.

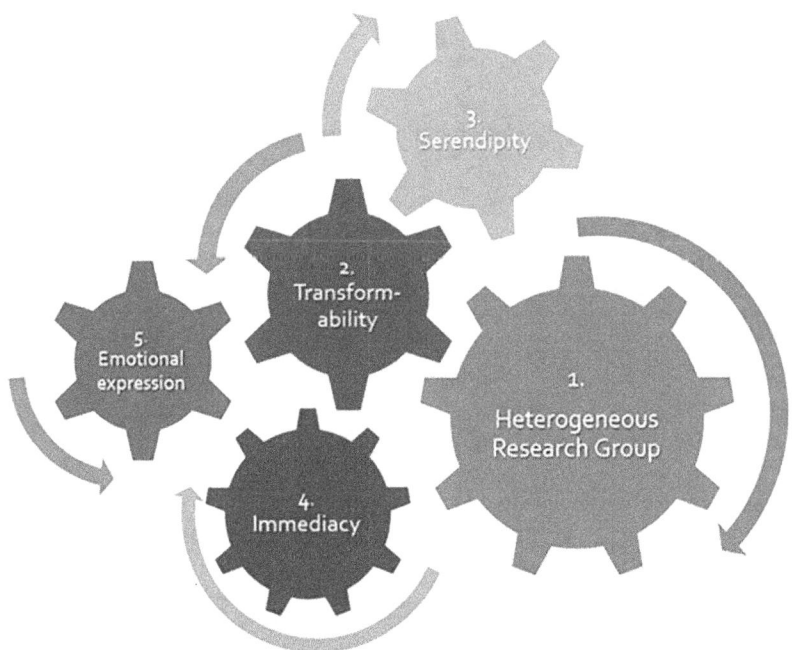

Figure 11.1 Distinguishing features of the dynamic walking tour methodology: a comprehensive framework

Heterogeneous Research Group

The affordances and limitations of participant observation and observer participation have been extensively discussed in scholarship spanning anthropology, sociology, and education (e.g., Bogdan & Biklen, 2007). In this study, the three groups of participants were situated in multiple places along the continuum between participants and observers: six graduate students and one university professor (all with a similar level of participation) held the role of observer participants; three local residents, of which one was a current graduate student and two were former graduate students, held the role of participant observers. Finally, six local residents—passersby and shop owners—actively participated in these interactions.

This heterogeneous research group complied with Brown and Durrheim's (2009) claims about the strengths of enhanced interaction with participants, by affording a multiplicity of perspectives on the role that language plays in the local landscape. These multiple perspectives, additionally, shed light on the LL's connection to issues of gentrification, tensions between the local Arab residents and the authorities, and the status of Arabic and Hebrew in the public space. Such multiple perspectives were central in forming the educational backdrop of this tour. For example, one of the participants who is a local resident of Jaffa and a former graduate student of the course led us to a newspaper shop where we met Ibrahim Khoury, an honorary resident of Tel Aviv-Jaffa who has worked to preserve the Arabic language and nationality by the teaching of Arabic and the provision of Arabic newspapers and literature. The following excerpt, translated into English from Hebrew, is from the interaction we had as a group with Mr. Khoury inside his newspaper shop:

Excerpt 1 (Translated from Hebrew)

> Shirin: This is one of the characters (in Jaffa) who preserve the Arabic language and the Arab nationality in this place. He is one of the symbols of Jaffa, of which we are proud. Ever since I was a little girl, my parents used to come in and buy newspapers and magazines, in Jaffa. You can look over there *(pointing at a pile of newspapers)*.

Elana: What does that say? *(pointing at a newspaper)*
Iman: It is from here, from Israel.
Elana: Ahh, it is translated; it must be from the North.
Iman: Yes, yes.
Elana: Wow, that is fascinating.
Ibrahim: I am an honorary resident of the city. *(Shows certificate).*
Elana: Wow, an honorary resident of Tel Aviv-Jaffa
Ibrahim: Because I keep, because I preserve the Arabic language.
Elana: Can you show it to us.
Ibrahim: And I taught Arabic and Mathematics.
Elana: Why isn't it written in Arabic here? *(Pointing at the certificate).*
Shirin: You need to ask the municipality.

Meeting this "language warrior," as one of the students called him, provided us with a diachronic perspective, an in-depth understanding of the history and importance of Arabic maintenance and preservation on this street. This interaction highlights how the local residents view the preservation of Arabic as parallel to preserving the Arab identity (Trumper-Hecht, 2010). This perspective would not have been available without the heterogeneous composition of the research group. The participant observers, local residents of Jaffa, initiated an opportunity for observer participants to meaningfully interact with local residents who hold historical knowledge of the language in the local landscape. Such interactions were invaluable learning opportunities made available by this unique feature of the tour.

Transformability

The dynamics of the tour also evoked the feature of transformability. All members of the heterogeneous group had the ability to interact, inquire, question, and attempt to transform the contested urban space. It allowed for an enhanced awareness of the languages in the linguistic landscape and the social implications of the visible and invisible languages. The local residents had mixed responses toward the representations of Arabic, Hebrew, and English displayed in the public space. Similar to Szabó and Troyer (2017), we gained emic perspectives, which reflected and justified a renewed need for language activism, to actively change the LL and strive for inclusion of what local residents see as their disappearing Arab language in a traditionally Arab town (see Figure 11.2).

For example, toward the end of the tour we entered a hardware store, the only store on the street that displayed an equal amount of Hebrew and Arabic on its sign. Nadeem, the shop owner and a former city-hall member, was indeed aware of the power relationship between Hebrew and Arabic and deliberately chose to keep both languages equally balanced on his storefront sign. Because this sign was unique, we decided to enter the store and inquire with Nadeem. Interestingly, this inquiry led us to learn about his initiative for using bilingual Arabic-Hebrew representation of the word "Welcome" (in Arabic, "Ahlan Wa Sahlan"). The following excerpt shows the moment in which we heard about this initiative and became excited about the prospect of collaborating with Nadeem in this real-world initiative for social change and transformation.

Excerpt 2 (Translated from Hebrew)

Shirin:	So, do you think that Arabic is disappearing, at least in the linguistic landscape or the signs, or do you think there is a larger awareness?
Nadeem:	No, I think there is awareness, there is a strong awareness.
Elana:	*(to Iman)*: That is just what you were saying.
Iman:	There are new [Arabic] signs.
Nadeem:	Yes, yes.

Shirin: There are new signs that have been added.
Nadeem: There are new signs that have been added, yes. And we have a new project that aims to put the words "Ahlan Wa Sahlan" on all the signs. To do it at our own expense, to put the words "Ahlan Wa Sahlan", that expression is acceptable to all.
Elana: Everybody knows them. So maybe we will start the campaign to produce buttons on which it says Ahlan Wa Sahlan.

All members of the walking tour had the ability to actively encourage social activism. As evident in the above excerpt, the participant observers and observer participants, all transcended from being passive observers to gaining additional insight into the complex social issues that arose in the contested space in Jaffa. As Troyer and Szabó (2017) emphasize in their co-constructed walking tour, the researchers in our tour could engage with locals in contemplating social actions and initiatives that would lead to transformation of the LL, rather than mere documentation of it. A similar situation arose when, as a group, we followed up on Iman's original documentation of a trilingual (Arabic-Hebrew-English) sign on a barbershop window. While approaching the shop, it became evident that the sign had been removed. If this walking tour had not included participant observers, who were local residents with inside knowledge and an active disposition to affect change, this observation would only have been documented and, at most, discussed among the researchers. However, because our walking tour included participant observers, we were able to act in the moment upon the discrepancies that we identified in the representation of language in the public space.

Furthermore, the dynamic nature of the tour presented moments, such as in the above example, where the group could witness an emotional response to the LL and empathize with the source of frustration (Garvin, 2010). As such, Shirin, a local Arab resident, felt compelled to act on the discrepancy she identified in the representation of Arabic in the barbershop (the alleged removal of the trilingual sign) and instantly entered the store to inquire further with the owner. Interestingly, the shop owner strongly advocated for the importance of such trilingual signs and explained that the sign had merely been sent to be repaired.

Beyond the heterogeneity of our group composition, which afforded us an insider's view rather than an outsider's assumption, this form of direct involvement in the field

Figure 11.2 Hebrew dominance on signage along Yefet Street

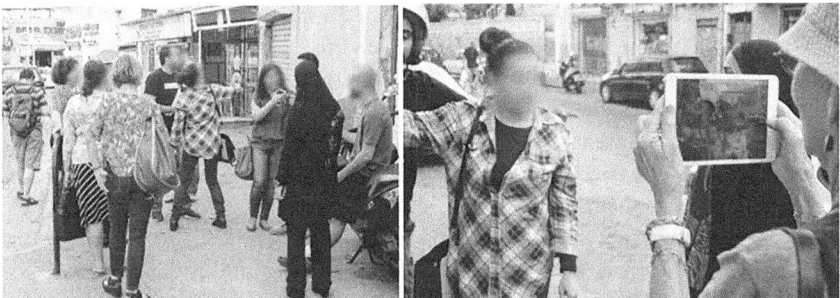

Figure 11.3 Members of the walking tour discussing the lack of Arabic on signage along Yefet Street

meant that we were also granted an opportunity to take part in processes of social transformation of the local LL. Such heightened and enhanced interactions in the field (see Figure 11.3) meant that we were not only learning about insiders' perspectives but were also granted an opportunity to enact change, which is arguably the epitome of educational work.

Immediacy

Building on Kusenbach's (2003) and Anderson's (2004) methodologies of "walking while talking" and the "go along interview," the flexibility of the route and heterogeneity of the group on our walking tour provided opportunities for enhanced interactions with people and spaces. The various members of the group engaged with participants directly without significant mediation. Initial caution between the groups transformed into sensitivity and empathy, with the participant observers creating a bridge between the local residents and the observer participants. By engaging with the locals through immediate presence, social and cultural markers were tangible and demanded participants of all backgrounds to assume responsibility for their actions and reactions.

Although at times these interactions raised concern among locals, the fact that we could interact with them on the spot due to the heterogeneity of the group meant that this concern could quickly transform into empathy and understanding. Interactions were thus less threatening and more authentic than those created by the lens of a documenting camera. As Shirin mentioned in her reflection, "You are the one who meets with naked reality, reality that speaks, that presents itself to us without forgery, without shame, and without hiding facts."

On one occasion, three of the observer participants were discussing the English-only signage of a particular store when the store owner approached them. This provided an immediate opportunity for the group members to ask him about his choice of language on his store's sign, at which point he fervently mentioned the decline in the status of Arabic among local Arab children and youth, as previously claimed by Shohamy and Abu Ghazaleh-Mahajneh (2012). As an example, he explained that his own son received an A+ in Hebrew but failed in his Arabic exam. To him, this epitomized the deterioration in the status of Arabic, which he solemnly regretted but had to take into account when considering the marketing of his business. Importantly, such an immediate experience of a local resident's predicaments was also powerful for the observer participants, who had to respond in the moment and consider the information not as detached empirical facts but as real-life concerns that they had to account for as well. Immediacy, thus, entailed a sense of responsibility, as the following example further highlights.

As the previous conversation with the shop owner continued, a passerby joined and soon became concerned that the group was surveying the area in order to assess the potential real estate value. A moment of suspicion was evident when he raised this question upfront, which was soon replaced by an elaborate explanation that the neighborhood is increasingly becoming gentrified.

The whole interaction with these local residents meant that we had to manage our response, in the moment, as participants with a variety of positionalities. This unplanned interaction afforded us an opening to engage in a deeper mode of participation, an educational opportunity to deeply inquire about the dynamics of this neighborhood. This consisted of a comprehensive understanding of different power relations as experienced by local residents, along with a responsibility to account for this understanding in the interaction with participants in the actual moment.

Serendipity

Alongside a few pre-arranged interviews that the participant observers organized with local shop owners, the tour was mostly conducted without a pre-formulated agenda. Considering the stringent time frame of graduate courses and research endeavors in particular, allowing for flexible time flow and the chance for tour destinations to change in the moment was a conscious decision by the group that entailed risks and a substantial amount of uncertainty. The rationale behind this decision played a major role in our insightful interactions in most of our examples in this chapter.

We believe that, in accordance with Brown and Durrheim (2009), the ability to participate in spontaneous interactions enhanced our ability to "unveil" social facts. Indeed, had we stuck to a preconceived plan, the tour would not have provided such deep understandings of the locals' perspectives or the transformative educational impact.

Serendipity meant that the group could linger or proceed along flexible routes and destinations according to their momentary interests. This allowed bottom-up knowledge to emerge through meaningful and spontaneous encounters. In the previous examples, our interactions with the shop owners and passersby were all spontaneous. Furthermore, the prolonged engagement in meaningful conversations and the willingness to linger until a sufficient understanding was achieved led us to comprehensively inquire about the variety of dimensions related to the representation of languages in the local LL. This included our learning about the context of sign changes (e.g., the barbershop), about the major endeavor to preserve Arabic and the concomitant deterioration of the language among youth, as well as the local initiatives for bringing about social change and transformation.

Emotional Expression

The focused attention on the LL during the walking tour interactions, in addition to the discussions among the participants themselves, heightened the emotions emerging from a variety of positionings and expressions of individual identities, not only from the local inhabitants (Shohamy & Gorter, 2008), but from all participants. They included identity expressions on a variety of levels and encompassed language, community, history, religion, nationality, loyalty, heritage, education, professions, etc. The dynamic walking tour proved to be an enabling methodology for researching emotional expression in LL (e.g., Ben-Rafael, 2009; Garvin, 2011; Leeman & Modan, 2009; Wee, 2016) and transforming it into learning opportunities. It revealed a heightened sense of the emotional dimension of participants' lived experiences, and by doing so it fostered caution and sensitivity in the researchers and demanded the researchers to be present in the moment.

The dominant arising emotions were pride, frustration, and concern. Both the local residents and the participant observers displayed a strong sense of pride over the importance of Arabic and its representation in the local linguistic landscape. This is manifested, for example, in Excerpt 1, in which the "language warrior," the Arab proprietor of a magazine and newspaper store, was very proud of his achievements in preserving the language. Also in the same excerpt, Shirin straightforwardly proclaimed that the shopkeeper was one of the symbols of Jaffa, of which she, among many other residents, were proud.

Even though pride was emphasized along with a sense of enhanced awareness of the importance of promoting the presence of Arabic in the local LL, a feeling of frustration was also evident among the participant observers and local residents. For example, when we encountered a major bakery business that had absolutely no Arabic representation on its signs, Shirin became visibly frustrated. The absence of her language clearly instigated an expression of emotion as a result from interaction with the LL.

Excerpt 3 (Translated from Hebrew)

Shirin: There is no Arabic here, the menu, the name, there is no trace of Arabic. Where is the Arabic? The proprietors are Arabic, the food is Arabic, the population is Arabic, the area is Arabic, even the little signs, with the new kinds of food, there is no Arabic at all. It is a shame, where is the Arabic identity? Not just the Arabic identity, the Arabic culinary identity?

The third and strongly linked emotion that arose was a deep concern about the disappearing representations of Arabic in the LL of Yefet Street in Jaffa. Souad in her reflection stated: "I don't have a problem with Hebrew, I just don't want it to come at the expense of the original language of the people." Also, Iman's reflection stated: "the reality check I made myself take, made it clear: Arabs are losing Arabic." This strong feeling of concern was evident in Iman's reflection of the walking tour, where she highlighted the grim reality of Arabic's deterioration and disappearance from the public space of her hometown. Nevertheless, this strong emotional response in the moment, as well as after the fact, has played a major role in Iman's active decision to "try harder in advocating the use of Arabic among Arab speakers in Jaffa, not instead of but alongside Hebrew." In accordance with Pink's (2015) claim, this study reiterates the rich potential of the sensorial process in methodologies that utilize walking to engender reflection.

These heightened emotional dimensions of the walking tour were central in directing all of the participants' involvement and engagement with people and places. In moments such as the examples above, the emotional responses of participant observers and local residents created both an immediate reaction among observer participants but also a lasting impression that fueled a desire for social change and betterment.

Conclusion

Contested urban spaces such as Yefet Street in Jaffa draw the interest of scholars for a variety of reasons. As researchers interested in exploring the visibility and representation of language in public space, LL scholars have understandably adopted the use of still photography of signs, interviews with passersby, video recordings of signage in public spaces, as well as (guided) walking tours and reflections (e.g., Garvin, 2010; Shohamy & Waksman, 2008; Szabó & Troyer, 2017). Our study adds to this tradition by offering an integrative and comprehensive framework based on a case of a walking tour in Yefet Street, Jaffa, to show the dynamic interaction of a variety of features that are not often incorporated together. Our aim was thus to clarify the particular affordances of an integrative walking tour methodology for understanding and learning about the complexities of LL in a contested urban space.

Our framework consists of five distinguishing features that we consider crucial for explaining the depth of inquiry that this walking tour produced. These interlocking features of heterogeneous research group, transformability, immediacy, serendipity, and emotional expression, worked together to produce a powerful and heightened educational engagement with a contested urban space, its inhabitants, and scholars situated in multiple places along the continuum between participants and observers.

The heterogeneous composition of the research group set the stage for an expansive inquiry based on insider and outsider perspectives, as well as on the invaluable access to the stories, predicaments, and social, political, and economic struggles behind the representation of languages in this contested public space. This unique access afforded an educational opportunity to interact, inquire, question, and attempt to transform the grim situation of the lack of representation for Arabic and the deterioration of its status among its speakers in the last neighborhood in Jaffa to be affected by gentrification.

Furthermore, the unplanned interactions with shop owners and passersby as well as the unfixed and flexible route of the tour promoted our proclivity to linger and engage more comprehensively with the people, stories, and social contexts behind the local LL. The serendipity of the tour meant that our interactions were not preplanned or scripted, but rather open-ended and fluid. Along with the heightened sense of caution and sensitivity set by the emotions of pride, frustration, and concern, that were continually stoked, such a disposition arguably established the immediate quality of our interactions. This in turn fostered a sense of responsibility for our actions and reactions, both in the moment and in reflection.

The predicament of Arabic in Jaffa and the complexities of the Arab residents' linguistic practices are an overlooked yet burning issue in contemporary Israeli society. In this unique case study of a walking tour, the LL functioned as a spark that ignited multiple understandings of a complex social reality. By concurrently producing the interlocking features of heterogeneity, transformability, immediacy, serendipity, and emotional expression, this walking tour highlighted the fact that LL is never esoteric, but rather a living construct in people's lives. Understanding this construct in a variety of situated perspectives played a crucial role in cultivating our mutual desire for bringing about social change in the contested public space of Yefet Street, Jaffa. As one of the participants reflected, "I realized I had been living in a parallel universe." It is our hope that through multifaceted scholarly engagements with LL that incorporate the five features we presented, enhanced awareness of such parallel universes could ultimately lead them to amalgamate.

Note

1   It should be noted that this study was conducted before the Nation-State Bill was passed.

References

Abu Ghazaleh-Mahajneh, M. (2009). *Attitudes towards the status of the Arabic, Hebrew and English languages among Arab students at the university*. MA Thesis, Tel Aviv University [in Hebrew].

Amara, M., & Schnell, I. (2004). Identity repertoires among Arabs in Israel. *Journal of Ethnic and Migration Studies*, 30(1), 175–93. doi: 10.1080/1369183032000170222

Anderson, J. (2004). Talking whilst walking: A geographical archaeology of knowledge. *Area*, 36(3), 254–61. doi: 10.1111/j.0004-0894.2004.00222.x

Ben Rafael, E. (2009). A sociological approach to the study of linguistic landscapes. In E. Shohamy & D. Gorter (Eds.). *Linguistic Landscape: Expanding the Scenery* (pp. 40–54). London: Routledge.

Ben-Rafael, E., Shohamy, E., Hasan Amara, M., & Trumper-Hecht, N. (2006). Linguistic landscape as symbolic construction of the public space: The case of Israel. *International Journal of Multilingualism*, 3(1), 7–30. doi: 10.1080/14790710608668383

Bogdan, R., & Biklen, S. K. (2007). *Qualitative Research for Education: An Introduction to Theories and Methods*. New York: Pearson.

Boyatzis, R. E. (1998). *Transforming Qualitative Information: Thematic Analysis and Code Development*. Thousand Oaks, CA: Sage.

Braun, V., & Clarke, V. (2006). Using thematic analysis in psychology. *Qualitative Research in Psychology*, 3(2), 77–101.

Brown, L., & Durrheim, K. (2009). Different kinds of knowing: Generating qualitative data through mobile interviewing. *Qualitative Inquiry*, 15(5), 911–30.

Garvin, R. T. (2010). Responses to the linguistic landscape in Memphis, Tennessee: An urban space in transition. In E. Shohamy, E. Ben-Rafael, & M. Barni (Eds.) *Linguistic Landscape in the City* (pp. 252–71). Bristol, UK: Multilingual Matters.

Garvin, R. T. (2011). *Emotional Responses to the Linguistic Landscape in Memphis, Tennessee: Visual Perceptions of Public Spaces in Transition*. Indiana, PA: Indiana University of Pennsylvania.

Golan, A. (1995). The demarcation of Tel Aviv-Jaffa's municipal boundaries following the 1948 war: Political conflicts and spatial outcome. *Planning Perspectives*, 10(4), 383–98. doi: 10.1080/02665439508725830

Goldhaber, R. (2007). The perception of spatial isolationism in Jaffa. In E. Rekhess (Ed.), *The Arabs in Israel. Together but Apart: Mixed Cities in Israel* (pp. 63–72). Tel Aviv, Israel: Tel Aviv University. [in Hebrew].

Goldstein-Havazki, R. (2011). A travel diary in Jaffa: Development of linguistic landscape awareness and attitudes among teenagers. Unpublished MA thesis, Tel Aviv University.

Hicks, D. (April 2002). Scotland's linguistic landscape: The lack of policy and planning with Scotland's place-names and signage. In *World Congress on Language Policies, Barcelona* (Vol. 20, pp. 16–20). Barcelona, Spain.

Hochschild, A. R. (2012). *The Managed Heart: Commercialization of Human Feeling*. Berkeley, CA: University of California Press.

Johnson, M. (2018). *The Aesthetics of Meaning and Thought: The Bodily Roots of Philosophy, Science, Morality, and Art*. Chicago, IL: University of Chicago Press.

Knesset. (2018). *Basic Law: Israel—The Nation State of the Jewish People*. Retrieved from https://knesset.gov.il/laws/special/eng/BasicLawNationState.pdf

Knesset. (2020). *Constitution for Israel*. Retrieved on February 2, 2020 from https://knesset.gov.il/constitution/ConstMJewishState.htm

Kusenbach, M. (2003). Street phenomenology. The go-along as ethnographic research tool. *Ethnography*, 4(3), 455–85. doi: 10.1177/146613810343007

Landry, R., & Bourhis, R. Y. (1997). Linguistic landscape and ethnolinguistic vitality: An empirical study. *Journal of Language and Social Psychology*, 16(1), 23–49. doi: 10.1177/0261927X970161002

Lefebvre, H. (1991). *The Production of Space*. Oxford: Blackwell.

Lee, J., & Ingold, T. (2006). Fieldwork on foot: Perceiving, routing, socializing. In S. Coleman & P. Collins (Eds.), *Locating the Field: Space, Place and Context in Anthropology* (pp. 67–86). Oxford, UK: Berg.

Leeman, J., & Modan, G. (2009). Commodified language in Chinatown: A contextualized approach to linguistic landscape. *Journal of Sociolinguistics*, 13(3), 332–62. doi: 10.1111/j.1467-9841.2009.00409.x

LeVine, M. (2007). Globalization, architecture, and town planning in a colonial city: The case of Jaffa and Tel Aviv. *Journal of World History*, 18(2), 171–98.

Monterescu, D. (2010). Spheres of transgression: The Israelization and Palestinization of urban space. *Zmanim: History Quarterly*, 110, 104–16 [in Hebrew].

Monterescu, D. (2011a). Estranged natives and indigenized immigrants: A relational anthropology of ethnically mixed towns in Israel. *World Development*, 39(2), 270–81. doi: 10.1016/j.worlddev.2009.11.027

Monterescu, D. (2011b). Identity politics in mixed towns: The Case of Jaffa (1948–2007). *Megamot*, 3(4), 484–517. [in Hebrew].

Monterescu, D. (2015). *Jaffa Shared and Shattered: Contrived Coexistence in Israel/Palestine*. Bloomington, IN: Indiana University Press.
Monterescu, D. (July 1, 2017). *The Arab-Jewish Battle over Street Names in Jaffa*. Haaretz. Retrieved from https://www.haaretz.com/israel-news/.premium-the-arab-jewish-battle-over-street-names-in-jaffa-1.5490673
Moriarty, M. (2014). Contesting language ideologies in the linguistic landscape of an Irish tourist town. *International Journal of Bilingualism*, 18(5), 464–77. doi: 10.1177/1367006913484209
Pennycook, A. (2009). Linguistic landscapes and the transgressive semiotics of graffiti. In E. Shohamy & D. Gorter (Eds.), *Linguistic Landscape: Expanding the Scenery* (pp. 302–12). New York: Routledge.
Pink, S. (2015). *Doing Sensory Ethnography*. London: Sage.
Rabinowitz, D., & Monterescu, D. (Eds.). (2007). *Mixed Towns, Trapped Communities*. London: Routledge.
Rubdy, R., & Said, S. B. (Eds.). (2015). *Conflict, Exclusion and Dissent in the Linguistic Landscape*. London: Palgrave Macmillan.
Rudnitzky, A. (2018). *Arab Population in Israel: Demographic, Socio-economic and Political Indicators*. Moshe Dayan Center, Tel Aviv University. Retrieved from https://www.iataskforce.org/sites/default/files/resource/resource-1588.pdf
Said, S. B., & Shegar, C. (2013). Compliance, negotiation, and resistance in teachers' spatial construction of professional identities. In B. S. Said & L. J. Zhang (Eds.), *Language Teachers and Teaching: Global Perspectives, Local Initiatives* (pp. 127–49). New York: Routledge.
Seals, C. A. (2015). Overcoming Erasure: Reappropriation of space in the linguistic landscape of mass-scale protests. In Rubdy R., & Said S.B. (Eds.) *Conflict, Exclusion and Dissent in the Linguistic* Landscape. *Language and Globalization* (pp. 223–38). London: Palgrave Macmillan.
Scollon, R., & Scollon, S. W. (2003). *Discourses in Place: Language in the Material World*. London: Routledge.
Shohamy, E. (2006). *Language Policy: Hidden Agendas and New Approaches*. Abingdon, UK: Routledge.
Shohamy, E. (2012). Linguistic landscapes and multilingualism. In M. Martin-Jones, A. Blackledge & A. Creese (Eds.) *The Routledge Handbook of Multilingualism* (pp. 550–63). Abingdon, UK: Routledge.
Shohamy, E. G., ben Rafael, E., & Barni, M. (Eds.). (2010). *Linguistic Landscape in the City*. Bristol, UK: Multilingual Matters.
Shohamy, E., & Gorter, D. (Eds.). (2009). *Linguistic Landscape: Expanding the Scenery*. New York: Routledge.
Shohamy, E., & Waksman, S. (2008). Modalities, meanings, negotiations, education. In E. Shohamy & D. Gorter (Eds.) *Linguistic Landscape: Expanding the Scenery*, (pp. 313–31). London: Routledge.
Shohamy, E., & Abu Ghazaleh-Mahajneh, M. (2012). Linguistic landscape as a tool for interpreting language vitality: Arabic as a "minority" language in Israel. In D. Gorter, H. F. Marten, & L. Van Mensel (Eds.), *Minority Languages in the Linguistic Landscape* (pp. 89–106). London: Palgrave Macmillan.
Szabó, T. P., & Troyer, R. A. (2017). Inclusive ethnographies. *Linguistic Landscape*, 3(3), 306–26. doi: 10.1075/ll.17008.sza
Tel Aviv-Jaffa Municipality (2013). *Socio-economical Research Report*. Retrieved from https://www.tel-aviv.gov.il/Transparency/DocLib6/%D7%94%D7%93

%D7%99%D7%A8%D7%95%D7%92%20%D7%94%D7%97%D7%91%D7%A8%D7%AA%D7%99-%D7%9B%D7%9C%D7%9B%D7%9C%D7%99%20%D7%A9%D7%9C%20%D7%AA%D7%9C-%D7%90%D7%91%D7%99%D7%91-%D7%99%D7%A4%D7%95,%202013.pdf

Troyer, R. A., & Szabó, T. P. (2017). Representation and videography in linguistic landscape studies. *Linguistic Landscape*, 3(1), 56–77. doi: 10.1075/ll.3.1.03tro

Trumper-Hecht, N. (2009). Constructing national identity in mixed cities in Israel: Arabic on signs in the public space of Upper Nazareth. In E. Shohamy & D. Gorter (Eds.) *Linguistic Landscape: Expanding the Scenery* (pp. 238–52). London: Routledge.

Trumper-Hecht, N. (2010). Linguistic landscape in mixed cities in Israel from the perspective of "walkers": The case of Arabic. In E. Shohamy, E. Ben-Rafael, & M. Barni (Eds.) *Linguistic Landscape in the City* (pp. 235–51). Bristol, UK: Multilingual Matters.

Wee, L. (2016). Situating affect in linguistic landscapes. *Linguistic Landscape*, 2(2), 105–26. doi: 10.1075/ll.2.2.01wee

Appendix 1

Original Hebrew Transcriptions

Excerpt 1

שירין: הוא אחת הדמויות המשמרות את השפה הערבית ואת הלאום הערבי במקום. הוא אחד הסמלים שאנחנו גאים בו לאורך כל ההיסטוריה של יפו. מאז שהייתי ילדה קטנה, ההורים שלי היו באים וקונים עיתונים וזורנלים ביפו, ומה זה *(מצביעה לכיוון עריסת עיתונים)* אם לא שימור השפה הערבית?
אילנה: מה זה אומר? *(מצביעה לעיתון)*
אימאן: זה מכאן, מישראל.
אילנה: אהההה, זה תרגום. כנראה זה מהצפון.
אימאן: כן,כן.
אילנה: וואו. מדהים.
(אברהים: אני יקיר תל אביב- יפו *(מציג תעודה)*.
אילנה: וואו, יקיר תל אביב.
אברהים: על השמירה שאני משמר את השפה הערבית.
אילנה: האם אתה יכול להראות לנו?
אברהים: וגם לימדתי ערבית וגם מתמטיקה.
(אילנה: למה זה לא כתוב בערבית? *(מצביעה לתעודה)*
שירין: צריך לשאול בעירייה.

Excerpt 2

שירין: אתה מרגיש שהערבית הולכת ו … ונכחדת, לפחות כאן ביפו? לפחות ברמה של המרחב הלשוני, השלטים? פחות, או שדווקא יש מודעות יותר?
נדים: לא, לדעתי יש מודעות, יש מודעות מאוד חזקה.

אילנה (לאימאן): את מה שאת אומרת, זה מה רואה? כן.
אימאן: יש שלטים חדשים שהוסיפו קצת, כן.
נדים: יש כמה שלטים שהוסיפו, כן. אנחנו יש לנו איזשהו פרויקט לשים את המילה "אהלן וסהלן" על כל השלטים – לעשות את זה על חשבוננו, אבל לשים אהלן וסהלן, זה מילה שהיא מקובלת על כולם ומאוד ...
אילנה: הם יודעים את זה.
נדים: כן.
אילנה: אז אולי, אולי נעשה קמפיין לייצר סיכות עם הכיתוב "אהלן וסהלן".
נדים: יאללה. בואי, נעשה את זה ביחד.

Excerpt 3

שירין: אין שום ערבית. התפריט, השם ... אין שום ערבית, אין זכר. איפה הערבית שלנו? למרות שהבעלים ערביים והאוכל ערבי והאזור ערבי. ואפילו השלטים הקטנים, החידושים באוכל, גם אין ערבית בכלל. וזה חבל. איפה הזהות – לא רק הערבית, הזהות הקולינרית הערבית, איפה היא?

Index

abortion in Ireland 198–9
activism 177–9, 186–7, 192
airports 99–101
   and biosecurity 100, 106–7
   and branding 109–11
   signage in 101–3
Arabic language 218–21
Auckland, New Zealand 98–109, 111
audience design 102, 117
authenticity 15–6, 24–5, 30–3

Banksy 1, 182–4
Brexit 133, 135–6

Chinese Language Week 105
Christchurch, New Zealand 99, 101–2, 107, 110
classroom(s) 1–4
community of practice 15, 25
Concordia Language Villages (Minnesota, USA) 14, 20, 33 (fn 2)
contestation and conflict 218–9, 223, 233
cultural appropriation 44, 52
   through language 110
cultural practices 15, 24–5, 31–3

deaf geographies/spaces 38–9, 46, 50–2
deaf peddlers 42–4, 52
dialogism 177, 184, 190–1
diary, diaries
   student travel reflections 58, 60–3, 70–2
discourse(s) 24–5, 31, 100
Drehu language 64, 69
dynamic walking tour 217–9, 221–33

Eighth Amendment (Ireland). *See* abortion in Ireland
emblems
   I-LOVE-YOU sign 43, 46
emotion, emotional expression 199–201, 205, 218, 223, 230–3

ethnography, ethnographic methods 15–19, 21–2, 26, 32, 123, 181–2
exoticism 108, 110–1
experiential learning 157, 160–2, 164, 168–9, 171–2

films
   history of deaf films 46
   impact on deaf people 46–7
fingerspelling 41–2, 48–9. *See also* sign language
flag(s) 60, 62–3, 67–9, 73, 188–9

Gallaudet University 48–50
German language 13–36
geosemiotics 60, 69–70, 202
Göttingen, Germany 178–9, 183, 185–6, 188–9
graffiti 183–5

healthcare, health communication 77–9, 86, 92–3
Hebrew language 218–20
heritage 144–8
heterogeneity 209–11, 217, 226–8
heteroglossia 26, 177, 185, 190–1
hospital(s) 78, 80–1, 86–93

immediacy 217, 229–30
immigration
   immigrant(s) 133–7, 140–5, 148
Indigenous community 157–59, 169–70, 172, 174
intertextuality 15, 16, 26, 34 (fn 3)

Jaffa, Israel 217–29, 231–3

Kanak people, Kanaky 57–9, 64, 66–9, 73
Kiswahili. *See* Swahili language
Kucapungane, Taiwan 158, 163–5, 167

language learning methods
  immersion 14
  multimodal literacy 159, 168, 171–3
  peripheral 118–9, 124–8
language policy 80–2, 103, 219–21
Lifou, New Caledonia 68, 72
linguistic appropriation. *See* cultural appropriation
linguistic landscapes (LL)
  definitions of 1–2, 58–9, 78, 157–9
Lviv, Ukraine 177, 180–2, 184–5, 189–91

Mandarin Chinese language 87, 100–7, 157–60, 163–5, 167
Māori language 108–12
marginalization
  marginalized languages 39–40
minority/minorities 136–7, 141, 144
mixed cities 218–9
mobile texts 102
multilingual sign(s) 158, 163–5, 167
multimodality
  of activist media 182–4, 188–9, 191, 207–12
  and signage 121–2
  in story house(s) 155, 157, 162, 168, 172–3
museum(s) 138–45, 147–9
  as educational tools 133–4
  post-museum(s) 137–8, 143, 145–8

nexus analysis 157–60, 171
Noumea, New Caledonia 57–61, 65–6, 68–9

Pacific, the 62, 66, 71
Paiwan language 155, 161–7, 171
phenomenography 3
playworld 18, 29
polyphony 177, 190–1
poetry (as signage) 189–91
post-disaster reconstruction 155–7, 160–3, 165, 167, 169–73

racial profiling 104
refugee(s) 133–5, 142, 145, 148
Rinari 155–7, 160–5, 169–73
Rukai language (Budai variety) 155, 161–7, 171

schoolscape(s) 1–3, 15–16, 18, 31–2
SeaCity Museum 138–41, 144, 147–9
semiotics
  and place, *See* geosemiotics
  semiotic aggregate 15, 22, 165
  semiotic landscapes 3, 59
serendipity 217, 230, 232
sign language(s)
  banning of use 40, 47, 52
  fingerspelling 41–2, 48–9
  in linguistic landscapes (SLLLs) 38–9, 41, 44, 46–50
  notation systems 41
sign(s)
  definitions of 19, 82–4, 97–9
social change 218, 227, 230, 232–3
Southampton, UK 134–6, 140–2, 144, 147–9
stance
  affective vs. epistemic 199–201, 207
sticker(s) 185–7
story house(s) 155, 157, 162, 168, 172–3
storybox(es) 139, 144–7
study abroad 57, 63, 70–1
superdiversity 136, 140
sustainability 156, 161, 163, 172–3
Swahili language 79–80, 84–92

te reo Māori. *See* Māori language
Tel Aviv–Jaffa. *See* Jaffa, Israel
tourism 100, 107–8, 111, 161
transformability 217, 227, 232
Turkey 119–20

walking tour. *See* dynamic walking tour
wayfinding 102–3
writing systems
  bias in favor of 40–1
  sign language notation 41

www.ingramcontent.com/pod-product-compliance
Lightning Source LLC
Chambersburg PA
CBHW072141290426
44111CB00012B/1937